Legal Reform in Occupied Japan

Legal Reform in Occupied Japan

A Participant Looks Back

BY ALFRED C. OPPLER

Princeton University Press, Princeton, New Jersey

Library of Congress Cataloging in Publication Data
will be found on the last printed page of this book

Publication of this book has been aided by a grant
from the Andrew W. Mellon Foundation

Printed in the United States of America
by Princeton University Press, Princeton, New Jersey

TO
CHARLOTTE
AND
ELLEN

◇◇

Foreword

The Allied Occupation of Japan was an experiment in directed political change. The avowed purpose was to "democratize" the essentially authoritarian political system of the erstwhile enemy nation. This was to be achieved by altering not only Japan's political institutions but also her political culture. Inevitably, the question arises whether such a massive interference of outsiders in the life of another nation can be justified, both legally and ethically. The planners of the Occupation found legal justification in the Japanese acceptance of the Potsdam Declaration and, subsequently, of the Instrument of Surrender. They saw sufficient ethical justification in the ends which the Occupation was to serve.

The first of these ends was peace. According to the directive of the U.S. Joint Chiefs of Staff to General MacArthur of November 3, 1945, the ultimate objective was "to foster conditions which will give the greatest possible assurance that Japan will not again become a menace to the peace and security of the world." To this end, measures were to be taken for "the strengthening of democratic tendencies and processes in governmental, economic and social institutions" and for "the encouragement and support of liberal political tendencies." Initially, democratization was considered to be instrumental for Japan's demilitarization in the interest of peace. A democratic Japan, it was thought, would also be a peaceful Japan.

However, the planners and executors of Occupation policy also considered democracy as a value in itself. Convinced of the superiority of democracy over other governmental systems, they felt justified in bringing the "blessings of liberty" to a population hitherto deprived of them. Underlying this justification in the minds of some was the assumption of a universality of human nature. General MacArthur stated this view succinctly: "History will clearly show," he wrote, "that the entire human race, irrespective of geographical limitations or cultural tradition, is capable of absorbing, cherishing and defending liberty, tolerance and justice, and will have maximum strength and progress when so blessed." The assumption of a universal human nature swept aside the question of the compatibility of the Occupation reforms with antecedent Japanese traditions and values. But to some observers, who did not share that assumption, the moral justification of the Occupation efforts hinged on this question.

Comparing Japanese and Western traditions and values, they saw them not only as different, but as different in their very essence and thus different in perpetuity. In particular, they saw individualism, the core value of democracy, as diametrically opposed to the traditional morality of Japan with its emphasis on the submerging of the individual in the group in the interest of harmony. Since they considered each value system as equally valid in its own sphere, they condemned the Occupation reforms as ethnocentric attempts to force alien values on a defeated, helpless nation. Such attempts, they felt, could only lead to results of a superficial and ephemeral nature. It may be noted that this view was based on the assumptions of a homogeneous Japanese culture, immune to the effects of social change.

In its endeavors the Occupation used law as an instrument of social change. The relationship between the social and cultural systems and the legal system is, of course, a hoary problem of jurisprudence. The discussion of this problem in the literature reflects the opposing views, outlined above. In the early nineteenth century, the famous debate between Thibaut and Savigny revolved to a large extent around these issues in dealing with the question of

whether the establishment of unified German codes was
compatible with the character of the people in various
regions. This debate had its counterpart in Japan toward
the end of the nineteenth century in the debate surrounding
the enactment of the family law provisions of the new Civil
Code. The same issues of compatibility were frequently
raised, explicitly or implicitly, in the postwar discussions—
including those in the Diet—about the new Constitution
and its implementation by legal and judicial reforms.

Judge Oppler played a prominent role in these reforms,
and his book is focused on them. When he joined the Government Section of SCAP in Tokyo in late February 1946,
it had already drafted the blueprint for Japanese democracy
which was to become the new Constitution. But the tasks
of implementing it, of bringing existing codes and laws
into agreement with it, of fostering the independence of the
judiciary, of protecting and promoting civil liberties, and
of developing the appropriate attitudes, was still to be done.
Honesty to himself, which is characteristic of him, compelled Judge Oppler to come to grips with the fundamental
questions which I sketched out above. They were before
him from the outset—as his early memorandum to his
division chief, cited in Chapter 7, shows—and they are
referred to again and again in his reminiscences. If I may
summarize his views, as I deduce them from his book and
from many discussions with him during our long association, I would state them briefly—and with apologies for
oversimplifications dictated by the need for brevity—as
follows:

A nation's value system is intimately related to its social
development. Social change engenders or at least makes
possible changes in values. Since social change affects various
population groups differentially, cultural homogeneity is
prone to break down as the society and its culture change.
In Japan, the effect of social change on the traditional
value system had already made itself felt in the twenties—
in the period referred to as "Taisho democracy"—but it had

then been counteracted by conservative efforts to maintain tradition by persuasion and coercion. In the immediate postwar years the trauma of defeat created an atmosphere of a "revaluation of all values." Under these circumstances, the Occupation "merely pushed forward existing reforming and liberalizing trends which would have effected similar results, though at a slower tempo," thereby helping "the progressive men and women of Japan in laying the foundations for a different and, as they expected, better society." As long as the reforms were likely to fit the existing or emerging social realities, as indicated by previous trends in their direction or by their support among the Japanese, they were not only justified, but beneficial. In other words, the justification for democratization was not that democracy was the best system for all of mankind, but that it might serve Japan in the second half of the twentieth century better than the myth-based authoritarianism of the past; the justification for raising the position of the individual vis-à-vis the collectivity was not that individualism was the highest good, but that many Japanese had begun to chafe under the constraints on the individual, imposed by tradition. Oppler's statements about the proper role of the Occupationnaire as "mentor," about his own role as "midwife" for the new Supreme Court, and about the function of his division in "suggesting and encouraging legislation designed to advance Occupation objectives," have to be understood, I believe, in this sense.

Since some of the existing laws had been designed to bolster the values of the past and were now thwarting the fruition of "existing reformist and liberalizing trends," they had to be repealed or revised. However, Oppler wrote to his superiors in the above-mentioned memorandum soon after he assumed his position, "other reforms, desirable though they might appear to the Western mind, should not be imposed by SCAP."

As a result of this basic stance, there was no wholesale "Americanization" of Japanese law, as less well-informed critics of the Occupation assert. Judge Oppler was not only too cosmopolitan in his background, but also too judicious to succumb to the parochial notions that American or Anglo-Saxon law, being superior to other legal systems, was in all instances a proper model for Japan. He was quite willing to contribute to the creation of an eclectic blend of legal systems, and he saw no difficulty in reconciling this eclecticism with the aim of "democratizing" Japan. Japanese democracy and its law, he was certain, was to be *sui generis*, not a carbon copy of the American variety. Since Japanese law, as developed after the Meiji Restoration, belonged essentially to the continental European legal tradition, his familiarity with that tradition was a special asset for the Occupation.

There were, of course, differences in the basic philosophy and in the operating procedures between and within the various sections of SCAP. The operating procedures in Oppler's divisions—first the Courts and Law Division of Government Section and later the Legislation and Justice Division of Legal Section—bore the imprint of his notions about the proper role of the Occupation. In his gentle way —and he was the gentlest "boss" imaginable—he insisted on the required sensitivity to Japanese desires and viewpoints. Naturally, the viewpoints of the various groups among the Japanese, with whom the division maintained contact, differed frequently, and in many cases these differences provided the parameter within which action was taken.

Given these restraints in objectives and procedures, Oppler could expect the reforms over which he presided to last—as, indeed, they did. One of the reasons was, as he recognized, that the restraints maximized the ego-involvement of the Japanese, who had cooperated in the reforms and who could then be relied on for their defense, once the Occupation was over.

I have concentrated on basic questions, related to the justification of the Occupation reforms, because I feel that even thirty years after the event evaluations of the entire

enterprise are often based on simplistic notions, barely sufficient to serve as rationalizations for the "gut feelings" of
the observers. It may be hoped that this book, written by
a thoughtful participant-observer, will substantially contribute to our understanding. The perspective of an official
below the section chief level is particularly propitious, because, as Judge Oppler notes, these officials enjoyed considerable freedom of action and exercised great influence
on their superiors.

The book abounds in interesting vignettes of Occupation
life and of the personalities of Japanese and SCAP officials.
As his long-time admirer and friend, I am glad that, being
partly autobiographical, it reveals something about the
personality of the author as well—his modesty, his lack of
arrogance, his wisdom and his generosity. I referred earlier
to his honesty to himself. During the Occupation he did not
allow his views to be determined by his superiors; he was
no other-directed organization man; he did not just do his
bureaucratic duty, but followed the dictates of his conscience in serving a cause in which he deeply believed.

Members of a new generation in the seventies may find
it difficult to recapture the image of the United States as a
selfless torchbearer of democracy which was widely held—
here and abroad—in the immediate aftermath of the Second
World War. They may, therefore, attribute the missionary
zeal of the early Occupationnaires to political naiveté, perhaps even to a misperception of the true and more sinister
purposes of the Occupation. However, the dedication to
democracy and to the cause of civil liberties of these American idealists was real enough, so that progressive Japanese,
emerging from a rather heavy-handed and at times somewhat paranoid authoritarianism, could see in them fellow-
fighters in a common cause, transcending nationality. It is
quite possible that Japan would have evolved into a democracy after defeat, even if there had been no Occupation.
But, if so, the process would probably have been longer,
more disruptive, and more painful. In other words, the

Occupation reforms, such as those described in this volume, alleviated the birth pangs of the new order.

More than a decade after the end of the Occupation, a progressive Japanese jurist—whose name occurs in Oppler's book—visited me at Stanford. Reminiscing about the Occupation, he praised those foreign reformers whose labors had been motivated by a sincere devotion to the cause of Japanese democracy. He felt that their successes had brought long-range benefits to Japanese society, and he regretted that political realities did not make it feasible to commemorate their achievements by erecting monuments to them. When I asked him whom he had in mind as deserving such an extraordinary honor, the first name he mentioned was that of Alfred Oppler.

Kurt Steiner
Professor of Political Science
STANFORD UNIVERSITY

Contents

◇◇◇

List of Illustrations

◇◇◇

Acknowledgments

This book for the most part represents reminiscences of the postwar legal reforms in Japan and other events that go back two decades or more. In describing them, I have been more or less dependent on my own memory and on the limited material I preserved when I retired from my Tokyo position. The book has been written in the solitude of my studio and there have not been those manifold consultations and discussions that acknowledgments usually mention.

Two scholars have, however, read the first very rough draft of my manuscript from beginning to end. I am deeply indebted to them. Professor Kurt Steiner, Institute of Political Studies at Stanford University, my former co-fighter for civil liberties in Japan, throughout the year 1974 engaged me in a lively correspondence in which he indefatigably gave me advice and made detailed suggestions. They were all the more valuable due to his intimate knowledge of issues in the occupation of Japan, some of which he has treated brilliantly in his publications. Professor Marius B. Jansen, East Asian Studies, Princeton University, prominent scholar of Japanese history, shared with me his wisdom and experience, especially clarifying important problems of organization of the book and pointing to weaknesses of the draft. He also had the kindness to open for me the door to Princeton University Press. If, as I hope, this is now a better book than the first version was, such improvement is largely due to the constructive criticism of these two friends.

Moreover, I wish to express my gratitude to Mr. Paul D. Moore, a graduate student of the University of Michigan, who is writing his Ph.D. dissertation on a related subject from the point of view of the political scientist. In the course of his research in the archives he discovered some of the memoranda submitted by me to my superiors in the Tokyo headquarters and provided me with copies and other relevant material. This refreshing of my memory has been a very welcome and significant contribution to the book.

My appreciation and thanks go also to Miss R. Miriam Brokaw, Associate Director and Editor of Princeton University Press. Representing the publisher, she has helped this inexperienced author with an unusual combination of broadmindedness, understanding, and patience.

Last but not least, I gratefully acknowledge the improvement of the manuscript resulting from the intelligent copyediting by Mrs. Margaret Case of the Press. On her advice, the substance has been condensed by deleting deviations. Though preserving the personal character of my English style, she has rendered it more concise and eliminated some of my Germanisms in it.

Legal Reform in Occupied Japan

◇◇◇

Introduction

It was with utmost reluctance that I began to write my memoirs. If my daughter had not urged me to do so, I would never have had the idea, since I did not want to look back into the past and to relive the various stages of my eventful life with its strange ups and downs in three parts of the globe: Germany, America, and Japan. My further objection that I do not feel important enough for such an undertaking was refuted by the argument that what mattered was not my person, but my experiences and observations. I yielded, mainly, to get away from the passive life into which my retirement had forced me, hoping that a creative activity might slow down the inevitable progress of senility.

To begin with, I did not think of publication, but merely wrote for the family. And write I did for years and years, trying to cover both my personal and professional lives, intimate private affairs as well as political events and official activities of a highly technical legal nature. At the end I had written three books, and produced a monstrous hybrid of autobiographical and historical opus. I changed my mind with regard to publication, and I believe now that some of it, especially my work in Japan, might be of general interest. Abandoning the original plan, I decided to give my Japanese period priority.

While the MacArthur occupation of Japan has been the subject of a number of books by scholars, little, if anything, has been written by participants below the top level about their own work and contacts with their Japanese counterparts. Such an account by one who was involved in the ambitious attempt of "democratizing" the legal system of an alien nation could possibly be a contribution to the history of the occupation. It is important that the few published accounts of others who had been active in different fields be supplemented before the participants have passed away.

The "missionary zeal" that I showed in Japan in connection with civil rights and the legal and judicial reforms will be better understood with some knowledge of my personal history. I may, therefore, be permitted to give the reader a very brief summary of my life and career.

I am a product of the nineteenth century, having been born in 1893 in Alsace-Lorraine, when it was part of Germany. My grandparents were still Jewish by religion. Although much traditional anti-Semitism prevailed at this time in Germany, my grandfather Oppler was an active medical colonel (*Oberstabsarzt*) in the Prussian army, and a decorated hero of the Bismarckian wars of 1864, 1866, and 1870. He died two weeks before I was born and was buried with all military honors. My father was a judge and ended his career as president of a court division in Berlin. Both my parents were already Christians, and my older brother as well as I were baptized when still in the cradle. We were brought up as Protestants.

I graduated from the *Gymnasium*, the type of German high school in which emphasis is laid upon classical languages and the humanities rather than upon science. The student who had graduated from this school may be compared to an American who has completed high school and his sophomore year at college. I studied law at the Universities of Munich, Freiburg, Berlin, and Strassburg, but the study was interrupted by four years of participation in World War I. In spite of my unmilitary nature, I advanced, though rather late, to the rank of lieutenant. As front combatant, I took part in the long and tiring battles around Ypres, Flanders, and Verdun. Initially a gullible victim of the German war propaganda, I eventually became disillusioned and in November 1918 welcomed the emergence of the Weimar Republic by joining the Democratic party. With the defeat of Germany, Alsace-Lorraine became French and, since we did not opt for France, our family was expelled from Strassburg and lost its home. We settled in Berlin, where my father had again obtained a judicial position.

After the first law examination and the prescribed three years as a judicial apprentice (*Referendar*), I passed the rigorous second one (*Assessor*) required for the judiciary and the bar in Germany. In 1927 I married Charlotte Preuss, a teacher and graduate student of Berlin University, whom I had met in the Dolomite Alps during a vacation. We have one daughter, Ellen, who has become an art historian. She studied at Smith College while her parents were in Japan. After graduation, she joined us in Tokyo, where she served with the military intelligence for several years. After a similar assignment in Germany, she took up graduate study and obtained her Ph.D. from Columbia University with distinction. At present, she teaches at Syracuse University as an associate professor.

I occupied various positions in the Prussian judiciary and administration. In the Ministry of Finance I worked as legal advisor on the financial settlement between the new Republic and the dethroned Hohenzollerns. I also served as public welfare counselor and as member of an intermediate administrative court in the regional government in Potsdam. At the ages of 38 and 39 I rose to top positions as associate justice of the Supreme Administrative Court (*Oberverwaltungsgericht*) and vice president of the Supreme Disciplinary Court (*Dienststrafhof*) respectively, both in Berlin. With Hitler's coming to power, this unusual career ended for political and "racial" reasons. I was demoted to a provincial position in Cologne, and later removed. The following years of the rising Nazi terror were the most sinister period of our lives. While my wife, as a so-called

1. The author as a justice of the Supreme Administrative Court, Berlin, 1931.

"Aryan," was not directly affected by the Fuehrer's insane racial policy, I was considered a Jew according to the infamous Nuremberg laws, deprived piecemeal of citizenship and all other rights, and finally reduced to the status of a dehumanized outcast. Reluctant to leave the country to which we were attached, we hoped to survive the Third Reich and waited much too long before we emigrated. My attempt to return to Alsace was unsuccessful. Prospects in the United States for a German jurist who could not speak English and was unskillful with his hands seemed to be hopeless. In our school we had learned Latin, Greek, and French, but English had been optional, and I had not studied it. Only when the "crystal night" of November 9, 1938 was followed by mass arrests of Jews and their detention in concentration camps, did I at long last realize that the horror would survive me and that I had to save my life. During these gruesome days and nights I hid myself in the home of a dear family friend, Louis P. Lochner, chief of the Associated Press in Berlin. This prominent American journalist and writer courageously gave shelter and assistance to numerous persecuted persons.

The coincidental fact that my birthplace had been in Alsace-Lorraine brought me under the French quota for immigration to the United States, and probably saved my life. This quota, unlike the German, was not filled up. While I therefore could be admitted immediately, my wife and child were not allowed by the American government to accompany me, since they came under the German quota. The necessity of separating from my family was the most bitter aspect of my emigration; it was quite uncertain whether we would ever be reunited. Still, my wife and daughter were not in immediate danger, and we had no alternative. I was advised by the consul that I could claim them on a preference quota as soon as I was able to support them in the United States.

My last weeks in Germany were full of harassment and anxiety. The Nazi bureaucratic agencies viciously delayed my departure and charged me all kinds of fees for the various permits I needed. When, in March 1939, I was finally ready to leave, the German army threatened to invade the remainder of Czechoslovakia. Expecting Allied counteraction, I reckoned with the beginning of another world war and a ban on emigration or complete stoppage of transportation to the United States. Chamberlain's appeasement policy still prevailed, however, and nothing happened from the allied side against the rape of that country. After a most painful farewell from my beloved ones, I could sail to the land of the free. I had to leave my golden watch behind, and was allowed to take with me only my wedding ring and ten marks, at that time about four dollars.

On the New York pier I was amicably welcomed by Dr. Alfred Cohn, an old Berlin friend, and his family. He had been wise enough to leave Germany early in 1933, and was now established as a physician. I was thankful for their taking care of the helpless refugee for one week in the fantastic metropolis.

Fortunately, I had close relatives in Brookline, Massachusetts. The widow of the well-known Harvard psychologist, Hugo Munsterberg, was the sister of my father. It was in her home that I enjoyed the loving hospitality of this aunt and her two talented daughters during the first difficult weeks in my new country. I realized soon, however, that to remain in this warm nest would not help my necessary adjustment to life in the United States, inasmuch as the three ladies spoke to me only in German. I was, of course, unable to find any job despite my desperate efforts. Still, time was cruelly of the essence if I wanted to get my family out of Germany while this was still possible. I was deeply worried and felt that only a miracle could help me.

The miracle happened. While looking for some modest employment in Cambridge, I met an exceptionally warm-hearted lady with a deep understanding for human suffering. Mrs. Justine F. Kershaw, daughter of Henry O. Houghton, co-founder of the Houghton Mifflin Publishing Company, invited me to be her guest in her beautiful summer residence of Merrywood in Marlborough, New Hampshire. In this genuinely American environment I spent half a year, from May to November, initially with no other duties than to learn English. This task was facilitated by the sociable disposition of the hostess, whose mansion was usually filled with interesting guests, all of them Americans. I spent part of my nights trying to acquire an English vocabulary, studying the *New York Times*, and after three months Mrs. Kershaw accepted my offer to reorganize the library at her estate. It consisted of many thousands of Houghton Mifflin books, and was accessible to the public. She also dictated her business letters to me. Thus I could now claim to have a job as librarian and private secretary of the lady, who supported my application for the entry of my family by a generous affidavit. While this request was processed, World War II broke out in September and weeks of great anxiety followed. Miraculously again, Charlotte and Ellen managed to board the last Italian ship that sailed from Genoa to the United States before Mussolini joined Hitler as belligerent. In December I could take them into my arms at the port of New York.

We settled in Cambridge and I found a modest job as a teacher of German at the Berlitz School in Boston. From October 1940 to April 1944 I worked in various positions at Harvard University, where I had been sponsored by Professor Carl Joachim Friedrich, the prominent political scientist. As resident consultant in the Graduate School of Public Administration, I did research and lectured on comparative government; as research assistant at the Bureau of International Research I concentrated on studies of the German civil service; and after World War II had started, I was instructor at the School for Overseas Administration, teaching enlisted men and officers German institutions in preparation for the occupation of Germany. In April 1944 I entered Federal Government service with the Foreign Economic Administration in Washington, D.C., where I assisted in studies on Germany and France. I wrote several civil affairs guides, handbooks, and other papers, some of which were published for the use of the forthcoming military occupation of Germany. My wife was admitted to the Harvard School of Education as a graduate student and received her degree as Master of Education in 1943. She accepted a job as a teacher at the high school in South Weymouth, Massachusetts.

At the beginning of 1945 both of us obtained the eagerly desired citizenship of our adopted country. This legally sanctioned the breach with the past we had factually already made long since.

This summary may suffice to give a picture in a nutshell of my background, so that I can now begin to tell the story of my Japanese adventure.

◇◇◇

CHAPTER ONE

Assignment to Japan

After V-J Day, the Foreign Economic Administration, having been a war agency, was dissolved, and we employees were temporarily transferred to the Department of State. Its personnel officer did not appear to have any interest in my German experience and I myself was fed up with German problems. Hence, I was delighted to be approached with the question of whether I would accept an assignment to Japan to serve in General MacArthur's Tokyo Headquarters, which ran the occupation of the defeated country. The prospect of getting away from the German past, of experiencing a different people and civilization, and of being able, perhaps, to help free Japanese society from some of the evils that had brought about militarist and authoritarian rule, appeared to me as a challenging opportunity. After discussing the offer with my wife, who was realistic rather than enthusiastic about it, I declared my willingness to accept the job.

Now the processing in the War Department started, and for at least two weeks I had to engage in the physical exercise of stamping the corridors of the labyrinth called Pentagon. After personal and medical checks had been completed, I was received by the colonel in charge of recruiting persons for the Japanese theater. He told me that I was to join the political unit, called Government Section, of the Tokyo General Headquarters (GHQ). He described to me the conditions under which I was to live, and painted a much rosier picture than the actual situation warranted. Among other things, he said I would be billeted in the first-class Imperial Hotel in Tokyo. He regretted that the "dependents" could not join the group assigned to Japan for the time being, but he expected housing for families to be finished in three months. I was to start in a P–5 position, corresponding to a major's rank.

As it turned out, only generals, full colonels in leading positions, and civilian VIPs enjoyed the accommodations of the Imperial Hotel, and my initial experiences with housing in Tokyo were not very encouraging. It also did not take three months, but a year and a quarter until my family was allowed to join me. Some of my colleagues who were processed by the same officer were exposed to similar optimism, and jokingly, we later used to call him "the world's greatest liar." Still, his motives may have been quite charitable. If I had known that the separation from my wife and child would last that long, I might possibly have withdrawn my acceptance of the offer, and I would have missed the best opportunity of my professional life.

I remember my interview with this man for another reason. When he did not give me any information on what I was supposed to do in Japan, I volunteered the confession that, although I had some familiarity with European affairs, I did not have any knowledge of things Japanese. As a matter of fact, this ignorance had bothered me since I had been recruited. "Oh, that is quite all right," the colonel answered. "If you knew too much about Japan, you might be prejudiced. We do not like old Japan hands!" I was somewhat baffled to observe the same phenomenon here as I had in the Department of State: here they wanted me because I did not know anything, and in State they were disinterested in my German background because I knew too much. Subsequently, when in Japan, I understood what the colonel had in mind. From the point of view of the military occupant, the democratizing program required reformers eager to build up something new. The old Japan hand, familiar with and often fond of the nation's past and tradition, was inherently more conservative and, to some extent, skeptical toward the reforming zeal of the occupation officials. It was for that reason that I subsequently found the old Japan hand an extremely useful counterpoise to the democratizing pioneer in myself as well as in others.

I still did not know what kind of work I would have to do in Japan, and did not have the slightest notion that my German legal background might qualify me for understanding the Japanese law, which was based on the Continental, and especially German, legal system. As I found out later, my transfer to Japan resulted from the Tokyo Headquarters' request to the Pentagon for a person of Continental, if possible German, juridical experience.

My departure was scheduled for the end of January 1946. Its worst aspect was the separation from my family. Again, there were to be thousands of miles between us, this time the Pacific Ocean—although I knew my wife and child were safe, in good hands, and could reasonably hope to be reunited with them soon, a situation quite different from the time when the Atlantic separated us. Nevertheless, there is always something foreboding in these goodbye scenes at railway stations, piers, or airports, a sudden moment of anxious thought lest one may never see his dear ones again. I was able to spend Christmas in Cambridge and say farewell to Mrs. Kershaw, whose age and condition justified some anxiety, and to my daughter, Ellen, now a senior in high school. Then my wife accompanied me back to Washington, and we enjoyed a few days together before she had to return on New Year's Eve to teach school on January 2nd. I accompanied her to Union Station, and when the waving goodbye had ended, I stood there, feeling utterly lonely and a little confused, but fully aware that a new chapter in my life had begun.

On one of the last days of January, I left the capital on a military airplane. At this time, after the war, there was a shortage of aircraft, and many of those available were de-

fective. Although I had priority 2, I was stranded in Honolulu for two weeks after landing on Hickam Field. I was
lucky enough to suffer this forced delay in one of the love-
liest places in the world. It was something like an interlude
between two worlds.

Finally, the flight went on. Shortly before Wake Island,
in the middle of the night, the pilot told us that one engine
no longer functioned and that we must stop there for re-
pairs. We stayed for hours in a primitive waiting room,
where coffee was served, and were relieved when we could
board the plane again. The takeoff seemed to be quite
regular, but when, after twenty minutes, I looked down, I
still saw the lights of Wake Island. We must have circled
above it all the time. We were not too happy when the
pilot reappeared and said: "We have the same engine
trouble again and must return!"

When we got out, it was two A.M. and pitch dark. I fell
over an iron bar and injured my foot so that I could not
walk. Wake Island had no housing, and I was carried into a
tent, where I lay alone, while my foot swelled painfully. It
was anything but pleasant, inasmuch as the tropical sun hit
me at six or seven o'clock in the morning and the heat became unbearable in the tent. What a letdown after I had
begun this trip in such an adventurous spirit! These morning hours seemed endless, but finally a jeep arrived and
carried me through the desert. Suddenly a real, small, and
newly built house emerged—the dispensary, where I was
dumped. A smiling medical captain stood in front of it and
welcomed me with real affection. "Congratulations," he
exclaimed, "I greet you as the first patient in our new dispensary!" I answered that I appreciated the honor, but that
my main concern was to get away from the island as soon
as possible and to continue my flight to Tokyo. After he
examined my foot he said that he could enable me to walk,
at least temporarily, if he gave me five injections with novo-
caine, after which I would have to use my foot for at least
two hours. I accepted this attractive offer and after the in-

jections were made with the cheerful aggressiveness of a
dentist, I began to pace the floor of the room up and down,
up and down, for two hours in the grisly heat, to which I
had not become accustomed even during a Washington
summer. It was a rude therapy, but it helped me to walk a
little, and in the late afternoon I was carried up the steps
of an airplane, direction Tokyo. When we took off, I did not
foresee that several years later I would have to land again
on Wake Island because of engine troubles. The flight to
Tokyo went off smoothly, and at dawn the contours of the
four Japanese islands became visible. Although my foot was
damaged, I felt a sanguine expectation of the new world
that awaited me in this third continent into which Providence and the Pentagon had sent me.

◇◇◇

CHAPTER TWO

Arrival in Tokyo

I had been among a group of men, some of whom were to join other sections of the headquarters. Future colleagues of mine in the Government Section were Andrew J. Grajdanzev and John W. Masland. Both were assigned to the Local Government Branch. Grajdanzev turned out to be a fanatic of decentralization and home rule. As a human being, he was a pleasant combination of kindness and intellectual sophistication. Masland, who was in Tokyo for only a short time, had nothing of Grajdanzev's lively temperament. He was a very balanced and knowledgeable scholar, somewhat withdrawn. He returned to his professorship at Dartmouth College, where he advanced to the position of provost. Since he was one of the most learned members of the Section, it is to be regretted that because of his brief participation in it, and because of his unassuming personality, no more use had been made of him. I visited him in 1961 in Hanover, New Hampshire, and was saddened to learn a few years later that he had died suddenly while traveling in India.

John M. Maki joined headquarters at about the same time as we did. Initially, he worked in the same branch as I did. Of Japanese descent, he had been adopted in childhood by an American couple, and could not have been more American in his attitude and mannerisms. He, too, resumed his academic career after a relatively short time, taught at the University of Washington in Seattle, and became vice dean of the College of Letters, University of Massachusetts.

His literary contributions to the political and legal history of contemporary Japan are invaluable, although I have sometimes felt that he is perhaps a little too much of a panegyrist of the Occupation. While beginning to tell the story of my work in Japan, I am deeply conscious of the temptation to yield to this danger out of loyalty to the group of which I am proud to have been a member.

Our navy plane landed on the main naval base of Yokosuka, whence we were taken in an army plane to Yokohama. There we were loaded into an open truck for transportation to Tokyo. On our way we experienced for the first time the horrible sights of aerial war destruction. Hardly anything but ruins had been left of the once flourishing harbor city of Yokohama. There was a deathlike silence, and the air was filled with a fine light rubble dust, which stained our clothes.

We were glad when we reached Tokyo, where the destruction was bad enough, too, but where at least some parts of the city had been spared in anticipation of the Allied occupation. This was evidently true of the area along the Imperial moat, where the impressive Dai Ichi Sogo building was located. Previously occupied by a giant insurance company, it now served as the seat of the General Headquarters (GHQ) under the American general with the title of Supreme Commander for the Allied Powers, abbreviated SCAP. This establishment, also named SCAP, was a microcosm in itself, born quite suddenly in the middle of an alien world. It had all the ingredients of a huge bureaucracy, with ambitious chiefs who were sometimes rivals for the favor of the top man. While in theory representing the Allied victors, the headquarters was in actuality almost completely American. It consisted of two main parts: first, the typical American general staff organization with its four G's (the Personnel, Intelligence, Operations, and Supply and Logistics Sections), an adjutant general, a judge advocate, and so forth; and second, a number of special "Sections," each of them responsible for a distinctive element of Occupation policy. In the approximate order of their importance, they were as follows: Government Section (GS), the political unit; Civil Information and Education (CI&E); Economic and Scientific (ESS); Legal (LS); Public Health and Welfare (PH&WS); Natural Resources (NRS); Diplomatic (DS); Civil Transportation (CTS); Civil Communication (CCS); Civil Property Custodian (CPC); Civilian Personnel (CPS); and Statistics and Report (SRS). There were also a number of service units, such as the Special Service Section and the Troup Information Section. The Sections were subdivided into divisions, and the divisions were usually further broken down into branches.

On February 23, 1946, I entered the 6th floor of the Dai Ichi building, where the Government Section was installed. I was welcomed with great warmth and cheer by Colonel Charles L. Kades, who was the most forceful official of the Section. In the daily routine of work we had to deal principally with him as superior.

The organization of the Section underwent repeated changes.[1] It was headed by brigadier, subsequently major general, Courtney Whitney. At my arrival it consisted of two divisions, a Korean and a Japanese; Kades was the chief of the latter. The Korean Division was later detached, which left only Japanese affairs in the jurisdiction of the Government Section. The units previously called branches under Kades' Public Administration Division then became divisions, and Kades was made deputy chief of the Section. Besides being a dynamic reformer, he had a delightful sense of humor. He may not have expected much of the badly limping fellow who reported to duty. As he told me later, an officer who witnessed my ordeal on the trip to Tokyo had characterized me as a nice guy, but expressed doubts about my usefulness by saying that I was accident prone.

[1] The most important ones took place before the summer of 1948 and are described in *Political Reorientation of Japan, September 1945 to September 1948*, Report of Government Section, Supreme Commander for the Allied Powers (Washington, D.C.: Government Printing Office, n.d.), II, 790ff. Cited hereafter as *Political Reorientation.*

2. Colonel Charles L. Kades, holding the draft prepared in the Government Section of a new Japanese Constitution.

It so happened that my start in Government Section
coincided with the most dramatic period of that institution,
when its members had just completed, in strict seclusion
and secrecy, the draft of a revised Japanese constitution
after it had become "evident that the Japanese Government
needed guidance and assistance to produce a document that
would embody the essentials of democratic government."[2]
I did not take part in this adventurous and amazing performance, which actually amounted to the writing of a new
basic charter within an unbelievably short time by a group
of pragmatic activists, none of whom was a well-known
constitutional scholar. The condition of my foot had wors-
ened to a degree that I had to be dispatched to a hospital,
where I spent my first ten days in Tokyo. I was still in bed
when a messenger from headquarters brought me a draft of
the document with a request for my comments. I made a
few suggestions and offered some criticism, but that was my
only contribution to the remarkable instrument of guidance
that was adopted by the Japanese government, initiated as
constitutional amendment by the Emperor, with few
changes enacted by the Diet (the Japanese Parliament), and
promulgated on November 3, 1946. It has survived until the
present day. Not one change has been made, in spite of the
criticism that it was imposed by the foreign victor and that
its Jeffersonian language and its individualistic as well as
egalitarian principles were alien to the tradition of Japan
and the mainstream of popular Japanese attitudes.

When, after my discharge from the hospital, I joined the
headquarters, the climax of the drama of constitution-
making was over and, together with other newcomers, I was
introduced to the chief of the Section, General Whitney. A
vigorously built person, whose facial expression appeared to
be a mixture of bonhomie, toughness, and shrewdness, he
emanated strength and self-confidence. His welcoming words
were characteristic of the man who, like a medieval knight

2 *Ibid.*, p. 790.

or samurai, had devoted his life to serving his Lord, Mac-
Arthur. He used the same lofty, if not bombastic, language
of which the latter was a master. His remarks also reflected
the constant awareness that MacArthur was a man of destiny
whom history had marked for great achievements.[3] Whitney
said: "I welcome you to Government Section and I con-
gratulate you on the unique opportunity destiny has given
you. While others can observe historical events, you will
take part in the making of history!" I was not yet accustomed to this grandiloquence, but retrospectively I must
admit that he was absolutely right and, to continue in the
same style, I am grateful to Providence for my part in it.

[3] This is evident also in Whitney's book: *MacArthur's Rendezvous
with History* (New York: Alfred A. Knopf, Inc., 1956).

◇◇◇

CHAPTER THREE

Personalities and Objectives

We, the newcomers, were not introduced to the Supreme
Commander himself. He remained aloof. Maybe we were
too small fry initially, but even after I had become division
chief with important responsibilities, I had little opportunity to deal with him personally. He was not the type
who, as Bobby Kennedy did after his appointment as attorney general, would walk through the office rooms and
have a few kind words for every employee down to the last
typist; and he would never invite his underlings to social
parties and receptions in the spacious former American
embassy building, his residence, as his successor, General
Ridgway, did. In the beginning of the Occupation, when
the Japanese people were suffering from cold and starvation,
such gatherings would have been in bad taste, but there was
nothing of this even after five years. He never even personally enlightened us as a group on his ideas and policies.
His official contacts, strictly in adherence to military usage,
were essentially limited to the chiefs of staff and, more
importantly, to the section chiefs, who were, to begin with,
military men, mostly generals, though not all of the regular
army.

The strange thing, however, was that the aura of admiration for the SCAP within headquarters was so infectious
that we did not mind all this, but interpreted it as the
rightful privilege of a great personality who has his own
determined way. It was more than a nimbus, since we came

to conclude, from our own indirect experience, that he was equipped with unusually statesmanlike qualities. He was certainly the right man to be leader of the Occupation of Japan, in which he had to be superior to the god-like Emperor. It was just his aristocratic aloofness[1] and his somewhat histrionic grandeur, reminding one of a Spanish nobleman, that caused his charismatic popularity with the Japanese people. Some of his qualities were definitely not typically American, but exactly those that made him controversial in certain quarters of the United States appealed to the Japanese. They admired his authoritative firmness and his sense of drama, in which they themselves were to play their part. Since he never traveled in the country, never vacationed in one of the beautiful sea or mountain resorts of Japan, but only moved from office to residence and vice versa, one may ask what his sources were for his knowledge and understanding of the Japanese nation. One explanation could be that he very frequently received knowledgeable visitors from outside the office, who provided him with information, although it was common knowledge that in these interviews he usually did most of the talking. Still, I, myself, have heard from one of them that he was surprised by the detailed knowledge of the general, who was blessed with an excellent memory. The same person had been very skeptical about the feasibility of democratization through military occupation under a general. After his interview, I found him deeply under the spell of MacArthur's personal charm. The visitor was the outstanding fighter for civil liberties, Roger Baldwin, whom the general had asked to help the Japanese in establishing their own Civil Liberties Union.

I may point out another phenomenon, namely, that the general, who personally was a Republican with a strong family tradition of conservatism, carried out his task of democratizing the Japanese nation with a fervor and in-

---

[1] The following witty comparison of the General with Mount Fuji has been ascribed to an American correspondent in Tokyo: "When the weather is clear, you can see MacArthur."

tensity that might have been expected only of an ardent libertarian.

I was fascinated when I read that none other than President Kennedy, a man of quite different temperament, became enchanted by the personality of MacArthur, with whom he interchanged visits as late as 1961, when the general was already eighty-one years old, and that to his great surprise he found that MacArthur was much more than a military man. It appears to me characteristic of the flexibility of the old fighter that he acted as an early Vietnam "dove."[2]

The fact remains that in the heyday of democratization, SCAP's reforms were criticized as radical by American conservative and reactionary groups, which, avoiding censure of the general himself, blamed the "excesses" on his

[2] Kenneth P. O'Donnell and David F. Powers in *Johnny, We Hardly Knew Ye* (Boston: Little, Brown and Co., 1970/72), p. 14 report as follows: "Like a lot of Navy veterans of the Pacific war, Kennedy had assumed that MacArthur was a stuffy and pompous egocentric. Instead, the President told us later, MacArthur was one of the most fascinating conversationalists he had ever met, politically shrewd and intellectually sharp. Later the President invited the general to the White House for lunch. They talked for almost three hours, ruining the whole appointments schedule for that day. I could not drag them apart. The President later gave us a complete rerun of MacArthur's remarks, expressing a warm admiration for this supposedly reactionary old soldier that astonished all of us. MacArthur was extremely critical of the military advice that the President had been getting from the Pentagon, blaming the military leaders of the previous 10 years who, he said, had advanced the wrong younger officers. 'You were lucky to have that mistake happen in Cuba, where the strategic cost was not too great,' he said about the Bay of Pigs. MacArthur implored the President to avoid a military build-up in Vietnam, or any other part of the Asian mainland, because he felt that the domino theory was ridiculous in a nuclear age. MacArthur went on to point out that there were domestic problems—the urban crisis, the ghettos, the economy—that should have far more priority than Vietnam. Kennedy came out of the meeting somewhat stunned. That a man like MacArthur should give him such unmilitary advice impressed him enormously." Although Majority Leader Senator Mansfield gave Kennedy the same warning, the politician in the President gained the upper hand over the statesman. According to the authors, he decided: "But I can't do it [liquidate Vietnam] until 1965—after I am reelected!" (p. 15).

civilian staff of "liberals," "New Dealers," or worse. Though eager to bring about a thorough transformation of Japanese society, MacArthur at no time treated the defeated nation with punitive vengefulness or acted as the triumphant victor.[3] This is one of the reasons why Prime Minister Yoshida Shigeru in his memoirs[4] has only praise and admiration for SCAP personally. He is less complimentary with regard to Government Section, which had the often unpleasant task of implementing SCAP's directives.

It was perhaps inevitable that a personality cult developed among MacArthur's top officials, several of them old friends from Philippine days—the "Bataan Crowd"—if the brilliance of his mind is considered together with his autocratic self-assurance, which demanded loyalty and compliance rather than argument and dissension. The far-reaching independence from Washington controls, which MacArthur claimed and actually enjoyed, and his success in staving off interference by other Allied nations, could very well have strengthened in him the feeling of his own infallibility, which his Tokyo environment so dangerously promoted. If so, the seed of the tragic conflict between him and President Truman, which ended his splendid career, is easily recognizable.

The details of the jurisdiction of Government Section including the functions of its various subunits, are spelled out in the various General Orders of the Chief of Staff cited in *Political Reorientation*.[5] The formulation of the Section's functions could hardly have been more apt to extensive interpretation; one may read, for example, the item: "make recommendations for the elimination of the feudal and totalitarian practices which tend to prevent government by the people." The choice of the title for the Section's history is illuminating; it was, indeed, the agency in charge of

[3] His address on the "Missouri" on the occasion of the signing of the Armistice signifies his "finest hour."

[4] See the *Yoshida Memoirs* (Boston: Houghton Mifflin Co. and Cambridge, Mass.: Riverside Press, 1962).

[5] See *Political Reorientation*, ii, 796, 797, 798, 801.

Japan's political reorientation, which included demilitarization, physical and psychological; the purge of undesirable
elements; governmental structure and functions; and most
other aspects of Japanese society, with the exception of
education and information, public health and welfare, agriculture and land reform, and economic matters other than
the relationship between government and business. The fact
that General Whitney was the closest and most trusted aid
to General MacArthur, which resulted in much jealousy on
the part of other chiefs—particularly of Major General
Willoughby, head of G–2—worked in favor of enlarging the
responsibilities of Government Section and of enhancing its
influence. In the staff memoranda the reform of the legal
system of Japan was even not listed. In the initial General
Order of October 2, 1945, the enactment of a new Constitution, which made a comprehensive revision of the law of
the land imperative, was, of course, not yet foreseen; but
even the General Order of February 13, 1947, which replaced it, mentions neither the Constitution, which had
already been promulgated on November 3, 1946, nor the
task of implementing its principles in the law of the land.

I was assigned to the Governmental Powers Branch,
headed by Commander Alfred R. Hussey, Jr. A memorandum of Colonel Kades, dated February 1, 1946, shortly
before my arrival, lists among the responsibilities of that
branch in paragraph 6 under item b, "the abrogation of
laws prejudicial to the achievement of occupation policies,"
and in item d, "the control of criminal and civil courts and
removal and replacement of unacceptable court personnel
and procurators."[6] As can be seen, the approach was still
predominantly negative, and the necessity of comprehensive
new legislation not fully realized. Apart from the removal
of judges and procurators, which became the task of the
Purge Division, the need to abrogate laws was visualized,
but not the need to guide the Japanese government and
recommend new enactments to liberalize the basic codes of

[6] *Ibid.*, p. 804.

law. Anyway, the cited activities were those with which I had to deal initially.

Hussey, my direct superior, was in civilian life a lawyer from Massachusetts, who wore his navy uniform with pride. He had an able legal mind and an excellent style in writing, but I found his approach toward the Japanese too authoritative and even a little bossy. Trained and experienced in Anglo-Saxon law, he lacked understanding of the Continental and Japanese legal systems, and it was obviously here that my contribution was to come in. My relations to Hussey were correct, but of rather an official nature. There was never between us the easy informality, the warmth of understanding, and the mutual enjoyment of a good laugh, that prevailed with the deputy of the Section, Charles Kades, whom most of us called "Chuck."

Of the other members of the Governmental Powers Branch, later Division, which saw repeated changes in personnel, I have already mentioned John Maki. There was also Dr. Cyrus Peake, a scholar and progressive thinker as well as a kind human being, with whom I soon became friends, and who proved helpful to me in the beginning of my work. He subsequently was, for a considerable period, the head of the Research Division in the Department of State, and later taught at a California university. I must also not omit Dr. Harry Emerson Wildes, a former journalist and "old Japan hand" with much knowledge of Japanese psychology. While not fully fitting into a bureaucratic organization, he was often a valuable source of information; his unorthodox and critical mind is also evident in his amusing but too negative book, *Typhoon in Tokyo*.[7] I always found his company stimulating.

Some professional women belonged to the branch. One was Dr. Eleanor M. Hadley, an economist. An able, dedicated, and imaginative worker, she specialized in the deconcentration of industry and trade, and particularly in the dissolution of the *zaibatsu*, the powerful combines that

[7] New York: Macmillan Co., 1954.

dominated the pre-Occupation economy of Japan. After she left Tokyo, she taught for some time at Smith College, and has published a scholarly book on her favorite subject.[8] In the later stage of her service in the Section, she worked closely with Thomas A. Bisson, special advisor to General Whitney. I liked him and considered him a strong personality of great intellectual integrity and idealism. He got into McCarthyite troubles, from which he suffered for a cruelly long time, although General MacArthur had supported him wholeheartedly. Both Bisson and Hadley provoked the displeasure and strong criticism of Prime Minister Yoshida on account of their uncompromising policies of economic deconcentration.[9]

I have a lively memory of Bisson's arrival in Tokyo because he came with Kenneth Colegrove, professor of political science at Northwestern University. No more different fellow travelers could be imagined, as far as *Weltanschauung* and political stance were concerned. Bisson became one of the more militant members of the Section, fully convinced that Japan as a patient needed serious surgery if her democratization was to succeed. Colegrove, on the other hand, approached the problems with scholarly caution, being basically a very conservative thinker, and, as I subsequently learned, radical rightist politician, without reformatory zeal. It was probably for this reason that not too much use was made of his expert advice. The trend was unmistakably toward more thorough reform. Colegrove joined the headquarters after the work on the new Constitution had been completed. I respected his erudition and found him personally pleasant.

When I arrived in Tokyo, most important personalities in the Government Section were in uniform, but not professional officers. As pointed out in *Political Reorientation*,[10] they held either temporary or reserve commissions, and their

[8] *Antitrust in Japan* (Princeton: Princeton University Press, 1970).
[9] See Yoshida's *Memoirs*, p. 154.
[10] See *Political Reorientation*, II, 793.

civilian backgrounds were truly varied. The law was represented, apart from General Whitney, by Kades, Hussey, and the intelligent and friendly Lieutenant Colonel Frank E. Hays, Kades' deputy and subsequently special advisor to the chief of the Section, all of them attorneys. Lieutenant Colonel Mile E. Rowell, my predecessor as judicial affairs officer, whom I never met, was also a lawyer. Captain Frank Rizzo, the clearheaded and soberminded head of the Opinions Branch, who, after occupying different positions of growing influence, succeeded Whitney as Section chief, was an investment banker. After the end of the Occupation, he remained in Japan, prominently engaged in inspection and testing business. He is the only member of the Government Section who has been awarded a high class Order by the Japanese Emperor.

Commander Guy J. Swope, head of the Legislative and Liaison Branch, subsequently chief of the National Government Division and of the Political Affairs Division, was a Pennsylvanian New Deal politician, who served one term (1938–1940) as Democratic member of Congress, and became governor of Puerto Rico. He also participated in the military government on Saipan and lectured at the Navy School of Military Government in Princeton, New Jersey. With that background he brought great political experience into his work, and he was also fortunate enough to benefit in his desk work from the help of two associates of a very different type of efficiency: young Lieutenant Milton J. Esman, a promising analytic-minded and thoroughgoing civil servant of refreshing candor, and Captain Justin Williams, who later took over from Swope the responsibility for the Diet and became chief of the Legislative Branch, and subsequently of the Parliamentary and Political Division. Dr. Williams had taught history and political science in the State College at River Falls, Wisconsin, where he headed the Social Science Department from 1931 to 1942, then joined the army and, after thorough training as well as teaching in various military government schools, joined the

Japan headquarters in October 1945. As one of the most
durable members of the Government Section, he continued
serving there until the end of the Occupation. He was not
only academically well prepared for his work of dealing
with the Japanese parliamentarians and functioning as the
clearing station for the submission to the Diet of legislative
bills (whether originating in the Japanese government or in
one of the SCAP Sections); he also qualified particularly
well for the job because of his flexible, diplomatic, and
sociable nature. He certainly belonged to those occupationnaires who worked with the Japanese and did not "kick
them around." He was always concerned with the independence of the Diet, and saw to it that its monopoly of
law-making would not be impaired to a greater degree than
important Occupation objectives required. Thus, he protected the legislative process from unnecessary interference
from other Sections or from his colleagues in Government
Section, as well as from the executive branch of the Japanese government. I shall have more to say about him when
describing my experiences in the post-Occupation period,
when our ways crossed again. Williams greatly benefited
from the work of his branch chief, Miss Helen Loeb, a pains-
taking and unusually perceptive analyst.

I have dwelt on Justin Williams at some length because
his division, as will be explained later, was the one with
which I had to deal most frequently. I am not prepared to
comment in any detail on some of the other leading personalities of the Section. Thus, I do not know enough of
Lieutenant Colonel Pieter K. Roest, chief of the early
Political Parties Branch, except that I remember him as
extremely liberal from the short time I knew him. Still, it is
my impression that his contribution to the achievements of
the Section was generally not valued as particularly great.
He was also an academician, a Ph.D. from the University of
Chicago in anthropology and sociology, who headed the
Social Science Departments at Reed College (Oregon) and

at the University of Toledo. He also served for some time in the United States Department of Agriculture.

Lieutenant Osborne L. Hauge, the Chief of the Information Management Branch and subsequently of the Public Affairs Division, one of the most likeable characters of the Section, was a college graduate, had been a newspaper editor, a director of publicity and promotion for the National Lutheran Church in New York, and an official of the Norwegian embassy. This background served him well in his assignment, which included information, liaison, and education. In all his functions he showed remarkable skill and enjoyed great popularity. Cecil G. Tilton, chief of the Local Government Branch, later Division, had several academic degrees and taught at the Universities of Hawaii and Connecticut as well as at military government schools. A pioneer of decentralization, he was the most conservative member of the group. Of somewhat excitable temperament, he could perhaps be characterized as occasionally aggressive, but he was by no means incompetent. I cannot say much about Lieutenant Colonel P. Marcum and his work in the Section, except that I have heard praise of his essential contribution to the drafting of the Civil Liberties Directive, SCAPIN 93 of October 4, 1945; nor do I know enough of his civilian background. He was the successor of Swope as chief of the National Government Division, and strongly reform-minded. Last, but not least, I must mention Major, subsequently Lieutenant Colonel and Colonel, Jack Napier, the only division chief who belonged to the regular army. He occupied various positions in Government Section, such as chief administrative and chief executive officer, and headed the divisions in charge of the purge. A self-made man without the educational advantages of others of us, he showed a great talent of adapting quickly, excelled in the field of administration, and brought to the supervision and operation of the purge all the qualities of cleverness and toughness that grim job demanded.

Whitney spent only part of his life as an officer in the regular army, and practiced law in the Philippines, where he became closely associated with General MacArthur. During the war Whitney was detailed by the latter to coordinate and direct the guerrilla organization against the Japanese enemy. According to MacArthur, he was ideal for such an assignment, "rugged and aggressive, fearless and experienced in military affairs."[11]

All the officers mentioned as chiefs, with the exception of Whitney, who remained a general until his resignation in 1951, and Napier, transformed themselves into civilians during the Occupation, after their commissions expired. Their civilian background and their return to that status appear to me significant as an explanation of the not very military spirit in Government Section.

As in most bureaucratic organizations, the important work in the preparation of decisions was done by the middle level in the divisions, and this group consisted mostly of civilians who had been offered their Tokyo jobs by the Department of the Army. This may also be part of the answer to the question raised by Roger Baldwin and other critics of how a military occupation could possibly bring the blessings of democracy to Japan's society. Not that the Section chiefs were figureheads. Some were, indeed; but Whitney was certainly not. Nevertheless, he was largely dependent on the loyalty and efficiency of those who laid the ground for his policymaking. One of the most gratifying aspects of our work was the awareness that we could, likewise, rely on his loyalty and that, if we were criticized in our sensitive work, we would have his full support as well as that of General MacArthur—a man in whom loyalty to those serving him was strongly, perhaps too strongly, developed. Whitney repeatedly expressed his confidence in his staff. Once I copied three sentences of one of his superlative praises. He wrote to another section chief: "I was particu-

[11] Douglas MacArthur, *Reminiscences* (New York: McGraw-Hill, 1964), p. 205.

larly pleased at your reference to the members of the Government Section. There was no finer group, personally or professionally, anywhere at any time. In fact, I have often referred to it as capable of efficiently administering any task under the American flag."

The hyperbole so characteristic of the MacArthur-Whitney style may be disregarded, but the fact remains that, on the whole, it was an able group, considering the haphazard manner of their recruitment. It may not be correct to call it a homogeneous group, since its members' motivations for serving in Japan, as well as their attitudes toward the Japanese people, varied considerably. In none have I discovered hatred, but with respect to the presence or absence of feelings of superiority or compassion there was a great deal of difference. Still, I would say that we had in common a belief in democratic institutions, interpreted within a wide range from a strongly liberal to a cautiously conservative viewpoint, and in the possibility of influencing an alien and completely different civilization. There also was in some of us a good portion of idealism, a term I do not use in the meaning of aloofness from reality.

This may be the proper place for a more detailed explanation of why I particularly devoted myself to my reformatory task in Japan with what I termed before as "missionary zeal." During the monarchical period in Germany, when I was young, I was deeply imbued by the typical German romanticism and, apart from my law study, followed mainly cultural interests, especially literature and music. It was characteristic of the young student generation of that time that political matters were greatly neglected. I now think that this unpolitical attitude, which most members of the higher middle class retained in their adult years, was one of the factors that brought about the various disasters of the German nation. As a matter of fact, in foreign affairs we by and large believed what our government told us. Thus, when I joined the army in 1914 at the age of twenty-one, I was convinced that the German cause was just and that the enemy nations had conspired to refuse us the famous "place in the sun," and to destroy us. In my patriotic ardor I was probably not much different from the Japanese boy combatant of twenty-seven years later, both of us victims of tradition and of the propaganda of our governments.

Years in the trenches gave me ample time to mature. The radical change from a sheltered life to the horrible experiences of the war forced my mind almost automatically into political thinking. I began to question the necessity of that Armageddon and, with the declining prospects of victory, doubts rose in me as to whether ours was the just cause; for I irrationally stuck to the idea that in the end only the just cause could be victorious. It was this belief that during the Nazi period saved me from desperation. The shock of defeat and surrender completed my metamorphosis from a hawk to a dove, as we would say today, and from a rather indifferent supporter of the throne to a republican and democrat. I had arrived at the conclusion that a parliamentary democracy with a reasonable separation of power and a system of checks and balances constituted the least imperfect form of government, in which the rule of law is best guaranteed.

The Weimar Republic, having failed at the end, is today subject to often unfair criticism. It is ignored or forgotten that, while it labored under gigantic adversities, such as communist and rightist upheavals, the restrictions imposed by the Versailles Treaty, and a most ungenerous Allied reparation policy, in no other time of previous German history had a comparable effort toward the achievement of individual liberties been made. There was no lack of men and women who served the cause of democracy with dedication, and I remain proud of having made my modest contribution in my judicial positions. Nevertheless, Weimar collapsed, ignominiously, as it seems. The controversial reasons for the success of Hitler are manifold and utterly complex. I will not attempt to discuss them here. Suffice it to say that the experience of the Nazi regime with its totalitarianism, nationalist paranoia, complete disregard of human rights, persecution and mass extermination of helpless minorities and political dissenters, made me better understand what had been going on in Japan before and during World War II. Quite naturally, the prospect of helping the Japanese in eradicating their milder variety of dictatorship strongly attracted me. In the meantime, the seven years spent after my immigration in the United States, part of it as a federal government employee, had brought me nearer to the American brand of democracy. The excessive capitalism with its corporative concentration of economic power often shocked me, and I have sometimes doubted the wisdom of the presidential system of government, as it developed in the United States. Still, the high political and legal principles upon which the American Constitution was based led to the expectations with which I had sought refuge in the land of the free, and has continued to be an inspiration. This, together with my European background, made a useful combination for my work in Japan.

MacArthur once met the argument that "the highest principles upon which rests our [American] strength and progress are ill fitted to serve the well-being of others," by emphasizing "that the entire human race, irrespective of geographical limitations or cultural tradition, is capable of absorbing, cherishing and defending liberty, tolerance, and justice, and will find maximum strength and progress when so blessed." In the same announcement he made it clear that the pattern of his course in the occupation of Japan lay deeply rooted in American history, and that he had "merely sought to draw therefrom the political, economic, and social concepts which throughout our own past have worked and provided the American people with a spiritual and material strength never before equaled in human history."[12] This was the spirit in which the Supreme Commander interpreted his mission.

[12] See *Political Reorientation*, II, 785.

I feel that his statement needs some qualification. First of all, while liberty, tolerance, and justice are ideals worth fighting and even dying for, the capacity to absorb, cherish, and defend them is not necessarily inherent in the entire human race, but depends upon the degree of development of a given society. The relative success of the Occupation efforts to promote these blessings in Japan has various reasons, the principal of which was the maturity of the Japanese civilization and the fact that we merely pushed forward existing reforming and liberalizing trends that would have effectuated similar results, though at a slower tempo.

The "imposition" of alien concepts and institutions on a completely different nation constitutes, indeed, the main charge with which critics impeach the Occupation. In his defense, MacArthur seemingly makes the same mistake as those critics; both treat the Japanese as completely homogeneous people: one implying that all Japanese, like all human beings, desire individual liberties, the others deploring the democratizing efforts of the Occupation on the ground that the Japanese, due to their ultranationalism and hierarchical tradition, have an aversion to fundamental human rights as extolled by the reformers. Both approaches have in common overgeneralization regarding a nation. I experienced a similar generalization at its worst during and immediately after World War II, when Vansittardism had it that there existed no decent German under the sun. In the case of General MacArthur, the optimism characterizing his statement may, of course, very well have been intended as a pat on the back and encouragement of the Japanese. As a matter of fact, the political attitude and behavior of the ethnically homogeneous Japanese have been much diversified. There were not always and only autocracy, militarism, and expansionism on the part of the rulers and docile submission on the part of the ruled, as even some occupationnaires believed. The victory of the democracies in World War I, and perhaps the example of the Weimar Republic, contributed to promising Japanese trends in the twenties toward a parliamentary government on the British pattern and a generally more liberal orientation.[13] Political parties had developed, which for a long time held their own against the military during the thirties.[14] Secondly, with due respect for the patriotic pride of the general, the exclusive use of the American pattern of democracy was not his wisest idea and has fortunately not been followed through. Still, since almost all occupationnaires were Americans, the danger that they disregarded other nations' democratic institutions was always close. I was soon to have that experience in the field of legal and judicial reforms. In view of the continental basis of the Japanese law, the attitude I sometimes met that what is all right for Ohio, Florida, or California must work out well in Japan was particularly unsound.

I shall subsequently explain why we were careful in introducing Anglo-Saxon concepts into the legal system of Japan. To the extent we did, I felt that we mostly proposed rather than imposed something. My inner justification—you may call it rationalization—of my assigned role as mentor was

[13] Intellectuals and students were strangely attracted by a rather doctrinal Marxism.

[14] The veteran liberals Ozaki Yukio and Saito Takao stand out for their opposition in the Diet to military expansionism. The latter was even expelled as a member following his criticism of the government's China policy. At times, when the young militarists resorted to assassination of dissenters, the advocacy of a moderate as well as of a peaceful course in foreign affairs required heroic courage. Among the victims of the repeated murders were not only parliamentarians, but also members of government, such as Premier Inukai Tsuyoshi, Admiral Saito Makoto (1935), and Finance Minister Takahashi Korekiyo (1935). The venerable Saionji, last *genro* (elder statesman), also on the blacklist of the conspirators, was lucky enough to escape in the February 1926 Incident. Minobe Tatsukichi, prominent professor at Tokyo Imperial University, who already in the twenties had propounded the theory, probably influenced by Hegel, that the Emperor was an organ of the state, was punished in 1935 with expulsion from the university and the House of Peers as a liberal who lacked respect for the imperial institution. Finally, Mrs. Kato Shizue, formerly Baroness Ishimoto, must be included in this honor list as a courageous fighter for women's rights.

that I, with the assistance of my colleagues, helped the progressive men and women of Japan to lay the foundation for
a different and, as they expected, better society. Their positive response was clearly distinguishable from a tactical
attitude of "going along," with mental reservations. In the
process we may have been revolutionaries, but we were not
wholesale destroyers of Japanese traditions, much of which
could be reconciled with what we envisioned. We were well
aware that the outcome could and should never be a replica
of the United States.

The endeavor of Americanization was completely out of
place when it was directed against delightful Japanese
customs that had no connection with any conceivable Occupation mission. I may mention, as an illustration, what I
observed in my billet. It was not the Imperial Hotel, but a
former fashionable clubhouse near the Dai Ichi building. I
shared my room with four young army captains, fine, but
noisy fellows, who disturbed my much-needed sleep. This
slight hardship was, however, compensated by pleasant
aspects of a typically Japanese environment. In the dining
room pretty waitresses in kimonos served our meals, and to
the delight of my musical ear a band played Beethoven,
Mozart, Schumann, Chopin, and Johann Strauss. During a
dinner, while listening to the music, an army officer sitting
at my table said: "Ridiculous that these girls run around in
kimonos; why shouldn't they wear Western style dresses?"
He also suggested that the classical music, which he found
boring, be replaced by a modern dance and jazz program. A
few weeks later his ludicrous ideas materialized: the kimonos disappeared and so did the classical music. The
tunes the Japanese got to hear from our GI radio sender
were not apt to promote their respect for American culture.

◇◇◇

CHAPTER FOUR

The Mechanics of Communications and Commands

The first problem was where to start, and I decided that I must make myself familiar with the organization, functions, and personnel of the Japanese courts, as well as with the status and attitude of the judges. A meeting with the president of the Supreme Court,[1] Hosono Choryo, was arranged in which we talked to each other through interpreters. Very soon I realized that we saw very much eye-to-eye and that this man would be an invaluable source of information for me and an ally in my future reform efforts. I was delighted to see the genuine, almost choleric fervor with which Hosono advocated the independence of the judiciary from the executive branch of the government, the innovation provided in the draft Constitution. I am not so sure whether he was personally democratic enough to treat his associates as though he were *primus inter pares* rather than boss. His temperament was impetuous and his mind uncompromising. With the permission of my superiors I spent several days with him in the countryside near beautiful Hakone Lake, for we had concluded that the atmosphere of the office with

[1] This Court (*Daishinin*) is frequently referred to as Court of Cassation, for example, in John M. Maki's *Court and Constitution in Japan* (Seattle: University of Washington Press, 1964) in order to distinguish it from the more prestigious and independent *Saiko Saibansho*, the Supreme Court established under the new Constitution. In the following I shall use the terms "old" and "new" Supreme Court.

its continuous interruptions hardly lent itself to acquiring the thorough information and informal clues I expected to receive. This was my first contact with the Japanese legal world, and I benefited enormously from his sincere type of communication. I shall always be grateful for Hosono's honesty. Having grasped that basic agreement existed between us on the necessity of liberating the judiciary, he completely discarded the prudent reserve that I was to meet so frequently during my early period of activity in Tokyo when communicating with Japanese government officials, as long as they were uncertain of my opinion on the subject of discussion. On the other hand, I was careful myself to distinguish expression of personal views from useful information.

It is perhaps characteristic that my first contact with the Japanese legal world was made in the most informal manner in strictly personal conversations at a meal or over a cup of tea. Throughout my Tokyo period such semisocial meetings took place innumerable times with Japanese judges, lawyers, professors, and government officials who had become close acquaintances or even friends.[2] There existed, of course, a multiformity of communications between GHQ representatives and the Japanese government. An explanation of the mechanism that developed may be in order.

Most frequently I met representatives of the Ministry of Justice (later Attorney General's Office), judges, and leaders of the bar associations. The initiative for these meetings came either from the Japanese or from me; in the latter case, if I wanted to speak to a government official, I could request his visit formally through the Japanese Liaison Office or just through a phone call by a Japanese-speaking employee of the Section. In the course of time I knew who in the ministry was in charge of a specific problem and could therefore ask for that official personally. The meetings usually took place in my office, but when we wanted to confer with the justices of the Supreme Court, we made it a

2 See Chapter 7 for examples of such personal relationships.

rule to meet them in their own official residence, the Court building.

In Japan most legislation consists of government bills drafted and submitted to the Diet by the cabinet. In many instances these drafts formed the subject of my discussions with ministerial officials.[3] Sometimes we were consulted on a member bill by parliamentarians, as happened in connection with the Habeas Corpus Law.

In important matters an assistant attorney general, accompanied by a whole staff of subordinates, would appear and ask for advice or decision. Other varieties of communications included standing committees, consisting of Japanese and American representatives, such as we used for the deliberation of the Court Organization Law and of the Codes of Civil and Criminal Procedure.[4] Agreements reached in such committees were not binding on the executive branch of the government, but carried with them enough authority to be adopted with little or no change for submission to the Diet. They usually were also approved by the SCAP, inasmuch as whenever his personal interest was assumed, his position was explored in advance.

There were few cases in the field of my responsibilities in which more formal communications on a higher level to the Japanese government were needed.[5] The most severe form of authoritative command was the SCAP Directive, abbreviated SCAPIN, a memorandum to the Japanese government ordering or prohibiting some action. The SCAPINs formed the Occupation law proper, which was supraconstitutional and not subject to any other Japanese law. This type of enactment was amply used in the first period of the Occupation in the fields of demobilization,[6] civil liberties,[7] and purge.[8] Since the system was one of indirect military

[3] Examples of numerous conferences with various officials of the Japanese government are offered in Chapter 11.

[4] See Chapter 7.

[5] This happened in the lese majesty case covered in Chapter 11.

[6] See *Political Reorientation*, II, 454.

[7] *Ibid.*, p. 463.   [8] *Ibid.*, p. 482.

government through the indigenous authorities, such a command had to be transformed into Japanese law. It had been felt undesirable to do so by statute, and thus make the Diet a kind of automaton. Therefore, the SCAP Directive was to be implemented by an imperial ordinance and, after the Constitution came into effect, by a cabinet order "pursuant to the acceptance of the Potsdam Declaration," also briefly called "Potsdam Ordinance."

After the initial Occupation surgery had been completed, a more courteous but no less authoritative command was preferentially used, namely, a "Dear Mr. Prime Minister" letter of General MacArthur.[9] Binding instructions could also be given the Japanese government orally by Section chiefs such as General Whitney, if the American official made it absolutely clear that he spoke for SCAP. In some instances "suggestions" approximating orders were made by General Whitney in a letter to the prime minister.[10]

[9] The absolute supraconstitutional power of SCAP was recognized by a decision of the Supreme Court of Japan of April 4, 1951, on the challenge of the purge of communists, even though this purge had been ordered not by a SCAPIN, but by a letter of General MacArthur to the prime minister. The somewhat ironic phenomenon that the Occupation could violate and sometimes did violate the principles of the very same constitution that it had produced and inspired is one of the contradictions resulting from a military dictatorship that aims at establishing democracy.

[10] For an example, see *ibid.*, p. 734.

◇◇

CHAPTER FIVE

The New Constitution

IMPOSED BY THE VICTOR?

The new Constitution was being deliberated in the Diet in 1946, and under the political circumstances there was no doubt that it would be enacted as the basic law of the land.

One of the most severe American critics of the way the new Constitution was produced, the late Harold S. Quigley, a thoroughgoing and knowledgeable political scientist, ridicules as sophistry "American belief that they [the Japanese] were free to reject a document prepared in the main in Government Section and enthusiastically endorsed by SCAP."[1] He touches on the much-debated question of whether or not the revised charter was "imposed" by SCAP on the Japanese government. My friend, Justin Williams, made an interesting attempt to disprove Quigley's thesis.[2] From a purely legal point of view, Williams is right when he emphasizes that SCAP did not "direct" the recalcitrant Japanese government to enact the Government Section draft, but that he merely made suggestions and gave guidance as to how to write a document complying with the requirements of the Potsdam Declaration. Such guidance was not contrary to SCAP's instructions from his home government and,

---

[1] See Harold S. Quigley and John E. Turner, *The New Japan* (Minneapolis: University of Minnesota Press, 1956), p. 94.

[2] Justin Williams, "Making the Japanese Constitution: A Further Look," *American Political Science Review* 59 (1965), 665–679.

strictly speaking, did not violate the Moscow Agreement by bypassing the newly established policy-making organization of the Allied powers, the Far Eastern Commission. According to the letter of the Moscow Agreement, this commission had to be consulted on "any directives dealing with fundamental changes in the Japanese constitutional structure." Professor Takayanagi Kenzo, chairman of the Cabinet Commission on Constitutional Revision, draws the same fine distinction between directive and suggestion.[3] Still, Quigley's point that in a military occupation this distinction becomes rather dim, is particularly strong when the suggestion, as it was, is followed by high praise of its substance by the Supreme Commander himself and, if not by direct threats, then by hints of the adverse consequences that non-acceptance might have. Commander Hussey, who first revealed the authorship of Government Section in his amazingly candid chapter on the Constitution in *Political Reorientation of Japan*[4] makes it clear that the cabinet, at least, was under pressure to accept the draft. He reports that on February 13, 1946, Whitney, while telling Foreign Minister Yoshida that there was no compulsion upon the cabinet to take further action, added that "failing action by the Cabinet, General MacArthur was prepared to lay the issue before the people himself." Nevertheless, it may be more correct to say that if there was coercion it came from the "international situation" rather than from MacArthur.

The letters of Generals MacArthur and Whitney to Takayanagi, who, with some other members of his commission, visited the United States in 1958 with the purpose of interviewing American participants in the drafting of the "MacArthur Constitution," show that this situation was explained to the Japanese as making speedy and affirmative action on the draft imperative. According to the interview-

[3] See Takayanagi's article, "Making the Japanese Constitution: What Really Happened" in the *Japan Times* of March 16, 1959.
[4] Vol. I, 106.

ers' communications,[5] SCAP was apprehensive about the interference of the Far Eastern Commission, which included Soviet Russia. Whitney states that "General MacArthur at the time was under strong pressure by some of the Allied Governments to pursue a much harsher—even brutal—course in the administration of the Occupation. Some even demanded the trial of the Emperor as a major war criminal." Whitney also observed that "this critical situation was well known to [Prime Minister] Baron Shidehara and Mr. Yoshida, then his Foreign Minister, whose cooperation with the Supreme Commander in his effort to protect the Japanese was magnificent." MacArthur himself wrote that the preservation of the institution of Emperor was his fixed purpose; that it was inherent and integral to Japanese political and cultural survival; and that the vicious efforts to destroy the person of the Emperor became one of the most dangerous menaces that threatened the successful rehabilitation of the nation. In his meeting with Prime Minister Shidehara on February 21, 1946, which Hussey does not mention, MacArthur emphasized his difficulties with the Far Eastern Commission and even expressed doubts whether he could keep his position much longer.[6]

In the light of these subsequent revelations, of which I was innocently unaware in February 1946, MacArthur appears now to have fathered the Constitution of Japan in the strange and complex combination of protector of the throne on the one hand, and reformer on the other hand—in both respects following American, though not necessarily Allied, policies. By playing both roles with remarkable virtuosity, he again showed his genius. The price the Japanese government had to pay for keeping the imperial institution and Emperor Hirohito personally was the acceptance of a far-reaching transformation of the governmental and socio-

[5] *Japan Times*, March 16, 1959.
[6] Theodore McNelly, *Contemporary Government of Japan* (Boston: Houghton Mifflin, 1959/63), p. 42.

political structures as well as of the Tenno (Emperor) to a mere "symbol of the state and the unity of the people." Takayanagi's commission, according to McNelly,[7] recalls that the cabinet was afraid that if it did not accept the SCAP draft, the Far Eastern Commission might force it to adopt a republican constitution abolishing the throne. Whether one might call it a more or less friendly persuasion or imposition by MacArthur, the cabinet was certainly not free in its choice to accept or reject the project. To be more precise, it was virtually out of the question for the Japanese government to respond with the refusal to do anything about a new Constitution. The Japanese could, however, suggest specific changes in one or the other provisions of the Government Section draft,[8] provided that the proposed change did not conflict with paramount political objectives of SCAP, such as the reduction of the role of the Emperor. It was mainly this issue that caused the initial shock to members of the cabinet. Only after the Emperor himself approved of the change did they decide to go along with SCAP. The coercion came from defeat and surrender, and from Japan's acceptance of the Potsdam Declaration, as even Williams implicitly admits.

To be sure, this declaration required that a peacefully inclined and responsible government should be established "in accordance with the freely expressed will of the Japanese people," but to ascertain this will would have been a difficult task. The Diet did not fully reflect it, since it consisted not only of the old House of Representatives—the

[7] *Ibid.*

[8] An example is offered in *The Constitution of Japan, Its First Twenty Years,* edited by Dan Fenno Henderson (Seattle and London: University of Washington Press, 1968), p. 251. The initial draft on property was criticized as having too socialistic a flavor and declared unacceptable by the cabinet which, indeed, obtained a milder version. Takayanagi, "Making the Japanese Constitution," p. 80, emphasizes that Government Section did not expect the Constitution to take the form of its proposals. He adds that Kades even expressed regret that not more amendments had been submitted in the Diet. Takayanagi observes: "The Japanese Government simply chose the easiest way."

new election took place only on April 10, 1946—but also of a Chamber of Peers: aristocrats, high taxpayers, and those with imperial appointment for meritorious services, including scholars. One may also ask the question of whether under a military occupation the Japanese were completely free to express their political will if it ran counter to a project they must have felt was inspired by the new master. Nevertheless, one had only to read the newspapers and speak to the man on the street, with university professors and students—I could do so mainly with the last two groups in English, German, or French—to realize that there were powerful movements among the people of enthusiastic support of Occupation objectives. As pointed out before, some of these movements had existed long before the war, but were repressed and became dormant. Their followers had welcomed MacArthur as liberator. The disaster into which her rulers had thrown Japan made a great number of other people ripe for a revaluation of all values. MacArthur, therefore, had some reason to believe that the majority was in accord with the principles of the new Constitution.[9] There was, however, a great deal of confusion as well as enthusiasm, and that would have made a referendum a questionable means of discovering the will of the people.

We have seen that the cabinet was not free in its reaction to the SCAP draft. Once the decision had been made to accept it, the newly appointed Premier Yoshida and his spokesman, Kanamori Tokujiro, vigorously defended the Occupation-inspired project in the long sessions of both Houses. The Socialist party, which was newly established in the House of Representatives, strongly favored the consti-

[9] Among Japanese scholars this question has, however, remained controversial. More recently, Sugahara Yutaka, characterized as "one of the most prominent figures in our judicial circles" by Saito Chu, in his article "Invalidation of Constitution," *Japan Times*, August 27, 1961, has emphatically maintained that the Constitution was imposed by the dictate of the victor, that it violated the Potsdam Declaration and, by destroying the tradition of Japan, the rules of international law. Apparently, this author calls for the invalidation of the Constitution.

tutional innovations, as was to be expected; but the
government was also supported by a coalition of the Liberal
and Progressive parties. One may, therefore, well doubt that
the members of the conservative parties, who must have
drawn their conclusions from the surprisingly revolutionary
position of their very unrevolutionary leaders, felt free to
abandon them on such momentous issues.

As a matter of fact, a frank discussion of the draft
developed in the House of Peers, where several aspects of
the draft were criticized. The members of the first chamber
made, indeed, a striking use of their right of free expression.
Still, there is quite a difference between criticizing proposed
legislation and voting against it. In the House of Representatives only the five members of the Communist party,
which favored the abolition of the Emperor, voted against
the bill; the number of favorable and unfavorable votes in
the House of Peers was not announced. Its president merely
stated that the required two-thirds majority had adopted
the project. Sato Tatsuo, chief of the Cabinet Bureau of
Legislation, who on the Japanese side got involved in the
drafting of the Constitution, assumes that not more than
four or five members voted against it. He identifies Sawada
Ushimaro as one of them. This former official of the defunct
Ministry of Home Affairs in his speech at the plenary session
said there was little necessity to make haste in adopting the
new Constitution, which, in fact, "is no better than a bor-
rowed suit of clothes, patched in too many places, and,
above all, insufferably misfitting." Sato adds the comment
that these sentiments were presumably more or less entertained by most members of both Houses who voted in favor
of the revision bill, but that they supported it in the belief
the early enactment of this democratic Constitution would
be best calculated to hasten the termination of the Occupation.[10] Sato, whom I have known as an intelligent
observer with a flexible mind, may have been too pessimistic

[10] Sato Tatsuo, "The Origin and Development of the Draft Constitution of Japan," *Contemporary Japan* 24, Nos. 4-6 and 7-9.

in his conjecture, which is apparently more correct if limited to most, but by no means all, members of the House of Peers. This chamber was mainly composed of the pre-Occupation "establishment," as we would say today, although a few liberals had been added more recently.

Kokutai AND HIROHITO

The retention of the Emperor had made the acceptance of the Constitution more palatable to most members of the Diet, but the more conservative ones were deeply worried that his reduction to a mere symbol deprived of governmental power signified the alteration of Japan's "national polity" or *kokutai*, according to which the Empire of Japan shall be reigned and governed by a line unbroken for ages eternal,[11] and which also connotates the deep "spiritual relationship" between the Tenno and his people, whatever this means. The mystical conception of a divine origin of the dynasty is based on the legend that Jimmu, traditionally regarded as Japan's first Emperor of the dynasty,[12] descended from the sun goddess, Amaterasu. The spokesmen of the government, which wanted to have the project enacted, tried hard to maintain that the document was a Japanese creation that did not bring about a break in the *kokutai*. The staunch supporters of the throne remained unconvinced, and they hated to see the Emperor deprived of his high economic powers by the provision of the Constitution according to which all property of the imperial household was to become state property.

In connection with *kokutai,* I was assigned the task of exploring certain problems involved in an amendment of the Meiji Constitution, which in Article 73 provided that "a

[11] Article I of the Meiji Constitution.

[12] G. B. Samson in *Japan, A Short Cultural History* (New York: Appleton-Century Crofts, 1943), observes on p. 28 that the officially accepted date of the foundation of the empire is purely traditional, and that even conservative historians do not uphold this chronology.

project to that effect shall be submitted to the Imperial Diet
by Imperial Order." While the draft Constitution actually
represented a revolutionary substitution for the old Constitution, the desire of SCAP and of the Japanese cabinet to
retain the imperial institution resulted in the policy of
sustaining the fiction of legal continuity. This was best accomplished if the new charter appeared as an amendment
to or revision of the Meiji Constitution. The question arose,
however, whether the power of the Emperor to initiate such
an amendment was unlimited or whether even he was bound
by the *kokutai*. In a memorandum to the Chief, Government
Section, dated August 25, 1946,[13] I concluded that no such
limitation exists, and that even if it should be recognized,
the acceptance of the Potsdam Declaration would have
altered the national polity. The same memorandum dealt
with a second question, namely, whether the Diet has the
right to modify or to supplement the imperial amendment
project or, as most Japanese scholars maintained, had only
the alternative of consenting to it or rejecting it. I arrived at
the conclusion that the Diet had the right to change the
project, and that even if this were denied, revisions by the
Diet made in conflict with the rule would be remedied if
and when the Emperor sanctioned and promulgated the new
Constitution, as revised by the Diet. The actual process of
constitutional change followed that line: the Emperor submitted to the Diet the project of amendment that was to
downgrade him, and the Diet felt free to modify and supplement it, although it made use of this right only to a very
limited extent.

Like several conservative interpellators in the House of
Peers, Professor Quigley believed that the Meiji Constitution was no bar to the attainment of Occupation objectives.[14] With all respect for his opinion, I cannot agree.
Even if the international considerations were disregarded, it

[13] The memorandum is published on pp. 662–666 of *Political Reorientation*, II.
[14] *The New Japan*, p. 94.

would have been irreconcilable with the revolutionary nature of this Occupation to put new wine into the old bottles. I particularly have in mind that the imperial institution in its Meiji version could not have been continued. The question of whether to abolish or modernize and democratize it must clearly be distinguished from that of the retention or removal of Emperor Hirohito as monarch because of his involvement in war and aggression. With regard to the institutional problem, I fully understood the position of those who in 1945 were opposed to any retention of the Tenno system under the ruling dynasty. They were concerned lest the undesirable features of the "Imperial Way" and emperor worship could, if exploited by a revanchist military clique, again breed "*kokutai* nationalism"[15] and the other isms we were eager to eliminate. The United States Initial Post-Surrender Policy for Japan in Part II, paragraph 2, explicitly states that the policy is to use the existing form of government, not to support it, and directs that "changes in the form of government initiated by the Japanese people or government in the direction of modifying its feudal and authoritarian tendencies are to be permitted and favored." The SCAP is also advised that he is not committed to support the Emperor.[16] The monarchy was retained because it accorded clearly with the will of the majority of the Japanese people, because it was likely to spare further bloodshed, and because it made the Occupation much easier. From today's vantage point, and in light of the unexpected response of the Japanese to the Occupation, it was probably a wise decision. Nevertheless, it was imperative that the imperial institution be deprived of its mythical halo and the pretension—unrealistic even in the Meiji era—that all power of government emanated from the Emperor, as the then-existing Constitution proclaimed.

[15] A term used by William P. Woodard, *The Allied Occupation of Japan 1945–1952 and Japanese Religion* (Leiden: E. J. Brill, 1972), p. 62.

[16] See *Political Reorientation*, II, 424.

The new beginning had to be anchored in a basic law that would place sovereignty in the people. There are many precedents in history in which a revolutionary change was followed and translated into legal language by a new Constitution.

The question of the fate of Emperor Hirohito as the monarch was also resolved in favor of continuity. From a purely juridical standpoint it was illogical to subject his generals and statesmen to punishment as war criminals and to spare the man in whose hand was supposed to have been the ultimate decision to enter the war. But apart from the reasons for retaining the Imperial institution as such, which equally appeared to call for keeping the present monarch, Hirohito had, indeed, shown himself amazingly cooperative during the first period of the Occupation. General Mac-Arthur was greatly impressed when the Emperor, in their first meeting, recognized his responsibility for what had happened.

On November 3, 1946, when I attended the solemn meeting of the Diet in which the Emperor promulgated the new Constitution, I saw the small and unassuming figure, and I thought how absurd our war propaganda had been to depict him as a despotic and hostile monster. It was equally difficult to believe in his divine sanctity, a belief that actually did not exist in the sense that the people looked at him as a god, as Western nations understand it. Historians have meanwhile agreed that, although he yielded to his advisors according to Japanese tradition, he did not want his nation to enter the war.[17] He had, however, the courage to overrule the bitter-end protagonists by deciding in favor of Japan's surrender. On New Year's Day, 1946, he called the belief that the Emperor is divine a "false conception." Although this Imperial Rescript may also have been issued under the pressure of the "political circumstances," there is little

17 The lonely opposite view, offered by David Bergamini in *Japan's Imperial Conspiracy* (New York: William Morrow, 1971), can be considered as rejected by knowledgeable scholars.

doubt but that Hirohito was more open to innovation than most of his ministers. He may even have welcomed the constitutional change that deprived him of a power he had possessed only on paper and not in fact.

The Japanese are very reluctant to discuss their Emperor. Thus the impression he made on the one American who had more insight into his attitudes and daily life than any other Westerner gains importance. This was Mrs. Elizabeth Gray Vining, the Crown Prince's tutoress, whom my wife and I met in Tokyo, and who became a dear friend of ours. This prominent Quaker is blessed with a keen mind, and in her numerous writings has shown a deep understanding of human nature. In her autobiography she gives a remarkable description of her life within the Imperial household,[18] and paints Hirohito in colors quite different from the picture of the poor little myopic fellow whose stereotyped reaction in a conversation was: *"so desuka"* (is that so?). It was, of course, known that his scientific achievements were significant, but what Elizabeth Vining emphasized was his natural dignity, his unresentful attitude when suffering humiliation, loss, or impoverishment, and his open mind. While this characterization may seem excessively panegyrical, and will probably be suspected as having been influenced by the friendliness she experienced from the imperial family, we know her well enough to be sure of her ability to draw the line between a detached objective judgment and her personal feelings. Her own role as tutoress proves that the Emperor was accessible to Western ideas, since it was he himself who expressed the wish to have an American teacher for his son, and, strangely enough, a woman. Mrs. Vining, who had frequent contacts with both men, speaks even of a "friendship between the Emperor and the victorious general," characterizing it as "a measure of the magnanimity of both men, but more remarkable in the case of the Emperor."[19] Surprisingly warm feelings for the Emperor were

[18] *Quiet Pilgrimage* (Philadelphia: J. P. Lippincott, 1970), pp. 227ff.
[19] *Ibid.*, p. 245.

also expressed by MacArthur to Mrs. Vining,[20] and may well have been one motivating factor in the general's policy as protector of the imperial institution and of the person of the monarch.[21]

Much later, Hirohito showed unprecedented broadmindedness by approving the marriage of the Crown Prince to a commoner. To me this event, so shockingly contrary to all dynastic ritual of Japan, was a gratifying illumination of how deeply Western ideas, such as those underlying the Constitution, had pervaded the nation.

We have concluded that the necessity of demystifying the imperial institution alone forbade the preservation of the Meiji Constitution. Waiting for a new one until the democratic food had been digested would not have done, either. This is self-evident in the area of fundamental human rights. To carry out the democratization of the codes of law first, and to enact a new Constitution afterwards would have meant to put the cart before the horse. We would still have been dependent upon the Meiji Constitution, which granted most civil rights to the "subjects" only "within the limits of the law." In other words, the legislature could at any time abridge or weaken them. SCAP was directed to establish fundamental rights. As long as no new Constitution existed, he used the instrument of a SCAPIN, as mentioned before, to confer on the Japanese people the blessings of civil liberties. It would, however, have been extremely awkward to continue their imposition by the fiat of the conqueror. Moreover, such SCAP directives might not have survived the Occupation. If, however, the needed reforms had to be legislated under the old Constitution, the Diet would have been free to enact restrictive statutes and to put SCAP into the position of vetoing them piecemeal, a

20 *Ibid.*, p. 252.

21 Woodard, *Allied Occupation*, p. 240, speaks of "the silent partnership of these two men," to which he attributes the unusual success of the Occupation.

most undesirable prospect. Therefore—and this applies to
most of the reform legislation in the field of my responsibility—it was essential to provide the Diet with guiding
principles in the form of a new basic law.

THE SUBSTANCE OF THE CONSTITUTION

The predecessor of the new Constitution, the Meiji Constitution of 1889, was intended to lay the legal foundation
for replacing an anarchic system of divisive feudalism with a
unitary state under the Emperor, restored to political power.
Drafting it involved a thorough search for a Western pattern appropriate to the needs of that Japanese era. It was
not astonishing that the choice made was Germany, which,
under Bismarck's leadership in Prussia, had completed its
unification after three victorious wars, and achieved much
of what the Meiji rulers dreamt of, politically as well as
economically. Prince Ito Hirobumi, who had visited Germany, was, indeed, greatly impressed by the personality of
the "Iron Chancellor." The transition from feudalism to a
constitutional monarchy in Japan could not, under the prevailing circumstances, be of a radical nature; looked at from
today's point of view, it was extremely conservative. Still,
when the Constitution was enacted, the judgment of prominent Western jurists seems to have been that it served its
purpose. The cautious conservatism that motivated its
drafters may well explain the fact that their model was not
the more liberal Constitution of the newly founded German
Reich of 1871, but the Prussian Constitution of 1850.

The Meiji Constitution vests the sovereignty in the
Emperor, from whom, at least in theory, emanate all governmental powers. This concentration in the monarch,
ideologically bolstered by the *kokutai* myth, resulted in an
outspoken executive supremacy over the bicameral legislature and the judiciary, which had no power to rule on the
legality of administrative acts. While one may admit that

when the instrument was enacted it showed progress over the *status quo ante*, it was discredited by the manner in which it had been applied in the thirties.

Inasmuch as I did not participate in the drafting of the postwar Constitution, I can hardly add anything new regarding its substance. Essential parts of it will be considered in connection with the implementing legislation. Suffice it to say here that it is one of the most progressive basic laws of the present time. Because of the nationality of its drafters in the Government Section, the Constitution has an Anglo-Saxon pattern. The retention of the monarchy, combined with representative government and parliamentarism, indicate the British model also evident in the structure of the legislative and executive branches. The American system is chosen, however, in the judicial realm. Set up as an independent third branch of the government, the judiciary is vested with power to review the constitutionality of legislative and administrative acts as well as with rule-making power. This check over the two other branches, in the United States the product of Chief Justice John Marshall's genius, was thus given the Japanese as a gift. It could be the most effective tool for building a true government of law.

The Diet as the legislative branch is declared to be "the highest organ of state power and the sole law-making organ of the state." It is bicameral, consisting of the House of Representatives with a term of four years, and the House of Councillors with a term of six years, half of whose members shall be elected every three years. The former is the more powerful of the two Houses, and in connection with important functions, such as legislation or designation of the prime minister, either it can overrule the latter by a two-thirds majority, or, if no agreement between them can be reached, its decision will prevail.

Executive power is vested in the cabinet headed by the prime minister and, in addition, consisting of other ministers of state. The prime minister is designated by the Diet from among its members. He appoints the ministers, the majority of whom must be chosen from among the members of the Diet. To guard against future political domination by the military, the Constitution requires all members of the cabinet to be civilians. The prime minister may also remove the ministers of state as he chooses; this power to hire and fire gives him a strong position, and somewhat compensates for the arrangement that not he but the cabinet is the chief executive.

The three branches of the government are not rigidly separated, but subject to various checks and balances. The cabinet is responsible to the Diet; more precisely, it must resign if the House of Representatives, and only this House, passes a resolution of no confidence or rejects a resolution of confidence, unless the House is dissolved by the Emperor, acting with approval of the cabinet. The judges of the Supreme Court are subject to popular recall, while the power of impeachment over all judges rests with the Diet. The judiciary, on the other hand, as we have seen, reviews the acts of the two other branches for their constitutionality.

As to the dissolution of the Lower House, a constitutional controversy ensued when, in 1948, Prime Minister Yoshida threatened to suggest to the Emperor the dissolution of the Lower House on the basis of Article 7 of the Constitution, which lists the dissolution among the functions "in matters of state" of the Emperor. The political opposition at that time maintained that the House could only be dissolved in the case of nonconfidence explicitly spelled out in the document, while the government held that this could be done for any other reason. Pursuant to a compromise, the dissolution was actually decreed after a nonconfidence vote.

The dispute was revived in 1951, as a result of public pressure on the government to have the House dissolved and new elections carried out after the coming into effect of the peace treaty. At that time I drafted a comprehensive memorandum, signed and used by the Section chief, in which I concurred in the predominant opinion of Japanese scholars that the dissolution power was not limited to the instance of nonconfidence. Ironically enough, the government, as well as the opposition, reversed their previous positions, which proved that their views were motivated by political rather than constitutional considerations. Eventually, the Yoshida government brought about the dissolution of the House in August 1952. A member of the opposition party appealed to the Supreme Court to invalidate the dissolution, mainly because it was not preceded by a nonconfidence vote. The Supreme Court refused to go into the merit of the claim for formal reasons. It pointed out that, being a purely judicial and not a constitutional court, as exists in West Germany and Austria, it can exercise constitutional review only within the limits necessary for judgment in relation to concrete legal disputes between the parties concerned. Justice Mano Tsuyoshi, in a lonely supplementary opinion, arrived at the unconvincing conclusion that the dissolution power is limited to the instance of nonconfidence.[22]

Under the postwar Constitution, sovereignty is vested in the people from whose will the Emperor derives his position. He is defined as "the symbol of the State and of the unity of the people." "Powers related to government" are explicitly denied him, since he is not the chief executive. What is left to him is the performance of functions in matters of state on behalf of the people, with the advice and approval of the cabinet. The phraseology, with its distinction between acts in matters of state and powers related to government, escapes clear legal analysis. Among the acts in matters of state there are listed convocation of the Diet and its aforementioned dissolution. Nobody could deny that these functions are "related to government." On the other hand, most matters related to government are simultaneously state affairs. Apparently, the prohibition regarding functions related to government is nothing but a corroborative repetition of the principle that the Emperor cannot make any final determination independently, but

[22] See Maki, *Courts and Constitution in Japan*, pp. 366ff.

needs the advice and approval of the cabinet. The inclusive list of the Emperor's acts in the Constitution indicates that the selection was motivated by the need for ceremonial solemnization of certain important decisions. Minister of State Kanamori, as spokesman of the government, referred to "functions which are appropriate of the symbol of the state and which are neither too much nor too little."[23] Anyway, whenever he acts, the real determination has always been made beforehand by the cabinet.

The Constitution emphasizes local government and decentralization, as well as popular voting for the heads of local governments and their assemblies. A chapter entitled "Rights and Duties of the People," which deals mostly with rights, grants an impressive and comprehensive catalogue of civil liberties to "all the people" or to "every person" without restricting these rights, as the Meiji Constitution did, by clauses such as "unless limited by law." The most important ones prescribe universal adult and secret suffrage; freedom of thought, speech, press, religion, and assembly; and a revolutionary change in the family law of Japan; here the guiding principles are exactly the opposite of pre-Occupation values, namely, "individual dignity and the essential equality of the sexes." Moreover, numerous important safeguards for the suspect, accused, and defendant in a criminal proceeding are included.

The emphasis in the document is undeniably on individual rights, and it may perhaps be criticized for being almost silent about the people's duties. The only provision that touches on this subject, apart from the reference to liability of the people to taxation, is the vague admonition that the guaranteed freedoms and rights shall be maintained by the people's constant endeavor, and that they "shall refrain from any abuse of these freedoms and rights and shall always be responsible for utilizing them for the public welfare." In light of the ideology of the real fathers of the

[23] Proceedings in the House of Peers, August 28, 1946 (*Official Gazette*, p. 13).

Constitution, who strove for the liberation of the Japanese from what they considered the police state of the past, it is not astonishing that no specific duties are spelled out. Whether there exist inalienable duties of "every person" that would require listing in a Constitution may well be doubted. Duties are usually described by ordinary legislation and are subject to constant change. The general clause in hortatory language, if understood as excluding abuse of the rights and limiting their use within the bounds of public welfare, places the burden of responsibility on the judiciary to decide what constitutes abuse and public welfare. This is a questionable test, since the danger always exists that the exercise of rights disfavored by the majority may be held to be an abuse or against the public welfare. Rights and freedoms must be especially protected when their use is unwelcome.[24]

Finally, unusual stress is laid upon the peaceful cooperation of the people with other nations, the horror of war, and on pacifism. These features are evident in the preamble and in the unique Renunciation of War clause, which also prohibits the maintenance of armed forces.[25]

Conspicuous by its absence is a grant of emergency powers to the cabinet as the executive. Its authorization to convoke the House of Councillors in an emergency session, if the Diet is adjourned, does not amount to such power. Measures taken by the first chamber under this authority are provisional until ratified by the next Diet. The drafters of the Constitution have deliberately avoided anything approaching devices such as martial law or *état de siège* that would allow abridgment or suspension of civil rights. Constitutional provisions of that type have frequently been abused for the establishment of dictatorial systems of gov-

[24] Actually, the Supreme Court has, in my opinion, applied the public welfare standard excessively, even in connection with prior restraint of freedom of expression, when a more refined criterion would have been desirable.

[25] For the origin of the war renunciation clause, see Chapter 17, note 1.

ernment, as, for example, by Napoleon III in France, and Hitler in Germany.

It might be of some interest to see the comments I, a completely uninfluenced newcomer who did not have any experience in Japanese affairs, made on the Government Section draft from my hospital bed on March 5, 1946. My handwritten notes have been discovered in the so-called Hussey Papers, File 58–A, in the Asian library at the University of Michigan.

Some of my doubts were based on an expectation that actually did not materialize during most of the post-Constitution period, namely, that as a rule the strongest party would lack an absolute majority in the Diet, and coalition blocs might hamper the generally reasonable expectation that the prime minister would be chosen from the strongest party. I did not favor, therefore, the proposed election of the prime minister by the unicameral Diet. Since he and his cabinet members were to be responsible to the Diet anyway, I considered this duplication of a check by the legislature over the executive as redundant. The obvious intention of making the Emperor a mere figurehead would lead to an extremely powerful legislative branch unrestricted by any veto, and a premiership with unusually broad prerogatives. I recommended a second chamber with the right of veto against laws enacted by the other chamber; this veto might be overruled by a two-thirds majority of the members of the latter. As for the prime minister, I did not share the political objections to vesting the real power of appointing him in the Emperor, who could not risk the selection of a person who did not enjoy the confidence of the Diet. To entrust the Emperor with this prerogative, however, would compel him to negotiate with the political parties, and thus integrate him in the democratic process. Finally, I argued against the secretarial system that the draft provided. In the United States this system, which makes the other members of the cabinet mere assistants to its chief, has worked well because of the two-

party system and the unique prestige of the popularly
elected president. In both respects the situation is different
in Japan, where the prime minister's power to hire and fire
could affect the freedom of his coministers to disagree.

Of my suggestions, only the addition of a second upper
chamber, the House of Councillors, materialized. This happened because the Japanese government also took exception to a unicameral system.

COMPARATIVE THOUGHTS

When I first learned of what happened in Government
Section and read the draft, my main concern was a comparative consideration connected with my German past. I
remembered the Weimar Constitution, which boasted similarly noble language and represented a very advanced basic
law, but which nevertheless did not grow into the guiding
emblem for a lasting democracy. In the Germany of 1919,
as in the Japan of 1946, the Constitution that so radically
changed the "national polity" did not arise out of a genuine
popular revolution, but resulted from defeat and surrender.
A closer acquaintance with Japanese attitudes has satisfied
me, however, that the similarity with Weimar was only
superficial. The unwillingness of the Germans to acknowledge their military defeat led to the *Dolchstosslegende*
(stab-in-the-back legend), according to which leftist and
pacifist influence inside Germany undermined the strength
and perseverance of the combatants on the front. The Japanese did not deceive themselves; they were too pragmatic
not to realize that the war had been lost militarily, and if
there had been any doubt, the atomic bomb would have
been the awesome proof. Hence, apart from small arch-
reactionary groups, I found little *Dolchstosslegende* among
the Japanese.

William Costello reports a master plan for scuttling the
Potsdam Agreement conceived by Ishihara Kanji, intimate
advisor of the first postwar premier, Prince Higashi-Kuni.

The accusation contained in the document proposing this plan seemingly resembles a *Dolchstosslegende*.[26] The document starts with the following words: "The cause for defeat lies in the extreme deterioration of morality among the people." Ishihara then hypocritically recommends complete compliance with the objectives of an occupation aiming at demilitarization and democratization as a plan "for winning an advantageous peace treaty." (The somewhat unrealistic renunciation of war and prohibition of the maintenance of military forces of any kind in Article 9 of the Constitution could easily have been explained as a Japanese proposal along the line of the Ishihara plan, had it not been Premier Shidehara, a man of an antimilitarist and liberal reputation, who allegedly sold the idea to SCAP.) The story of Ishihara's master plan illustrates only one element of Ishihara's manifold ideas that influenced a small but devoted group of followers. As Mark R. Peattie has shown, Ishihara was an extremely complex character with ever-changing attitudes. From a warrior who dreamed of an Asian victory in what he called "the Final War," he developed into almost a pacifist at the end of his life. Moreover, it was not merely the deterioration of the people's morale to which he attributed Japan's defeat, but also Tojo's conduct of the war, which he had opposed openly and vigorously. He never denied that his nation had been militarily beaten, and in that respect differed from the German protagonists of the *Dolchstosslegende*.[27]

A day after the promulgation, General Whitney requested me to write a comprehensive analysis of the new Constitution from a comparative point of view, with a deadline of one week. Since such a paper required thorough study of the constitutions of the most important nations, it was a formidable assignment, and I was directed to neglect all

[26] See *Democracy versus Feudalism in Postwar Japan* (Tokyo: Itagaki, 1948), pp. 97ff.

[27] See Mark R. Peattie, *Ishihara Kanji and Japan's Confrontation with the West* (Princeton: Princeton University Press, 1975).

other work and do it outside the office. I picked up a dozen
or more textbooks in various libraries and worked in the
undisturbed seclusion of my hotel room. It was a strenuous
effort, during which the hours of sleep had to be rigidly
reduced. I did my level best, and I met the deadline; still, I
doubt that my best was good enough. My own Section was
pleased with my work, but since it was to be published in
SCAP, Monthly Summation of Non-Military Activities in
Japan and Korea of November 1946, the Statistics and
Report Section had to be consulted. They tried to have
everything of a critical nature eliminated from the paper.
Kades left the decision to me as to how far I wanted to accept their "simplified" version. I did not change anything
of substance, but accepted a few of their suggestions on style.

Their attitude obviously betrayed a strong tendency
within the Occupation to see only unqualified successes.
This sensitivity to any criticism was a trait particularly
developed in General Whitney, who, considering the effect
on Washington, was irritated when the American press
corps reported anything not entirely positive.[28]

[28] While the Constitution has not been amended hitherto, changes
have been urged by influential elements of Japanese society. The most
remarkable study along such lines has been done by the aforementioned Cabinet Commission on the Constitution (Kempo chosakai). It
was established in 1956 and, after a thorough preparation, submitted
its final report, consisting of several hundred volumes, to the prime
minister in 1964. This report must be something like an encyclopedia
of constitutional problems, and also an invaluable source of information on Japanese life and attitudes.

I cannot cover this gigantic undertaking, but must refer to Robert
E. Ward, "The Commission on the Constitution and Prospects of
Constitutional Change in Japan," Journal of Asian Studies 24 (1965),
401–429; to John M. Maki, "The Documents of Japan's Commission on
the Constitution," ibid., pp. 475–489; and also to Takayanagi's and
Maki's contributions to The Constitution of Japan, The First Twenty
Years, pp. 71–114 and 279–299, respectively.

◇◇◇

CHAPTER SIX

The Courts and Law Division

A constitution is only a blueprint of pious principles and will remain ineffective as long as these are not implemented in the law of the land, which in Japan is codified, following the Continental system; and even the most progressive laws are of no avail unless they are willingly respected, vigorously enforced, and become an ingredient of the social fabric. Still, first things had to be done first, namely, the laying of the legal ground. While the Constitution was deliberated in the Diet, I realized with some awe that the tremendous task of bringing the legal and judicial codes into accord with the new charter would, within the setup of the Occupation, be part of my duties, which included almost everything else connected with Japanese legal affairs. As indicated before, there was within headquarters a Legal Section under Colonel Carpenter, but it was charged only with advising on American and international law, and the prosecution of minor war criminals. Japanese law and legislation was, until May 31, 1948, the exclusive responsibility of the Government Section.

During the deliberation in the House of Peers, Sawada Ushimaro showed a clear awareness of the difficulties facing the Diet under the new Constitution. He "brought up the important question . . . of the effect of an Anglo-American Constitution upon the body of Japan's law, drawn so largely from France and Germany. He himself likened it to that of an atomic bomb, crushing everything in its path. A complete revision of the codes would be required, a tremendous task. Adjustment to the new laws would be difficult for the people. With the executive deprived of its former extensive ordinance power, legislation would fall much more heavily upon the Diet."[1]

By and by my superiors realized what was involved. Within the Governmental Powers Division, I was made chief officer of a Legal Unit, and soon was given my first associate, Thomas L. Blakemore, who was to become a most valuable help and advisor to me. He had been with the Department of State, had studied the Japanese language for years in Japan, and was also well versed in Japanese law. After he left headquarters, he passed in the Japanese language the difficult examination that qualified him for the full practice of law before Japanese courts. As far as I know, he is the only non-Japanese who can boast this achievement. He is now one of the most successful attorneys in Tokyo. When he joined me, he was already an "old Japan hand." Hence, he had a better knowledge and a deeper understanding of the Japanese point of view than most of us, and while his resulting moderation was criticized by the most fanatic reformers, it was exactly his familiarity with Japanese attitudes that I appreciated. His mastery of the language served us particularly well in our negotiations with the Japanese, since he could catch those fine nuances of their remarks that we would have missed if dependent upon an interpreter who was not a lawyer. In general, we were fortunate in having Americans of Japanese descent as interpreters, so that we were not dependent on the English-speaking liaison officers whom the Japanese brought to our meetings.

In carrying out the reforms, I had been given a kind of blanket authorization to make decisions, except in cases in which I felt that the political importance or other sensitivity of the matter called for a decision on a higher level. While I frequently sought the advice of Colonel Kades, who in his

[1] Quoted in Quigley and Turner, *The New Japan*, p. 159.

wonderfully informal manner was always willing to discuss problems with his associates, a formal procedure for obtaining approval was seldom necessary. If it was, I would not only report but also propose what should be done, which shows the influence on policy-making of the man on the working level.

One incident may illustrate the amicable relationship between Kades and me. At some time—I do not remember exactly when, but it must have been when changes in the draft Constitution were still possible—Kades, a New Yorker, played with the idea of introducing the election of judges, as is the practice in his home state. I emphatically objected, since I was convinced that at this immature state of the development of political parties it would be disastrous to draw the judiciary into the turmoil of party politics. Under the prevailing circumstances it would not be the proper way of getting qualified judges. Kades thought the matter important enough to bring it up in one of the meetings of the whole professional staff of Government Section, over which General Whitney presided. The latter was won over to Kades' idea, and indicated that he was in favor of election of judges. I then got up and argued against it. After some discussion, Whitney asked for a vote of the approximately sixty persons present. I was the single dissenter; all others voted yes. Genuinely sorry that I lost this battle so definitely, I asked Kades a few days later whether he had taken up the question with the Japanese. He said: "No, we just cannot do it over your dead body."

Confidence in me was growing, while the work increased. Within less than a year and a half, my position was upgraded in terms of "simulated" military rank from that of major to one of full colonel or even brigadier general. Anything like this in the States would probably have been vetoed by the Civil Service Commission, but in MacArthur's realm the impossible was made possible when he willed it.

More important, however, was the organizational change that took place in November 1946, after the promulgation of the Constitution, when the scope and urgency of implementing legislation were fully comprehended. After I had delivered my comparative analysis of the new charter, I was allowed to "revive Oppler's constitution," as a brief note in my calendar expressed it. Kades, always considerate, sent me for a week to the beautiful mountain resort of Gohra so that I could recover from the strain of the work and the loss of sleep. A short time after I returned to Tokyo, it was decided to separate my Legal Unit from Governmental Powers Division, and to elevate it to a new division under the name of Courts and Law Division, with me as the head. Personal considerations may also have motivated this step. Inasmuch as Commander Hussey did not too frequently interfere with our work, his power to do so had become somewhat theoretical.

I was, naturally, elated by this change, which was initiated by Kades and approved by Whitney and MacArthur. It reflected the broadmindedness of these men. Here I was, a very new American, formerly a national of a country with which the United States had just been in an atrocious war, and speaking with a German accent! The promotion of such a person to division chief within the political Section of a military headquarters is certainly not customary, to put it mildly. Here again, the pragmatic approach was evident. It was my familiarity with Continental law, and nothing else, that brought about the conviction of Kades and the generals that I might be qualified for the job.

The next concern, however, was to staff my new division. It was recognized that we badly needed additional lawyers. The second one who joined me was Arthur McCormick, an attorney from Cleveland, Ohio. Not a particularly hard worker and occasionally somewhat disorganized, he excelled in his writing style and, being of a very pleasant personality, he proved efficient in the field of human relations. I could therefore use his diplomatic talents advantageously for negotiations with the Japanese.

While McCormick was recruited from the United States,

I was in the fortunate situation of being able to select most of my other associates personally, on the spot. Among lawyers in other Sections of SCAP it had become known that there were vacancies in my division, and what could be more tempting than the experiment of influencing the whole legal system of another nation? It was this magnetism that led Howard Meyers to me. He served in the Counter Intelligence Division of SCAP's G–2, and was eager to be transferred to the Government Section. We had several meetings, and I soon realized that his penetrating legal mind and his enthusiasm regarding the reform work would greatly benefit my division. After some difficulties were overcome, CID approved his transfer, and I have never regretted my efforts to add him as the fourth lawyer to the division. He did a fine job, particularly in the field of criminal law. At the end of the Occupation he joined the Department of State, where he still serves in an important position.

Dr. Kurt Steiner, a lawyer from Vienna, was also interested in joining me. He served in another Section, and I met him first when, together with a WAC lieutenant, Ethel Weed, we discussed questions of the family law in the Civil Code. Miss Weed was primarily concerned with the equality of women, of which she had been a constant and effective advocate in the Civil Information and Education Section. I would have loved to have Steiner join my division. I soon discovered that he and I had many things in common: the European background as well as the pioneer spirit. I could not, however, obtain his transfer during the reform period, but succeeded in getting him as my associate much later. My expectations had been fully justified. A man of education and intellectual culture, he exhibited remarkable gifts in propagating civil liberties among the Japanese. He was also well versed in the Japanese language. After the end of the Occupation, he received his Ph.D. in political science at Stanford University, where he now holds a full professorship. He has written several books on Japanese affairs, especially on questions of local government and family law.

Two other lawyers came to me from the Occupation of Korea, where my old friend and colleague from the FEA period in Washington, D.C., Dr. Ernst Fraenkel, worked as a kind of advisor to President Syngman Rhee. When they were on leave in Tokyo, they visited me, having been told by Fraenkel about the opportunities in my organization. They both had been reserve officers: Walter E. Monagan, Jr., a major (later lieutenant colonel and colonel), and Richard B. Appleton, a captain. Otherwise, the two could not have been more different in temperament and character. Monagan was somewhat the type of a general staff officer: level-headed, self-confident, discreet, and reserved, devout Roman Catholic, and more on the conservative side than the rest of us. He subsequently served in the Department of Defense. Appleton, on the other hand, was tremendously extroverted, vociferous, and outspoken. Due to his intense energy, he was an indefatigable worker. Both men proved to be jurists far above average, and became efficient members of the team. Monagan was especially competent in the difficult area in which economic and legal problems intermingle. Appleton did excellent work in the field of criminal procedure and in the preparation of exchange of persons programs, which will be described later.

I was also given an administrative officer, Captain Frank C. Novotny. Also a lawyer in civilian life, he was a most conscientious and reliable aide, who, apart from relieving me from much troublesome routine work, contributed a great deal to the achievement of the division. With his unassuming character and imperturbability, he was often the moderating element when tempers got too hot among us. The need for continuous research, obvious in view of the nature of our work, was greatly aided by our legal analyst, an intelligent college graduate, Jeanne Conners, a thoroughgoing and dependable worker. Of the interpreters I wish to mention only Corporal Tanaka Masayoshi, whom I remember as having been particularly helpful.

I have deliberately dwelt on the personalities of my associates during the most important period of my activity as chief of the Courts and Law Division of the Government Section, because they deserve credit for any achievement resulting from our reform work. What we were assigned to do was not the type of legal work in which a lawyer is usually engaged, but it represented policy making on a high level, for legislation is policy making. Others may judge more objectively, but I, for one, believe that it was a good team, and that I was fortunate to have had these fine and dedicated coworkers. Among us there was a give and take. While they learned from me to understand Continental and Japanese law, I familiarized myself through them with the Anglo-Saxon legal system. It was just these different legal backgrounds that had the effect that the changes we brought about in close cooperation with the Japanese legal world were not blindly copied from Anglo-Saxon jurisprudence, but were the fruit of an endeavor to combine the best features of both the Continental and Anglo-Saxon systems.

◇◇

CHAPTER SEVEN

The Legal and Judicial Reforms: A Cooperative Effort

In approaching this task, I had, as far as method and procedure were concerned, a wait-and-see attitude. I realized
that much depended on the response or lack of it on the
Japanese side. With respect to the substance of the reforms,
however, certain basic ideas on law and society occupied
my mind and inspired me. Being fifty-three years old, I was
a senior member of the Occupation. If I had learned anything in an eventful life ever close to legal problems, it was
that the conception of "law and order" as used in the
United States, meaning protection of the individual from
illegal invasions by other persons into his rights, is only
half the answer, as long as no solution has been found to
the problem of who "controls the controllers." After all,
they are human beings subject to any human weakness, be
it lust for power, partiality, intolerance, or corruption. My
activities as judge of the Prussian Supreme Administrative
Court during the Weimar Republic had been an appropriate training along the line of such control. While limited by statute in its jurisdiction, that court reviewed,
among other things, the legality of administrative acts. The
central government was immune from this review, but police
regulations and acts, as well as ordinances of regional and
local chiefs, could be, and were, frequently invalidated. It
might surprise the reader to learn that even in the pre-

Weimar Kingdom of Prussia liberal elements were built in the structure of the government, and that my court, which was founded in 1875, emanated from this mildly liberal tradition. It is needless to emphasize that my later observations under the Nazi regime, in which all legality in a substantive sense had vanished, deepened my conviction that protection of the individual from illegal and arbitrary acts of the legislature and the executive is just as important as his protection from murder and burglary. This conviction served me in good stead in my task of helping the Japanese implement the principles of their new Constitution. They had given great importance to safeguards of individual rights against illegal interference by the government, and had introduced control over both lawmaking and executive disposition by judicial review. Professor Dan Fenno Henderson described the change pursued by the Occupation as a transition from a "government *by* law" to one of a "government *of* law."[1] Looked at from another point of view, it was also a step away from collectivism toward individualism.

I have described the cooperative efforts we used in our negotiations with the Japanese on the reforms in several articles.[2] They also deal with the substance of the new laws, and so do some writings of my associates.[3] It may not be an

[1] See *Political Development in Modern Japan*, edited by Robert E. Ward (Princeton: Princeton University Press, 1968), pp. 415 and 455. Takayanagi similarly points out that the new Constitution replaced the rule by law under the old Constitution by the rule of law, or of government under law or due process of law; see *Law in Japan, the Legal Order in a Changing Society*, edited by Arthur Taylor von Mehren (Cambridge, Mass.: Harvard University Press, 1963), p. 14.

[2] "The Reform of Japan's Legal and Judicial System," *Washington Law Review* 24 (August 1949), 290ff.; "The Judicial and Legal System." *Political Reorientation*, I, 186–245; "Courts and Law in Transition," *Contemporary Japan* 21, Nos. 1–3 (1952), 19–49.

[3] Thomas L. Blakemore, "Post-War Developments in Japanese Law," *Wisconsin Law Review* (July 1947), Part I, pp. 632–653; Richard B. Appleton, "Reforms in Japanese Criminal Procedure under Allied Occupation," *Washington Law Review* 24 (November 1949), pp. 401–430; Howard Meyers, "Revisions of the Criminal Code of Japan during the Occupation," *Washington Law Review* 25 (1950), pp. 104–134; Kurt Steiner, "Post-War Changes in the Japanese Civil Code," *Washington*

exaggeration to say that the method of full and free discussion has been unique in a military occupation, and certainly did not prevail in all other Sections of headquarters. For instance, according to my information, the Japanese negotiators in the conferences on revision of the Commercial Code later sharply criticized the high-handed manner in which the conference was chaired by an official of the Anti-Trust and Cartels Division of the Economic and Scientific Section, which had primary jurisdiction over this reform. Our method was time-consuming, to be sure, but it enabled us to see the various aspects of a planned enactment and may have prevented us from reforming in too much of a hurry. It did not take long until the Japanese representatives of the Ministry of Justice, the public procurators, and the men of the bar and the universities on the committees found out that we were not without understanding of their legal system, due to Blakemore's knowledge of Japanese law and my Continental legal background. Soon they felt free to express their opinions frankly. There was only one authoritative demand: compliance with the constitutional principles. Still, the question of compliance or violation was more often than not in twilight and open to discussion. It is astonishing in how few instances we had to resort to the fiat of the conqueror. The most sensational of these was SCAP's demand for the abolition of the lese majesty provisions in the Penal Code, which he considered contrary to the principle of equality before the law. The story will be told in Chapter 11; this demand was not made in the form of a SCAPIN, but, as pointed out before, by a letter from MacArthur to the prime minister. The demand was implemented in the Diet legislation, with the revision of the Penal Code by completely eliminating the lese majesty provisions.

Another less spectacular example, in which we insisted

Law Review 25 (August 1950), 286–312; Steiner, "The Revision of the Civil Code of Japan: Provisions Affecting the Family," Far Eastern Quarterly 9 (February 1950), 169–184.

on a change in the law, pertained to the same Code, namely, its unequal treatment of the sexes in case of adultery. Here, the violation of the Constitution was so clear that it was even not necessary to bring the matter to the attention of SCAP. The existing law provided for punishment of the wife and of the other party to the adultery. A husband who was unfaithful with an unmarried woman was not subject to punishment. The principle of equality of the sexes, we told the Japanese, left them the alternative of either making adultery equally punishable for both sexes, or of abolishing it as a criminal offense. Characteristically enough, the Diet decided in favor of abolition. After all, it consisted mostly of males, and the habit of keeping a mistress was probably more customary in the case of Japan's married men than in other nations, since the choice of spouse was made by the family elders and often not based on mutual affection.

Our influence on the implementing legislation was exercised at various levels and in different forms. On the working level, we were consulted by ministerial officials in charge of the first drafting, and we had more or less informal conferences with members of cabinet committees and other committees that deliberated on the bills.

Article 98 of the Constitution provided that all laws contrary to its principles would become null and void at the date of its enforcement. After the promulgation of the document on November 3, 1946, the Japanese government realized that a complete revision of the basic codes of law within the remaining six months was absolutely *ultra vires*. To fill the resulting legal vacuum, it was decided to submit to the Diet provisional bills "For the Temporary Adjustment Pursuant to the Enforcement of the Constitution." They contained only the most elementary changes required by the new constitutional principles. This emergency measure was used mainly for the Civil Code and the procedural codes. Since it was to serve as a guideline for the courts in a transitional period, it was legislation in unusually broad and even intentionally vague terms, to leave much to judicial interpretation. A date for the expiration of these provisional laws was provided. They were subsequently replaced by regular legislation for the complete revision of the codes.

The device of temporary law was obviously not available for the implementation of the structural provisions of the Constitution regarding the judiciary. Courts had to function immediately in their new setup after the enforcement of the instrument. Therefore, the Court Organization Law had to be, and was indeed, passed within the six-month period between the enactment and coming into effect of the Constitution on May 3, 1947. This was the first codification in which we resorted to the method of formal conferences with the Japanese. We did so because of the limited time available, which required intensive concentration, and the importance of implementing and strengthening the constitutional principle of independence of the judiciary. Blakemore and I, who alone represented the Occupation, frequently had to mediate between the representatives of the Ministry of Justice and the judges, among them President Hosono.[4] The former were reluctant to give up the supervisory power of the executive branch of the government over the judges, while the latter occasionally went too far in their proposals. Among the younger officials of the ministry, several were in full sympathy with our democratization efforts, particularly Naito Yorihiro, who subsequently was transferred to the secretariat of the Supreme Court, and is now chief judge of a high court. Another was Higuchi Masaru, also a judge, and later a member of the Supreme Court Mission.[5] He diligently recorded our discussions on the Court Organization Bill. Even in the higher brackets of the ministry I experienced unexpected understanding of

[4] Tanaka Kotaro, chief justice of the Supreme Court, in a pamphlet, *The Democratization of the Judicial Administration in Japan* (Tokyo, 1959), p. 3, observes that with regard to "the reforms of the judicial branch there was always comparatively smooth cooperation between the occupation authorities on the one hand and the Japanese Government authorities and judicial circles on the other."

[5] See Chapter 22.

our objectives. Thus, I found Okuno Kenichi, chief of the Civil Affairs Bureau in the Ministry of Justice and subsequently Supreme Court justice, open-minded and cooperative.

Outside my official activity I was fortunate in establishing friendly personal contacts with prominent Japanese jurists, which greatly improved my grasp of their legal conceptions, and must be mentioned here as a contribution to the cooperative reform efforts. One such friend was the outstanding constitutional scholar of Tokyo University, Miyazawa Toshiyoshi, whose profoundly liberal attitude made him a kind of spiritual ally. I greatly benefited from the interchange of ideas with this wise and learned man. Another was a young professor of law, also of Tokyo University, Kawashima Takeyoshi, a courageous critic of the feudal features of Japanese society.

I followed the principle of listening to the views of knowledgeable jurists of all political shades. Among the professors who also participated in the law drafting panels were Suenobu and Wagatsuma Sakae, experts in civil law, and Dando Shigemitsu and Kaneko Hajime, experts in criminal and civil procedure respectively. During the Occupation, I never met Professor Takayanagi Kenzo, who after the termination of the Occupation played a leading role in the Commission on the Constitution. I was all the more surprised when I read the incorrect remark he made more than twenty years later that none of the Occupation lawyers had a knowledge and understanding of the Continental legal system.[6]

As far as the judges were concerned, I kept close contact with several members of the old Supreme Court, among others Nemoto Matsuo. Some of them, but neither President Hosono nor Nemoto, subsequently became justices of the new Supreme Court. As for the new Supreme Court members, Chief Justice Tanaka Kotaro and I became friends and had frequent exchange of ideas after the Supreme Court

6 See *Washington Law Review* 43 (June 1968), p. 972.

3. The author conversing with Chief Justice of the
Supreme Court, Tanaka Kotaro.

Mission in 1950. I shall say more about him in connection with that mission. A very close personal relationship developed between me and Associate Justice Kuriyama Shigeru. He had not been a jurist before, but was the only member of the new Supreme Court with a background different from those whose careers had been connected with the law. A prominent member of the diplomatic corps, former ambassador to Belgium, he approached legal problems with a somewhat freer and less analytical mind than most of his brethren. I found in him a great deal of common sense.

I also repeatedly discussed the legislative program with leaders of the various bar associations, particularly with the dynamic and impervious Mano Tsuyoshi, who subsequently played an important role as an associate justice of the Supreme Court, and with the amiable and well-balanced Tsukasaki Naoyoshi, later vice president of the Court. Another leader of the bar whom I liked personally very much was Kondo Rinji, a man with a healthy criticism of archaic Japanese attitudes and a forward-looking and constructive approach towards the future. He subsequently became the first president of the newly established Family Court in Tokyo, and advanced to president of the Hiroshima High Court. Finally, throughout the Occupation I entertained close relations with the late Senoh Akira, one of the best-informed, wholeheartedly progressive lawyers I met in Japan.

Within my official activity the method of free discussion with representatives of all circles of the Japanese legal world came into full play in connection with the very comprehensive and extremely complicated reform of criminal procedure. Here it was our task to implement the numerous safeguards provided by the Constitution for those involved in criminal prosecution. From the point of view of democratization, this was particularly important legislation in a country where the rights of such persons had been neglected. We established a high level committee, consisting of officials of the Attorney General's Office (successor to the Ministry of Justice), members of the Supreme Court, chief procurators, legal scholars of the universities, and representatives of the bar associations. Since the subject of the deliberations involved fundamental human rights, we invited leaders of the newly founded Japanese Civil Liberties Union. These conferences, which I chaired, and which lasted long hours almost daily for several weeks, took place in the spring of 1948, when my staff had been increased. We were then only four Occupation lawyers,[7] often facing thirty-odd Japanese.

During the preparatory drafting stage several questions had been satisfactorily resolved in conferences with the Attorney General's Office and various committees. There remained, however, about sixty controversial issues. After having agreed upon our own position among ourselves, sometimes after lively arguments between Continentalists and Anglo-Saxons, we formulated these for the use of the Japanese in problem sheets. We most often aimed at reasonably balancing individual rights with the needs of an effective law enforcement.[8] It was, indeed, the old dilemma so

[7] The American side was represented by Blakemore, Meyers, Appleton, and myself (see Chapter 10).
. [8] As far as I know, the only American writer who covers these meetings is Chalmers Johnson in his fascinating book, *Conspiracy at Matsukawa* (Berkeley and Los Angeles: University of California Press, 1972). On p. 36 he lists the Japanese participants of the negotiating committee on the basis of his studies in the National Archives, Washington, D.C. I wish to add that, apart from the presence of representatives of the Japanese Civil Liberties Union (Unno Shinkichi), the participation was actually changing and that usually more Japanese were present than his source indicates. Thus I remember that occasionally Tanimura Todaichiro, formerly vice minister of justice and subsequently associate justice of the Supreme Court, was with us. As for the participation of occupationnaires, Johnson on page 37 makes the amusing mistake of stating that "when the Japanese demurred at a proposed reform, representatives of Government Section present at the meetings, who usually took a more hard-nosed attitude than Legal Section officials, would often deliver a little impromptu lecture on American civics." Actually, the reform of criminal procedure, like the other major legal reforms, was carried out exclusively within the jurisdiction of Government Sec-

familiar to our own country and its Supreme Court, namely, civil liberties versus law and order; in a process of implementing new constitutional safeguards of a previously neglected type, the emphasis was inevitably on the rights. Nevertheless, the composition of the committee was a certain guarantee that neither of the two horns of the dilemma was ignored. The public procurators, particularly Baba Yoshitsugu and Hashimoto Kanzo, were vigorous fighters for law and order, mostly supported by the ministerial officials; the lawyers, who for the first time were consulted on legislation, as well as the civil liberties leaders, emphasized the individual safeguards. The judges and the law professors were usually divided in their individual approach, Justice Mano Tsuyoshi representing the progressive, and Professor Dando Shigemitsu, outstanding expert in the field, the more conservative point of view.

In the early period of my activity in Japan I frequently found it difficult to obtain the frank opinion of a Japanese in conversation because of his reluctance to disagree, which seemed to violate the ethical demand of politeness. It was our greatest satisfaction that we were able in these conferences to overcome the initial stiffness and restraint of our discussion partners, after they had realized that we not only wanted to give them a hearing, but were genuinely eager to learn from them. As chairman, I particularly enjoyed and encouraged debate between them, which put me into the welcome role of moderator. We Americans, far from playing the role of Occupation bosses who knew everything better,

tion, to which I belonged as Chief of the Courts and Law Division, during the meetings. Shortly afterwards, as described in Chapter 19, my division with its personnel was transferred to the Legal Section, where it assumed the name of Legislation and Justice Division. Before this transfer the Legal Section had nothing to do with the Japanese law and none of its members participated in the conferences, which on the Occupation side were held by my associates and myself. There could, therefore, have been no differences in attitudes between members of the two sections. We, the Americans, who conferred with the Japanese as members of the Government Section, only afterwards transformed ourselves into members of the Legal Section.

used persuasion rather than fiat. Soon we felt and acted as
international colleagues in law. The debate was often vigorous, and occasionally witty. I even tried to submit controversial questions to voting, but the Japanese did not like that,
lest the minority would lose face. Thus, since, we avoided
imposing our view, results had to be reached patiently by
compromise, and, indeed, we arrived at agreements or
compromises in all the problems under discussion. It would
be naive, however, to deny that two factors contributed to
the auspicious atmosphere in these conferences: first, the
traditional Japanese penchant for harmony and compromise; and, second, the awareness of all participants that
reformatory action was necessary. At the risk of appearing
overoptimistic, I may add that the majority of the Japanese
even felt that it was desirable.[9] Like all pioneers, we were
optimistic with regard to the survival of our reforms after
the end of the Occupation; but without this optimism,
which at least up to the present has proved warranted, we
would have been paralyzed.

In controlling subsequent new enactments and revisions
of law, we did not repeat the procedure of conferences in
standing committees also used in the revision of the Code of
Civil Procedure, since the reform work on the main codes

[9] *Ibid.*, pp. 35ff., expresses skepticism in connection with a similar
description in my 1949 *Washington Law Review* article of the relationship between the American and Japanese conferees. While in other
respects I find Johnson's criticism fair and sometimes valuable, here he
significantly misquotes me. I wrote that after initial reluctance and
coolness on the part of the Japanese "the relationship between the
occupant and the occupied seemed eventually to be forgotten over the
feeling of an international fellowship among jurists who have in common the ardent concern for the improvement of a law." I have never
denied that we had the final authority, nor have I ever maintained that
"reform of criminal procedure came about primarily on the initiative
of the Japanese." Some of the reforms were, of course, mandatory to
implement either the requirements of the new Constitution or an
established SCAP policy, such as the decentralization of the police. The
latter must have motivated the remark I allegedly made on what
Johnson calls the separation of the procurators from the police—not
during the revision of the criminal procedure, but more than a year
before, when the Occupation atmosphere was quite different.

had been completed. Also supervision of the Japanese government had been increasingly relaxed, generally speaking. We continued, however, to influence legislation by more informal means. Our relationship to those in charge of the drafting had reached such a degree of mutual trust that they often sought our advice on their own volition.

Less than two months after my arrival in Tokyo, in a memorandum for Colonel Kades, chief of the Public Administration Division, I called the attention of my superiors to the enormity of the task involved in the implementation of the principles of the new Constitution.[10] First, I pointed out that it was in accordance with the general policy of SCAP to leave the revision of the law to the Diet and the drafting to the Japanese governmental authorities. If this were done, I wrote, any progress in the liberalization of the legal system would be more valuable and lasting than could be achieved by SCAP directive. This did not mean, I continued, passivity on the part of the Occupation forces. Their task I defined to be: (a) to see to it that laws prejudicial to the objectives of the Occupation be abrogated and to prevent legislation of this kind; (b) to suggest and encourage legislation designed to advance the objectives of the Occupation. The memorandum then stressed the need for differentiation in the degree of our insistence. It should be inexorable, I proposed, when issues of disarmament, elimination of monopoly capitalism, and defeudalization were concerned. Other reforms, I added, "desirable though they might appear to the Western mind, should not be imposed by SCAP. . . . We should promote gradual development toward long-range objectives by inspiration and advice rather than by pressure." I elaborated on the nature of the Japanese law, which is not based on common, but on civil law, and follows mainly German and French patterns.

[10] Memorandum dated April 11, 1946; Subject: Steps to be taken by the Government Section in connection with the Legal Reforms Planned by the Japanese Government (File 58-A of the Hussey Papers in the Asian Library of the University of Michigan, Ann Arbor).

"Although we may be inclined," I wrote, "to consider the Anglo-Saxon legal system superior to the Continental, we should resist any temptation to replace hastily one by the other. The Japanese would not be able to work an artificially imposed system which differed fundamentally from what they have practiced up to the present time. As a matter of fact, among certain legal groups and business circles, there has been a trend toward the American pattern of law in the last twenty years, and it is obvious that the political and economic situation resulting from the defeat of the Axis powers will greatly strengthen this tendency. However, a transformation of the whole legal system can be achieved only gradually."

This Memorandum illuminates the spirit in which I approached my reform work and, as I must claim, by which I was guided throughout the Occupation period to the best of my capability. It should give credibility to my repeated emphasis upon my preference for advice and persuasion over fiat.

CHAPTER EIGHT

Institutional Reforms

In starting with the substance of the legal and judicial reforms, some very general remarks on the history of the great Meiji codification may suffice for our purpose.[1] I shall restrict myself to emphasizing that the far-reaching adoption of Continental law after the Meiji restoration could well be compared to the reception of Roman law in Europe of the fifteenth and sixteenth centuries. The modernization of Japan's legal system was at that time held necessary to improve her international prestige, and particularly to free her from the extraterritoriality of the big powers and other handicaps resulting from the unequal treaties. The basic codes covered in this and the two following chapters closely followed the Continental, and overwhelmingly the German, pattern, with occasional mixtures of French elements. The main reason for choosing the Continental instead of the Anglo-Saxon legal system was, of course, the pressure of the political situation, which required prompt action. This was made relatively easy by taking over—so to speak—on a silver platter the codified German law as a whole. But it is a sound assumption that the definite preference for Germany was also motivated by the Meiji leaders' admiration of that nation during its promising Bismarckian period.

Two main objectives were behind the legal and judicial reforms under the new Constitution: first, to create an

[1] For a brief summary of prewar legal history, see my remarks in *Political Reorientation*, I, 188ff.

independent judiciary; and second, to implement the safeguards of fundamental human rights of an individual, be it
generally as a citizen or as a member of the family (especially as a woman), or as a suspect, accused, or defendant in
a criminal process. The substance of these reforms has been
analyzed in part by the aforementioned articles written by
my associates and me.[2] Moreover, in my subsequent chapters problems pertaining to various aspects of the reform
will be discussed repeatedly in a more pragmatic form. Since
the temporary laws were superseded by the final enactments,
they have merely historical value and will not be covered in
the following analysis.

THE JUDICIARY

Under the existing system, which I knew well from Germany, the courts were subordinated to the Ministry of
Justice. While the latter could not interfere directly with
the decisions of the judges, its powers to appoint or to propose appointment, to promote and transfer them, as well as
the superior prestige of the public procurators—comparable
to our state or federal attorneys—as administrative officials
under the ministry, were all very much apt to influence the
judicial functions indirectly. This was particularly true in
political cases, when the procurators served as watchdogs
over the attitudes of the judges. Rewards and punishments
lay especially in the power to promote or not to promote.

This treatment of the judiciary as just another group of
civil servants essentially affected its prestige among the
people. There were, in addition, functional reasons why
judges ranked lower than high administrative officials. I
have in mind particularly the allergy to litigation of the
Japanese, born out of their traditional ideal of harmony.
This resulted in their preference for settling their disputes
through mediation, conciliation, and compromise instead
of fighting for their rights in court, which was frowned on as

[2] See Chapter 7, notes 1–3.

quarrelsome individualism. Criminal cases did not overflood the courts either, because of Japan's modest crime rate, which has been explained by the strong control of the individual by the closely knit family and by the local community. In this respect the authority of the public procurator to refrain from indictment, and his inclination to do so unless he had gotten a confession or a case he otherwise could not well lose, also reduced the number of criminal processes. The little use made by the Japanese of their judicial system finds its most striking illustration in the very small percentage per capita of lawyers. Still, the judges of Japan, although their social prestige did not measure up to the importance of their responsibilities, enjoyed a reputation of integrity and even of a degree of personal independence. I learned that Hosono himself had shown gratifying backbone against interference attempts of Premier Tojo during the war.[3] Nevertheless, if the democratization of Japan was to be of any success, it appeared unrealistic to rely on the personal independence of individual judges, which would always require an unusual degree of courage and ethical responsibility, as long as swimming against the current meant risking one's career.

What was needed, especially for a nation in which executive authority had been paramount, was complete organizational as well as functional independence, combined with enhanced powers and prestige of the judiciary. In providing these, the fathers of the Constitution may not have appreciated the appealing side of the Japanese predilection for harmony and compromise, but undoubtedly looked at it as a reflection of a collective type of society. The strong individualism that penetrates the instrument favored a different attitude, namely, the resolution of the citizen to fight for his right when it is challenged or violated. The elevation of the judiciary to a separate branch of the government with the power of judicial review justified the expectation that such a change would eventually occur, and that the Japanese

[3] See Chapter 11.

people would make increasing use of their courts. The citizen could now litigate, as he had not been able to do before, in an area where the road to conciliation is virtually blocked, namely, against his government. The judiciary must, in my view, be independent not only from the executive, but also from the legislature, notwithstanding the latter's impeachment power. I emphasize this independence because Article 41 of the Constitution, which declares the Diet to be the "highest organ of state power," has sometimes been interpreted as granting the legislative branch a kind of superiority over the others. Thus Maki maintains that the article "clearly . . . places the Diet over the Court."[4] The same was asserted by the Judicial Committee of the House of Councillors, when it claimed the right to investigate court decisions. I have repeatedly rejected the idea that Article 41 confers superior rank on the Diet and gives it powers not explicitly spelled out in the document within the framework of checks and balances.[5] It is my view that the characterization of the Diet as the highest organ has symbolic rather than legal significance: it calls for reverence to the directly elected representation of the people, in whom sovereignty rests. To hold otherwise would actually make the Diet omnipotent and open the door to a parliamentary dictatorship certainly not intended by the drafters. This "highest organ" phrase may also very well have contributed to the reluctance of the Supreme Court to invalidate laws as unconstitutional. Henderson speaks of the "dual supremacy" (of Diet and courts).[6]

The seven articles of the Constitution that deal with the judiciary left much to be implemented, strengthened, and

[4] See John M. Maki, *Court and Constitution in Japan; Selected Supreme Court Decisions, 1948–60*, with translations by Ikeda Masaaki, David C. S. Sissons, and Kurt Steiner (Seattle: University of Washington Press, 1964), p. xxxviii.

[5] See my article in *Contemporary Japan*, pp. 25ff. and 32–33, and my review of Maki's book, *Court and Constitution in Japan*, in the *Washington Law Review* 39 (August 1964), p. 655.

[6] See *Political Development in Modern Japan*, p. 441.

added. The charter referred certain matters to subsequent legislation, such as the number of Supreme Court judges, the organization of the inferior courts, the retirement age of all judges, and the popular review of the appointment of Supreme Court judges. It is silent on other matters, such as the qualifications of Supreme Court judges. Most of the gaps have been filled out by the Court Organization Law of April 16, 1947, but additional implementation is contained in specific laws—for instance, the People's Examination of Supreme Court Judges Law of November 29, 1947; the Impeachment of Judges Law of the same date; and the Law Concerning the Status of Judges and Other Court Officials.

The Supreme Court under the new Constitution (*Saiko Saibansho*) is not a revised edition of the former, *Daishinin*, but a new creation, with new prerogatives and responsibilities. Under the Meiji Constitution the judiciary was part of the executive and not an independent branch of the government. It could not possibly have the power of judicial review, since that Constitution, as gift of the Emperor, was not subject to interpretation by the courts.[7] The new Supreme Court, according to the Court Organization Law, consists of the chief judge and fourteen associate judges, compared to the thirty-two judges of the *Daishinin*. This greatly increased the burden of work for the members of the new Court, and indeed contributed to the subsequent continuous and serious backlog of cases. But considerations of prestige, as well as the intention to avoid the clumsiness resulting from too large a decision-making body, motivated the preference for a smaller number.

Reasons of prestige were also behind the constitutional provision that the Emperor is to appoint the chief judge. This puts him on the same level as the prime minister. The associate judges of the Supreme Court are appointed by the cabinet and, of course, since the Emperor's action is merely a rubber stamp of a decision already made, the cabinet also has the actual power of appointing the chief judge. From

[7] See Maki, *Court and Constitution in Japan*, p. xvii.

the point of view of judicial independence, one may well regard this method as a weakness, in view of the danger that the cabinet could select personalities it expects to see eye-to-eye with it or to cause minimum trouble. The temptation to do so is well known in connection with the appointment power of the president of the United States. In my own view, however, there was hardly a better alternative at the time of the drafting of the Constitution. As pointed out before, I did not favor at all, even during the following years, election of judges by the people, which would have involved them in party politics. Similar considerations applied, though to a lesser degree, to an arrangement like the American check on the presidential appointment by the Senate. We nevertheless felt that because of the tremendous importance of a proper selection of the members of the highest tribunal, the cabinet should at least be advised before its determination. Hence, the Court Organization Law provided for a high-level consultative committee. But in the process of appointment we experienced a Japanese phenomenon with which we had not reckoned. The cabinet, being afraid that any deviation from the committee's proposals would cause its members to lose face, accepted them altogether. This actually meant that the appointment power had shifted from the cabinet to the committee, a result not in harmony with the Constitution. Consequently, the committee was later abolished.[8]

That leaves the popular review as the only check on the appointment of Supreme Court judges. According to the

---

[8] For details see *Political Reorientation*, I, 235–36. There were actually two such committees; the first one, which had acted in a very unsatisfactory manner, was dissolved. For further criticism of the selection of Supreme Court judges see Thomas A. Bisson, *Prospects for Democracy in Japan* (New York: Macmillan, 1949), p. 84. He also notes that many observers were disturbed by the fact that the newly appointed Chief Justice Mibuchi Tadahiko had served for fifteen years as chief legal advisor to the Mitsui Trust Company after his retirement from judicial service. I myself was not happy about this choice. Bisson also voiced apprehension lest the occupation reforms would be declared unconstitutional by the Court as soon as the Occupation's control was removed. This, however, did not happen.

Constitution, the appointment shall be reviewed by the people at the first general election of members of the lower House following the appointment, and must be repeated after a lapse of ten years and every ten years thereafter. The implementing law provides for a printed ballot for the first time in Japanese history. I thought that this check was also primarily of a symbolic rather than practical significance. It *encourages reverence for the sovereignty of the people, to which even the members of the highest tribunal should be subject.* It may also imply that with its new power of judicial review, the Supreme Court is entrusted with a highly political prerogative, the abuse of which in extreme cases ought not be left unchecked. It is, indeed, only in such cases that the review could possibly become effective. It would require the unusual situation of a court decision that has aroused the indignation of the masses, who are otherwise little interested in judicial decisions and hardly willing or able to distinguish between the attitudes of majority, concurring, or dissenting judges or to evaluate their abilities.

As I have pointed out before,[9] the referendum might possibly serve as a useful check on the executive in case the cabinet abuses its appointment power, for instance, by selecting an incompetent judge for political reasons or by "packing" the Court. While I was in Japan, it was usually the Communist party that urged its followers to vote newly appointed judges out. None has ever been removed, and those favoring recall constituted a tiny minority.[10]

The inferior courts consist of the collegiate high courts,

[9] See my article in *Contemporary Japan*, p. 28.

[10] In the Commission on the Constitution it was noted that the vote for dismissal was usually under 10 percent of the total votes, the largest having been 12.5 percent.

In December 1971, an unusual campaign for the rejection of a Supreme Court associate judge, Shimoda Takeo, former ambassador to the United States, was started by about 250 representatives of the National Council for Independence of the Judiciary. The step was supported by the two leftist parties and by some labor unions. The appointee was held to be unqualified because of his "hawkish" views and his alleged statement that judges should be obedient to the executive branch of the government. See *Japan Times*, December 12, 1971.

normally composed of three members, but in cases of insur-
rection of five; the district courts, composed of either three
judges or one; and the single-judge summary courts. The
former local courts have been abolished. With the exception
of the lowest level, the organization corresponds essentially
to the previous one of appellate and district courts. The new
district courts have, however, taken over the jurisdiction of
the abolished local courts. The summary courts are limited
to petty cases in civil jurisdiction, and in criminal affairs to
small offenses formerly handled by police courts, which also
were abolished as suspected tools of the police state. A subsequent innovation was the establishment of family courts,
consisting of Domestic Relations and Juvenile Divisions.
The first function in marital and parental affairs and regarding custody of children and guardianship, thus taking
over responsibility formerly entrusted to the family council
under the old family system; the second constitute genuine
juvenile courts, replacing agencies outside the judicial organization and under the Ministry of Justice.

The judges of the inferior courts are also appointed by
the cabinet, but this must be done from a list of persons
nominated by the Supreme Court. Thus, the Constitution
bestows the actual power of appointment upon the highest
Court, which now controls the personnel policy affecting the
other courts.

There is a difference in the guaranteed tenure of judges.
The judges of the Supreme Court may continue in office
until they reach the statutory retirement age of seventy
years, unless judicially declared mentally or physically incompetent, or removed by public impeachment or popular
review. The judges of the inferior courts, however, whose
limit of tenure is age sixty-five,[11] according to the Constitution, "shall hold office for a term of ten years with the
privilege of reappointment."

The drafters in Government Section, who were predominantly concerned over the independence of the judiciary

[11] Subsequently extended to seventy for Summary Court judges.

from the executive, did not consider it necessary to protect the judges of the inferior courts from arbitrariness of the Supreme Court in connection with what amounts to its reappointment power. Still, the nonreappointment of a judge of the Kumamoto District Court, Miyamoto Yasuaki, produced something like a crisis within the judicial family in 1971. The Supreme Court, under the chief judgeship of Ishida Kazuto, had refused to inform Miyamoto of the cause for its action, but the general assumption seemed to have been that his membership in the Young Lawyers Association (*seihokyo*) had made him appear undesirable.[12] This organization, allegedly left of center, had frequently criticized the government, and the chief justice had gone on record to say that membership in it was considered inadvisable for judges. I think the excitement was the result of the fact that the Supreme Court, out of a typically Japanese courtesy, had regularly, with very rare exceptions, proposed the continuation in office of judges of the inferior courts after ten years, and that this was probably a politically motivated case of nonreappointment. The judges had more or less grown convinced that they had a right of reappointment, although the Constitution clearly speaks of a privilege. Without going into the merit of the position of the Supreme Court, which would not be possible since the reason for it was not revealed, I may remark that the question of a judge's political attitude is sensitive and controversial. While in my view membership in a political party or other organization, as long as it has not been declared illegal, is his constitutional right,[13] a certain restraint appears proper when it comes to militant political activity, particularly for an extreme rightist or leftist movement. Engaging in it may well be based on idealism, but often betrays a fanaticism ill·suited for a judge, who must always be able to see both sides of a problem. That is exactly what the fanatic is un-

[12] See *Japan Times*, February 16, and March 6 and 9, 1972.
[13] This was also the position of the German Disciplinary Courts for public officials during the Weimar Republic.

able to do. The Court Organization Law in a provision, the constitutionality of which may be doubtful, explicitly prohibits judges from engaging "actively in political movements." The demand of the affected judge and his supporters that the Supreme Court reveal the reason for the nonreappointment was not without merit. The secrecy used in this case was not in line with modern principles of personnel policy that favor, if not a hearing before a disadvantageous determination, at least an explanation afterwards.

Further events during the chief judgeship of Ishida Kazuto have shown another potential danger to the independence of the individual judge. To be sure, the Constitution provides in Article 78 that judges shall not be removed except by public impeachment, unless judicially declared mentally or physically incompetent to perform official duties, and that no disciplinary action against them shall be administered by any executive organ or agency. Such action, consisting of a fine or reprimand, for example, may, however, be taken within the judicial branch, in the final instance by the Supreme Court and even against its own judges.[14] If this power is not used very sparingly and wisely, one might fear lest a huge new bureaucracy culminating in the Supreme Court replace the Ministry of Justice as an institution, threatening the freedom of the individual judge.[15]

[14] The disciplinary punishment of four associate justices of the Supreme Court is described in the third section of Chapter 19.

[15] A tempest was caused by the disciplinary actions (reprimands) in 1969 and 1970 against two judges of the Sapporo District Court. Fukushima Shigeo was in charge of a case in which a large group of citizens challenged the government for the construction of a missile base for the Self-Defense Forces on the ground that the maintenance of these forces violated Article 9 of the Constitution, the war renunciation clause. Chief Judge Hiraga Kenta had advised Fukushima in a private letter to decide that the complaint was not justiciable. He had expressed the same view to the senior judge of Fukushima's division in a memo, a copy of which the latter received from that judge. News reporters got hold of the letter, and Fukushima made a copy of the memo available to them. The two documents were thereupon published. In the pend-

As for impeachment, the chapter of the Constitution covering the Diet requires that an impeachment court be set up from members of both Houses for the purpose of trying those judges against whom removal proceedings have been instituted. The Judges Impeachment Law of November 20, 1947, makes it clear that impeachment is only the ultimate weapon, by restricting its use to grave violation or neglect of official duties or conduct, inside or outside the office, "absolutely inconsistent with the dignity and integrity which the office requires." Nevertheless, impeachment remains a powerful check by the legislature over the judiciary. The institution of removal action—in other words, the indictment function—has been assigned to an impeachment committee consisting of twenty members of the lower House. A two-thirds majority is necessary for a resolution to proceed with the impeachment. Any person may lodge a request for impeachment with the committee.[16]

---

ing case Fukushima granted the plaintiffs a temporary injunction, but the *Sapporo High Court* reversed this ruling. Both judges were reprimanded, Hiraga because of his two attempts to influence the decision of his junior colleague, and Fukushima because he had caused the publication. Meanwhile, the affair had taken a political coloring. Ultrarightists had criticized the punishment of Hiraga, attributing it to machinations of the allegedly subversive Young Lawyers' Association, of which Fukushima was a member. A petition was submitted for his impeachment to the Diet Impeachment Committee. It ruled favorably but suspended the proceedings. The same committee rejected, however, an impeachment request from the Sapporo Bar Association against Hiraga. This different treatment aggravated the political polarization ensuing from the incident.

Fukushima, who had submitted but then withdrawn his resignation, was, however, not disciplined on the basis of the article in the Court Organization Law that prohibits judges from engaging actively in political movements, possibly because of doubts whether the Young Lawyers' Association was a political movement and subversive. He continued in his position at the Sapporo District Court, and in 1973 decided that the Self-Defense Forces were unconstitutional. (See Chapter 17, n. 2, below.)

[16] It is remarkable how abundantly and often unreasonably the Japanese have made use of the impeachment weapon against judges since the enactment of the Judges Impeachment Law. According to the *Japan Times* of July 16, 1970, about 2,400 requests for indictment of a

The court of impeachment itself is composed of fourteen members, seven from each House. Here again, a two-thirds majority is required for removal. The trial must be public. Once removed from office, a judge is excluded from judicial positions, but the law generously holds a door open for the recovery of qualification from the impeachment court.

What are the professional requirements for judges from Supreme Court justices down to assistant judges (the start of the judicial career after completion of study and training)? In the higher ranks the emphasis is on long legal, and particularly judicial, experience and tenure. For the Supreme Court judges, the Court Organization Law demands "persons of broad vision and extensive knowledge of law," at least forty years of age. Unfortunately, the traditional respect of the Japanese for their senior citizens has hitherto prevented the appointment of any person even in his forties. The average age of members of the Supreme Court has remained constantly high.[17] While I write this, I am myself an octogenarian, but I have never thought and do not think today that wisdom necessarily increases with old age. When it happens, it is a blessing, but not infrequently the mind narrows with the arteries and old judges are not always flexible enough to adapt themselves to changing conditions.

---

judge have been filed, but only four judges have actually been tried and only two of them were found guilty. Thus, twenty-nine persons, mainly what the same press report calls intellectuals, filed such a request against Chief Justice Ishida, charging him with violating judicial independence and imposing unconstitutional controls. Ishida had said in a public statement that extreme militarists, anarchists, and avowed communists were undesirable as judges. He also had expressed the view that utmost caution should be applied in the exercise of constitutional review of laws and administrative acts. The impeachment committee refused impeachment, in my opinion justifiably so, although the remarks about judicial review lacked wisdom, in light of the Chief Justice's sensitive position.

[17] According to David J. Danelski in *Comparative Judicial Behavior*, edited by Glendon Shubert and Danelski (London: Oxford University Press, 1969), pp. 129–130, the average appointment age has been sixty-one years and four months, and only four of the twenty-eight justices appointed from 1948 to 1965 have been less than sixty years of age.

I now think that we made a mistake by not giving at least the middle-age generation a better chance. We should have balanced the requirements of a minimum age and of a higher maximum age of the judges of the Supreme Court by a provision that of the fifteen judges at least five must be younger than fifty years of age when appointed.

A majority of ten of the fifteen judges are subject to rigid qualifications. They must have held positions of president of a high court or judge for at least ten years, or positions as judge of summary courts, public procurator, lawyer, professor, or assistant professor of law in universities for at least twenty years, either in one position or cumulative. Somewhat milder requirements have been set up for the holders of some special positions, among them those of assistant attorneys general, who are administrative officials.[18] The recognition of long experience at the bar was especially gratifying, since it enhanced the prestige of the lawyers. The length of tenure in the various above positions prescribed by the law has contributed to the old age of the members of the highest tribunal.

Five of the fifteen judges may be selected from among outstanding personalities who have had no long careers in positions connected with jurisprudence. The cabinet has regrettably made use of this promising latitude only sparingly. Occasionally, a well-known diplomat, for example, Kuriyama Shigeru, has been appointed.

[18] Kawashima Takeyoshi in *Comparative Judicial Behavior*, p. 115, believes that Occupation authorities may have erred about the liberalizing effect of the appointment of professors and administrators. I do not recall that we expected administrators to have such an influence on the bench. Since the regular courts assumed the power to determine the legality of administrative acts, we were rather motivated by the consideration that the Supreme Court should, besides legally trained persons, have experienced administrators as its members. As for professors, I doubt that one can generally label them as "conservative." If those on the Court with academic backgrounds proved so, the reason seems to me that in the selection of justices to the highest tribunal the government gave preference to conservative scholars. I have no doubt that a less conservative government would easily find liberal members of the academic world, like Kawashima himself.

There are also complicated qualification requirements for high court presidents and judges, the general rule being previous tenure of at least ten years in positions connected with law. Only the appointment to a summary court is somewhat easier to obtain.

As for the assistant judges, the Court Organization Law merely provides that they shall be appointed from among those who have finished study as judicial apprentices. This leads us to the education and training for the legal profession.[19] Without our suggestion, on the initiative of the Japanese drafters of the law, the same rules now apply to lawyers (previously excluded from the Legal Training Institute after the university examination), as to judges and procurators. This innovation again benefited not only the prestige but also the quality of members of the bar. The requirements for the law candidate are very rigid, and a highly selective system takes care that only the very able and knowledgeable make the grade. Even in prewar times judges and procurators performed their duties with efficiency. If I was ever critical of the Japanese judiciary, the reason was never that I found it wanting in erudition and sophistication, but rather that I did not always agree with their slowness, over-cautious ideological attitudes, and their strictly analytical methods of interpretation—although, here again, generalization is wrong and unfair in light of the great differences between individual judges.

First of all, the aspirant for the legal profession must pass the difficult national higher civil service examination for the judiciary. According to John Maki, only one in twenty-two candidates passed it in the six years from 1952 to 1957.[20] The candidate need not necessarily be a graduate of a university, but usually is. Even if he is a graduate, he must do a great amount of private study, since the law departments of Japanese universities, differently from ours, provide only

[19] For an excellent analysis, see Abe Hakaru in Von Mehren, *Law in Japan*, pp. 155ff.
[20] See *Court and Constitution in Japan*, p. xxxiv.

a general and essentially theoretical knowledge of law, besides other disciplines such as political science. Among those who have passed the examination, a selection of judicial apprentices is made in another stiff test conducted by a commission whose members are appointed by the Ministry of Justice. The very few who succeed in this test are then appointed judicial apprentices under the jurisdiction of the Supreme Court. The institution through which the Court fulfills this most important responsibility of preparing future judges, lawyers, and procurators for their profession is the Legal Training and Research Institute, which also performs other duties, particularly research.

Two years of judicial apprenticeship are prescribed. This system of practical training for the legal profession follows the German model of the education of the *Referendar*, as the student who has passed the first state examination in law is called. I have myself undergone a similar training in Germany, and have always thought that for the Continental European aspirant—and the same is true of the Japanese—it is an excellent method of learning what his university, with its emphasis upon analytical scholarship, cannot offer, namely, how the law is actually applied in the courts, and how it can be used by the lawyer and public procurator. While the apprentice spends an initial and concluding part of the two-year period in the institute, with courses given by selected members of the profession, who also test whether he has benefited adequately from his assignments, the assignments themselves are really the meat of his practical training. He must serve for fixed periods of time in a court, in a procurator's office, and with a lawyer. This is where he can observe the business of litigation and the various stages of a criminal trial, and where he learns how to draft a judgment, an indictment, or an appeal. At the end of the two years, another examination is required before the door is finally opened to the coveted judgeship, procurator's office, or to the bar. All candidates usually pass this also difficult examination, a fact that proves how careful the selective process of the appointment of apprentices has been. The state provides a salary during the apprenticeship.

According to the Constitution, the whole judicial power is vested in the courts, and extraordinary courts are excluded. This monopoly is enhanced by the demand in the Court Organization Law that all legal disputes shall be decided by the courts, meaning the regular courts. The result was not only the abolition of police courts, which would have disappeared in any case, but also the end of the Court of Administrative Litigation. Although, because of my own background, I could have been expected to regret the elimination of that court, I welcomed it. There was no substructure of inferior courts, and the administrative court, due to the "principle of enumeration," had very limited jurisdiction. According to this principle, an administrative act could be challenged in the court only if this was explicitly permitted by statute. There was not much willingness of the judges to decide against the government, and no adequate rules of due process of law were applied.[21] The Japanese court, therefore, never reached the independence and prestige of its European counterparts, particularly the French *Conseil d'Etat* and the Prussian Supreme Administrative Court. There was no popular demand in Japan for a new experiment with administrative justice.

In considering the load of manifold responsibilities of the *Saiko Saibansho*, the present Supreme Court, one must keep in mind that they include several nonjudicial tasks. Apart from the activities connected with the training of the would-be jurists, the Court performs legislative functions. At first sight, there seems to be a contradiction in the Constitution. Although Article 41 declares the Diet to be the sole law-making organ of the State, Article 77 vests the Supreme Court with the rule-making power, under which it determines, among other things, the rules of procedure and of practice. This has been interpreted by some judges in our conferences as meaning that the reform of the Codes of Civil

21 See Von Mehren, *Law in Japan*, p. 240.

and Criminal Procedures should not be enacted by Diet legislation, but by rules of the highest tribunal. It was, however, resolved that the fundamental framework of these revisions should be laid down by the legislature as the "sole law-making organ," and that the Court should provide the necessary details and fill in the gaps by supplementary rules. In the course of time innumerable such rules of a highly technical and minute nature have been issued. The interesting question of whether a Supreme Court rule may change or abolish a statutory provision has not yet been decided.

The Constitution also mentions the administration of judicial affairs as subject to the rule making. The Court, acting here as judicial assembly, performs functions such as organization of the inferior courts, training of the judges, their appointment and promotion, internal discipline of the courts, and "matters relating to attorneys," the latter consisting mainly of decisions regarding admission to the bar. The public procurators are also mentioned as subject to the rule making, but since they are administrative officials under the Ministry of Justice, this can mean only that the rule making of the Supreme Court pertains to their role before the courts. In all the administrative tasks the routine work is done by the Secretariat General of the Supreme Court, headed by a secretary general of high rank and staffed by qualified persons, mostly judges. Its subdivisions correspond to the various functions of the courts. To be assigned to this organization enhances the prospects of advancement, and its officials have, indeed, frequently been promoted to judgeships in high courts and even in the Supreme Court.

The new responsibilities of the Court made it imperative to relieve it from too heavy a burden, particularly in a period of transition to a new Constitution and completely new laws. First of all, it was resolved that the Court does not need to sit on all cases in its full composition. This led to the establishment of three petty benches consisting of five judges each. Constitutional questions must, however, be decided by the grand bench presided over by the chief judge, unless the petty bench can follow precedent. The grand bench consists of the whole court, but nine members constitute a quorum.

Another relief was granted by a change of the appeal system that limited the jurisdiction of the Supreme Court. Space does not allow me to elaborate on this complex matter.[22] Suffice it to point out that the Japanese law distinguishes between *koso* and *jokoku* appeals and *kokoku* complaints. Upon *koso* appeal, the higher court examines both issues of fact and law. Previously, it required a complete trial de novo (retrial) by the appellate court, but in criminal procedure this has been dispensed with, and the scope of reexamination by and large left up to the court.[23] *Jokoku* appeal is primarily restricted to constitutional questions and challenges of the compatibility of the decision with judicial precedents. The Supreme Court, upon *jokoku* appeal, may, however, go beyond that limitation and admit cases involving an important problem of the construction of law. This provision has been compared with our American writ of certiorari. The latitude of the Supreme Court to rescind a judgment reaches further in criminal procedure. The law lists a number of reasons, among them even "gross error in finding facts," and "gross injustice of punishment." Thus the Court is here virtually free, though not legally bound, to change or invalidate any decision that it deems unjust.

Kokoku complaint is directed against a ruling of the lower court. It can be made to the Supreme Court only if the constitutionality of the ruling is challenged.

The simplification of the appeal system consisted, apart from the changed nature of the *koso* appeal, in the reduction of trial instances. Cases starting in the local courts often

[22] For details see Maki, *Court and Constitution in Japan*, pp. xxv–xxvii.
[23] See the article of Appleton in *Washington Law Review* 24, 427–428.

went through four instances, with *koso* appeal to the district court, a second *koso* appeal to the appellate courts, and *jokoku* appeal to the Supreme Court (*Daishinin*). The frequent abuse of the right to appeal and the slowness of the procedure under such a system had the consequence that civil suits as well as criminal cases sometimes lasted up to ten, if not fifteen, years. To remedy this situation, and the unbelievable backlog, the new procedural laws permit only three instances. In civil procedure, the Supreme Court has been relieved from decisions on petty cases initiated in a summary court. Decisions of these can now be appealed by *koso* to a district court and by *jokoku* from the latter to a high court. The Supreme Court would deal with such a case only if a constitutional question were involved. In criminal procedure the limitation to three instances has been obtained by eliminating the district court as *koso* appeal instance against judgments of the summary court. Appeals from both district court and summary court decisions go now to a high court, whose judgment is subject to *jokoku* appeal to the Supreme Court.

The introduction of individual dissenting opinions, especially in the Supreme Court, by the Court Organization Law is, as I have emphasized before,[24] an almost revolutionary innovation in a country where expressed disagreement has often been considered bad taste. It is certainly preferable to the earlier system, well known to me from my former experience as a German judge, according to which only the majority decision reaches the public, while the views of the minority remain a secret. Their publication in Japan could also serve the useful purpose of helping the people form a judgment on the individual Supreme Court justices and thus to enable them to exercise reasonably their right of review of the appointments. Most importantly, the dissenting and even the concurring or, as the Japanese prefer to call them, the "supplementary" opinion of today frequently becomes the majority decision of the Court tomorrow, and

---

[24] See my article in *Contemporary Japan*, p. 41.

thus may serve as pioneer in the development of judge-made law. Kawashima, who looks at such opinions as proof of individualism, notes that they have increased with passing time.[25] This corresponds to my own observation. Mostly I see, however, the names of the same judges making vigorous use of the expressed dissent: namely, Mano Tsuyoshi, Fujita Hachiro, Kotani Katsushige, Kawamura Matasuke, Okuno Kenichi, and, to a lesser degree, Kuriyama Shigeru.[26]

PUBLIC PROCURATORS AND ATTORNEY GENERAL

The separation of the judiciary from the executive branch of the government affected both the procurators and the Ministry of Justice. The changed position of the former is reflected in the Public Procurators Office Law, which was enacted simultaneously with the Court Organization Law. The procurators, whose education corresponds to those of the judges, as we have seen, are now strictly administrative officials under the Ministry of Justice. Their function before the courts is the public action or indictment in criminal cases. In the trial they represent the state as a party on a level equal to the defense attorney. They also act for the public interest in certain domestic relations cases. The organization of the procurators' offices parallels that of the courts, with supreme, high, district, and local procurators' offices. Heading the Supreme Procurators' Office is the procurator general who, in his relationship to the ministry, enjoys a great deal of independence. Thus, the ministry may not directly give orders to a procurator, but must do this through the procurator general.

The procurators are also appointed officials. Here again, some check on their appointment and continuation in office was considered advisable. A Committee for the Examination

25 See *Law in Japan*, p. 114.

26 Danelski, *Comparative Judicial Behavior*, pp. 121–156 in what he calls "The Supreme Court of Japan, an Exploratory Study," offers an interesting analysis of the background and attitudes of the justices.

of Qualifications of Public Procurators, consisting of members of both Houses of the Diet, the procurator general, and representatives of the ministry, the Supreme Court, the bar associations, and the law schools, serves this purpose by periodic examinations that could result in the removal of a procurator found unsuitable.[27] Besides this personal check, a functional one was set up by the Law for the Inquest of Prosecution,[28] in the form of a popular investigation of cases in which the procurator has failed to prosecute. The inquest has been characterized as a mild or embryonic form of grand jury; it has in practice played only a modest role in terms of percentages, but has served as a relatively effective check.[29] Although its finding does not constitute a true bill of indictment, but is of an advisory nature, it could, if unfavorable, have undesirable consequences for the procurator's career, inasmuch as it is publicly posted and brought to the knowledge of his superior and of the Qualifications Committee. One of the reasons for establishing this check was the latitude given the procurator by the Code of Criminal Procedure to dispense with the indictment because of the character, age, and situation of the offender, the nature of the offense, the circumstances under which it was committed, and the conditions subsequent to the commission. This provision, which will be discussed in connection with the Code of Criminal Procedure, lends itself to favor-

[27] Established by amendment of the Procurators Office Law, dated May 1, 1948.

[28] Law of July 12, 1948. For details see Howard Meyers, "The Inquest of Prosecution," Harvard Law Review 64, No. 2 (1950), 279–286.

[29] According to statistics provided Judge Hattori by the Secretariat General of the Supreme Court for the period from 1948 through 1960, the inquest reviewed 18,748 cases. The decision of the procurator not to indict was found proper in 72.6 percent of the cases and improper in 9.2 percent (see Hattori Takaaki in Law in Japan, p. 135). For devices by which procurators protect themselves from this check, see Chapter 20. In 1951 the Supreme Court expressed its strong opposition to the rumored abolition or curtailment of the inquest to the cabinet. In a memorandum I emphasized the significance of the institution as one of the few devices of direct democracy, and suggested that GHQ support the position of the Supreme Court.

itism—discovering which was thought to be the main purpose of the inquest.

The change brought about by rendering the judiciary independent from the Ministry of Justice altered the nature of the latter. The conclusion from this change was drawn by the law of December 17, 1947, establishing the Attorney General's Office (AGO), which was enacted simultaneously with the new Police Law pursuant to a "suggestion" of the Supreme Commander in form of a letter to the prime minister.[30] It replaced the minister of justice by an attorney general, who is a member of the cabinet serving as its supreme legal advisor. As such, he took over the functions of drafting and editing legislation and cabinet orders, which were previously exercised by the Cabinet Bureau of Legislation. This bureau was abolished "in the interest of governmental efficiency and economy." Actually, the efficiency of its staff did not leave anything to be desired, at least from the point of view of the pre-Occupation regime. It consisted mostly of jurists trained in the law school of the Imperial University. The reason that SCAP took exception to the bureau was rather that it had developed the habit of checking not only on the formulation and legal correctness, but also on the policy of proposed legislation, thereby exercising an influence incompatible with the principles of the new Constitution and the position of the Diet under it.

Within the Attorney General's Office several bureaus, each headed by an assistant attorney general, reflected the various responsibilities of that authority. They were concerned with legislation, prosecution, research and opinion, litigation, and execution.

It is obvious that this reorganization along American lines not only constituted a modernization, and drew the logical consequences from the independence of the judiciary, but beyond that was of high political importance. With the abolition of the Home Ministry and the democratization and decentralization of the police, it did away with two

[30] See *Political Reorientation*, II, 705–706.

powerful agents of the former police state. The emphasis in the law on civil liberties gives expression to the idea that the state, besides controlling its citizens, has the obligation to protect their rights. Awareness of this obligation was shown by the initiative of the first attorney general, Suzuki Yoshio, in establishing a Civil Liberties Bureau within his office. This bureau works in the field through civil liberties commissioners.[31]

LAWYERS

Although not without political influence, the legal profession enjoyed little social prestige in Japan, even less than the judges, and was subject to tight supervision by the Ministry of Justice, exercised by the procurators over the bar associations. While disbarment and other disciplinary punishment of lawyers were entrusted to a disciplinary court connected with the appellate courts, the minister of justice could open the procedure. I have already mentioned the shockingly small number of lawyers in Japan,[32] a phenomenon caused mainly by the aversion of the people to litigation and by their preference for compromise and out-of-court settlement. In court trials the customary role of

[31] While the AGO law was not handled in my division, it had to be discussed here, since it appears inseparable from the legal and judicial reforms. This is one of the very few Occupation-induced legal-judicial innovations with regard to which the clock was subsequently turned back to some extent; the Cabinet Bureau of Legislation has been restored, and the Attorney General's Office has again become the Ministry of Justice—without, however, an essential change of its responsibilities.

[32] That diminutive size of the bar has not increased sufficiently. As Andrew Horvart reports in *Mainichi* of December 5, 1972, Japan has fewer than 8,000 lawyers—that is, fewer than one for every 13,000 people, while there is one for about every 700 Americans. Tanabe Kohji in *Law in Japan*, p. 83, n. 33, similarly stresses the paucity of Japanese lawyers in 1960. Hattori Takaaki, describing the status of the pre-Occupation bar, points to the lack of confidence in the ability of the legal profession (*ibid.*, p. 128). The fact that lawyers were not admitted to the same training as judges and procurators may have contributed to this distrust.

lawyers was not that of courageous fighters for the rights of their clients. In criminal cases, their advice to the defendant was often, even in doubtful instances, not to deny guilt, but to plead mitigating circumstances in order not to irritate the presiding judge. It was clear to us from the beginning that the liberation from governmental control of the bar had to follow the creation of an independent judiciary. Our contacts with the leaders of the bar associations made us see the potentiality of an eventual development of Japan's bar to a protagonist of civil rights.

The revision of the Lawyers' Law was, however, delayed until June 10, 1949, and thus turned out to be the last important reform within the jurisdiction of my division. The reason for the delay was that the question of the degree of independence to be granted the bar was for a lengthy period a controversial subject among the leading bar associations, the Attorney General's Office, and the Supreme Court. Here we did not have to push anything, since the bar associations themselves showed a gratifying zeal to achieve the greatest possible degree of independence. We had, however, the satisfaction of being continuously consulted by their leaders, who were interested in the American system of an integrated bar. We restricted ourselves to information, and in this function MacCormick proved particularly useful. The Lawyers' Law was introduced as a member bill by a lawyer, who was a member of the Diet.[33] Without going into any detail, it may be pointed out that the position of the bar associations was finally accepted. The law provided that a bar association be established within the area of each district court. A Japan Federation of Bar Associations was to be the nation-wide top organization, with the various bar associations as well as the individual lawyers throughout the country as its members. Admission to the bar must be made through the local bar association

[33] Hattori in *Law in Japan*, p. 136, states that it was enacted with the support of the bar and "clearly represents 'a step forward' for the bar as a whole."

4. The author, Arthur McCormick, and George Koshi discuss the Lawyers' Law with members of a Tokyo bar association.

that the candidate wants to join. The application is then forwarded to the federation, which keeps a name list of all lawyers. Registration in this list is a prerequisite for admission to the bar. If, however, the local bar association refuses to forward the application, the candidate may complain to the federation, which decides on the merits of the case. Against its finding, the person adversely affected may appeal to the high court. The only function left to the Supreme Court is the admission of foreign lawyers.

In September 1951, a representative of the Japan Bar Association asked me to write an article on the future of the Japanese bar in the Peace edition of *Hoso Koron* (Legal Review).[34] In this article, I pointed out that, although Japan's lawyers had enjoyed the status of full autonomy for only two years, they had, under the guidance of the Federation of Bar Associations, given proof that freedom from outside control means increased responsibilities. The federation, I wrote, had worked out a code of ethics for the legal profession; created a Civil Liberties Committee, and shown considerable initiative in the protection of civil rights; expressed opinions on legislation and judicial administration; promoted legal aid to the poor; encouraged the establishment of Practicing Law Institutes to train lawyers in the revised law and procedure; and engaged in many other significant activities. Women lawyers had organized their own bar association and specialized in family law and those legal aspects that affect women's status. Moving on to the future, I professed belief in the basic brotherhood of all those who serve the law. I somewhat sanguinely visualized future bar associations that would include judges, procurators, and legal scholars in their membership.

[34] Translated and published in the *Nippon Times* of October 5, 1951.

◇◇

CHAPTER NINE

Reform of Substantive Law

CIVIL CODE[1]

The old Civil Code of 1898 was patterned on the Code Napoleon and on the German Civil Code, in the process of the adoption of Continental law after the Meiji Restoration. The objectives of the Occupation did not call for a change in the three first books of the Civil Code, namely, General Provisions, Real Property, and Obligations. They have remained unchanged, a fact that also disproves the assertion that the Occupation completely Americanized the Japanese law. It was only in the fields of family and inheritance law covered in the fourth and fifth books that fundamental changes were required to have constitutional principles such as dignity of the individual, equality of sexes, free choice of marriage partner, and freedom of movement implemented. Here the adoption of Western patterns had been carefully avoided in the Meiji reforms, and semifeudal customs had been retained, in spite of already remarkable opposition.

The family system under the old Code was characterized by the institution of the "house," that is, a clan unit distinguished from the Western type of nuclear family consisting of father, mother, and unmarried children. The head of the house, most often the oldest male of the clan, wielded important powers over the sometimes large number of other

[1] For more details, see the two articles of Kurt Steiner listed in Chapter 7, n. 3.

members, who did not necessarily live together with him. When they did, the customary "three generation household," as R. P. Dore terms it,[2] would consist of the husband as head of the house and his wife; his eldest son and the latter's wife and children; his unmarried sons and daughters; and his unmarried younger brothers and sisters. When the brothers married, they sometimes also remained in their older brother's house, but more often they founded so-called branch families, which retain a certain deference to, if not economic dependence on, the main family. Daughters, when they married, left the house of their father and became members of their husband's house. Marriage was not considered the fulfillment of the partners' love, but rather as means for the preservation and perpetuation of the family. Neither the boy nor the girl could freely choose the partner, but the match was arranged by the parents through a go-between on the basis of considerations of the family's benefit rather than the happiness of the young couple. Seeking such happiness was frowned upon as egoism. The bride had to undergo a kind of apprenticeship under the frequently strict and unpleasant guidance of her mother-in-law, an apprenticeship called "learning the ways of the family." The *yome*, as the new daughter-in-law was named, had, in addition, often enough to suffer from the instruction and nagging of her unmarried sisters-in-law. Thus, from birth to death, a Japanese female had to be a patient servant, mostly to a male, be it her father or the head of his house, or her husband or the head of his house. Even as widow, she remained a member of her husband's house and subject to control by its head. Of course, none of these dependencies were as hard to bear as the period of training by the mother-in-law. After her eldest son had grown up and married, she would herself become a training mother-in-law of his bride, and one should assume that the remembrance of her own mother-in-law troubles should prevent her from using the

[2] See R. P. Dore, *City Life in Japan* (Berkeley and Los Angeles: University of California Press, 1958), p. 123.

same harsh methods. But according to all observation, this usually did not happen.

Here it may be mentioned briefly that the inequality of the wife extended to the legal arrangements for the administration of her property, divorce, and inheritance.

The "head of the house" was, as a rule, a grandfather. When he died, his eldest son, to whom the younger children owed respect even before, succeeded him in the headship. Although emphasis is upon male superiority, widows—if childless or during the minority of their children—may become heads of the house, and so may daughters, although if they later marry the headship usually falls to their husbands. To have a male heir, a father may adopt a young man who is to marry his daughter, and who then takes the family name.[3]

As for the powers of the head of the house, his approval was required for almost all important decisions in the lives of the members, such as change of residence, marriage, divorce, and adoption. Since property and inheritance were tied up with the house, a feature of particular importance in case of the agricultural farm, refusal to obey the head, which could lead to expulsion from the house, had serious economic implications, apart from the social ones. This was all the more notable as the powers of the head of the house were to some extent counterbalanced by his obligation to support needy members of the family. Incidentally, this economic cohesiveness might also benefit a retiring head of the house. When he grew very old or sick and needy, he would resign the headship in favor of his first-born son in the expectation of receiving support from him.

One may say, then, that the principal elements of the house system included primogeniture, male superiority, and social and economic cohesiveness. It is necessary to add

[3] Adoption was, however, frequently abused for obtaining cheap child labor or forcing girls into commercial prostitution. I saw to it that the family courts paid continuous attention to this danger when dealing with applications for adoption.

respect for the ascendants, symbolized in ancestor worship and the demand of filial piety. This demand could lead to serious conflicts of loyalty, for instance, if the parents did not get along with their daughter-in-law and urged their son to divorce her. In the strict spirit of the house system, he was expected to give in to his parents' wish or command, even if he loved his wife.

All this was a reflection of Confucian philosophy, which neglects the individual and his "inalienable rights" in favor of a hierarchical setup. In Japan, the imperial system itself was a product of this philosophy. At the top of the pyramid, the emperor towered as a kind of super-pater familias over the state, with the family below. The individual was far down, with duties to all levels of government and family, and with pitiably few rights. There existed a variety of personal dependencies, as we have seen, within the family unit, and, moreover, in the relationship between *sensei* (teacher) and pupil, or between *oyabun* (boss) and *kobun* (underling). These dependencies were praised by traditional-minded Japanese as "beautiful" because of the corresponding mutual loyalties they engendered, a remnant indeed of feudal attitudes, such as also prevailed in medieval Europe. The Constitution laid the legal groundwork for liberating the Japanese people from what its Occupation drafters as well as many Japanese believed were antiquated bonds.[4]

But this raises the sociological question: were they really antiquated? More specifically, was the house system still a vital ingredient of Japanese society, or was it already obsolete when we worked on the revision of the Civil Code? One of the most brilliant attempts to answer this question for the year 1958 has been Dore's book, *City Life in Japan*. The author, in introducing his description of the family system, makes the interesting remark that it "is not a de-

[4] See, for instance, the statement of Minister of Justice Kimura quoted by Steiner, "The Revision of the Civil Code in Japan," p. 175. I remember Kimura as a not overly liberal official. His position appears all the more significant.

scription of how most people behave today, nor even of how most (only some) people think people ought to behave today. It is rather a description of how most people think most people used to behave and everyone used to expect people to behave."[5] To some extent, this observation was already true of the early Occupation period. While this whole field of social and moral attitudes resists simplification, one may accept as valid, even for this period, Dore's findings that in Tokyo and in other large cities, especially Osaka, the family system was essentially weakened and undermined. It was, indeed, my impression as early as 1947 that it was virtually obsolete among blue collar workers, and not vital at all among office employees. The extensive replacement of men by women in men's jobs during the war economy and the increasing admission of women to the higher forms of education had contributed to the fading, though not the complete disappearance, of the Confucian myth of female inferiority.

In agricultural areas of rural Japan, the house system actually survived much more strongly, inasmuch as its principle of primogeniture prevented the fragmentation of the small farm. Certain aristocratic and upper-class families also continued to cultivate the traditional system, which had found its purest—and most rigid—application among the Tokugawa samurai. It is, therefore, not surprising that conservative members in the Diet during the discussions on the Constitution took exception to the utterly individualistic Article 24,[6] which, indeed, engendered more debate in the Diet than any other part of the Constitution except for the articles dealing with the Emperor.

Still, the old family system was moribund even without the pressures accompanying the making of the Constitution; it would only have died a slower death. In 1898 there were

[5] P. 96.
[6] Article 24 reads: "With regard to choice of spouse, property rights, inheritance, choice of domicile, divorce, and other matters pertaining to marriage and the family, laws shall be enacted from the standpoint of individual dignity and the essential equality of sexes."

already reformists who favored a more individualistic approach to family law in the old Civil Code. But the overriding reason for the rather radical abolition of the old system that followed with the revision of the Code was what Dore characterizes as the confusion after defeat, "catastrophic to the old morality."[7] I have called it "the revaluation of all values." After the people had suffered the shock of seeing the whole seemingly gigantic fortress of military and political power break down ignominiously, the feeling of "damn what you have adored and adore what you have damned" was very much in vogue. Going beyond political and military values, this skepticism—and with it, the open-mindedness to innovations—extended to societal and moral values.

To return to the legal aspects, the existing Civil Code embodied the old house system and was obviously in sharp conflict with Article 24 of the Constitution. After the latter had come into effect, that system was, at least legally, doomed to elimination or emasculation. One may say that the real decision was already made with the enactment of the Constitution. Still, when the very broad principles of Article 24 had to be implemented in the law of the land, particularly in a revised Civil Code, there remained definite possibilities of nuances. Realizing the sensitivity of this private family sphere, we assisted in the drafting of this aspect of the reforms in a carefully restrained manner, limiting ourselves to informative advice when such was requested. While we never urged the complete abolition of the house system,[8] we watched with eager interest how the

[7] Dore, *City Life in Japan*, p. 162.

[8] In an article of the *Asahi Evening News* of August 22, 1959, "14 Years since Surrender," it is explicitly recognized that the "amendment of the Civil Code was not subjected to pressure from the Occupation authorities," and the earlier-mentioned Okuno remarked: "I want to make it clear that we did not receive any instructions or directives on this matter." The same article quoted, however, two former officials of the Ministry of Justice, who made less friendly comments on the revision of the Code of Criminal Procedure. Since they both looked at it

Japanese would adjust it to the principles of the Constitution. They did a more thorough job than we had expected. The attempt to save at least the institution of the house, though deprived of features irreconcilable with the new individualism, was defeated in the committees in favor of its complete abolition as the family unit. We were told that this more radical solution was vigorously advocated by three women leaders. They had ample reason to fight, since women were the largest population group to benefit.[9]

The principal and fundamental change enacted by the revised Code of December 12, 1947, lies, of course, in the replacement of the "house" by the "conjugal" Western family centered around father and mother with their unmarried young children. The powers of the head of the house disappeared with the abolition of the house system. There is, however, some sentimental remembrance of ancestor worship in Article 897 of the new Code, which exempts the ownership of genealogical records, of utensils for religious rites, and of tombs from the rules of succession, and provides that it devolves upon the person designated by the ancestor or by custom "to hold as president the worship to the memory of the ancestors."

The legal sanctions against a young man and woman who, in disobedience to their elders' will, follow their own heart in choosing a spouse are gone. The new Code allows them to do so without any permission of a house head. The parents' consent formerly needed for the bride up to the age of twenty-five and for the bridegroom up to thirty years is now required only for minors. The customary go-between *has certainly not vanished from the Japanese scene, but it is* now easier for the daughter as well as the son to say no to

---

from the one-sided point of view of the prosecutor, they did not sufficiently appreciate the necessity of strengthening the rights of the accused, as required by the new Constitution.

[9] It is interesting that the women lawyers' group, with whom I conferred on these family questions, favored the retention of the house system without the powers of the head.

the proposed engagement.[10] The inferior position of the wife with regard to her legal capacity in the management of her property was also abolished. While formerly any important disposition she made of it without the approval of her husband could be voided, she is now free to manage her personal property and dispose of it.

Inequalities on account of sex have, moreover, been deleted in connection with divorce. In that area, the women suffered particular discrimination. The ancient custom permitting the husband to dismiss his wife by sending her a "note of three and a half lines"[11] must have been the source of much tragedy. Even when it came to judicial divorce, her position was inferior to that of her husband. The unequal treatment of adultery in the criminal law, which I have described before, had its parallel in the divorce law of the old Code. Adultery was always a ground for divorce when committed by the wife. She, however, could demand divorce only if the husband had been convicted of a sexual crime. Equalization has been adopted in this field, too. In consistency with our self-restraint with respect to domestic relations, we did not object to the retention of the traditional divorce by agreement, although we were aware of the danger that due to her subordinate position, which we did not expect to disappear overnight, this institution would continue to work to the disadvantage of the female partner. Even though she might not have been willing to choose the unenviable status of a divorcée, she more often than not agreed formally to the divorce, as we had found out, under the pressure of her husband and of her in-laws, with whom she usually, though now no longer necessarily, had to live. We saw to it, however, that a judicial check on the voluntary nature of the agreement was introduced in the revised law.

[10] Dore, in *City Life in Japan*, p. 157, expresses the optimistic view that "the greatest single change in Japanese family institutions lies in the increased importance attached to the emotional relationship between husband and wife."

[11] See Steiner, "The Revision of the Civil Code in Japan," p. 182.

As for inheritance, there was previously the distinction between succession into the house and succession into personal property. In succession into the house, which now no longer exists, the male was generally given preference over the female members. With regard to succession into personal property, the surviving spouse did not inherit anything as long as there were lineal descendants. Under the new Code, the wife as well as the husband, when succeeding with such descendants, are entitled to a legal share of one-third, a more generous rule than that provided in the German Civil Code, where the share is only one-fourth.

Parental power, previously exercised by the father, is, pursuant to the reform, in the hands of both parents. The family court, to which considerable authority is assigned, would decide if and when the parents could not come to an agreement in matters involving the welfare of the child.

These illustrations show that the radical revision of the Civil Code, with its sociological implications, represents a very important—if not the most important—part of the reform legislation, since it affects the intimate life of every Japanese man and woman. While not perfect, the reform surpassed our hopes, and appeared quite apt to open the way to a freer individual in a freer society. That does not mean that we expected collectivist attitudes to change rapidly into individualist ones, but we knew that this legal foundation would greatly help the progressive elements of the population to advance their ideas. The victory of these elements in the process of the legislative change encouraged us, and confirmed our previous impression that the traditional institution of the house was doomed, at least as a legally prescribed mode of life. Whoever wanted to stick to it as a "beautiful" custom could, of course, do so, as long as others who rejected it were not forced into it by law. Up to now, twenty-five years later, reactionary attempts to restore the old family bonds have failed.[12]

[12] For instance, Kishi Nobusuke, as chairman of the Liberal party's Constitutional Revision Committee in 1953, made a statement to the

My *expectation* is that the trend has been continuously in the direction of abandoning family institutions that do no longer fit into the highly industrialized modern Japan with its economic miracle. The presence in the country of innumerable American officers, soldiers, and civilians over several years, the tremendous influence of Western culture upon the Japanese people, the attraction of the big cities, the definite improvement of women's position in society, and the increase of marriages based on love—all these developments cannot fail to result eventually in a conformity of popular attitudes with the reformed law.

Closely related to the revision of the Civil Code, the Family Registration Law of January 1, 1948, replaces the old house registration *(koseki)* with one of the small Western-type family unit. Formerly under the jurisdiction of the minister of home affairs, the *koseki*, with all its minute information, served as a fitting instrument of the police state. But since the Japanese law has traditionally made registration the prerequisite legal confirmation and effectuation of most important events in human life, such as birth, recognition, adoption, marriage, divorce, death, and disinheritance, an impossible confusion would have ensued if we had insisted on its disappearance.[13]

CRIMINAL CODE[14]

The Criminal Code, which also leaned heavily on European models, did not require a thorough mending, since it was a

---

effect that Article 24 may be subject to revision; this statement met, however, wide criticism. Prime Minister Ikeda, in the early sixties explicitly rejected the idea. Furthermore, Takayanagi in *The Constitution of Japan, Its First Twenty Years*, p. 100, reports that in the Commission on the Constitution some—mostly male—members recommended the restoration of the old family system and that he himself opposed it as harmful because of conflict with the changes in sociological ideas.

[13] For details see my contribution to *Political Reorientation*, I, 217–219.

[14] For details see the article of Howard Meyers, "Revision of the Criminal Code of Japan During the Occupation."

relatively advanced piece of legislation. Although it was enacted as early as 1882 and needed some modernization, there were few provisions irreconcilable with the new constitutional principles. We have already mentioned that the revised version, enacted on October 14, 1947, adjusted the whole chapter called "Crimes against the Imperial Family" to the principle of equality before the law as well as to the changed position of the Emperor as a symbol. The dramatic events leading to the abolition of these sanctions against lese majesty will be reported in a subsequent chapter. It has also been described how the unequal treatment of wives and husbands in cases of adultery was deleted in the Code. SCAP's insistence that nobody should enjoy privileged protection before the law resulted in our also approving the deletion of the provisions in the Code subjecting crimes against heads of state and envoys of a foreign power to more severe punishment than those against other people. While the retention of the lese majesty chapter would have been politically undesirable under the circumstances prevailing in the first years of the Occupation, the legal question of whether privileged protection in criminal law of a person or category of persons under specific conditions violates the constitutional principle of equality was subsequently under judicial review. In a famous patricide case,[15] the Supreme Court had to deal with the articles of the Code prescribing more severe penalties for inflicting death or other bodily injury on lineal ascendants than for committing the same offenses against other persons. It might appear inconsistent that in spite of SCAP's abolition of lese majesty we left these provisions untouched. We did so out of the same consideration for the sensitive area of family relations that underlay our self-restraint in the revision of the Civil Code. As was to be expected, the majority of the Court upheld the constitutionality of the unequal treatment on the basis

[15] The judgment of October 11, 1950, is translated into English in Maki, *Court and Constitution in Japan*, pp. 134–139. For an analysis see Kurt Steiner, "A Japanese Cause Celebre: The Fukuoka Patricide Case," in *American Journal of Comparative Law* 5 (1956), 106ff.

of natural law, declaring the relations between close relatives "the great fountainhead of human ethics," and also
holding, among other points, that the requirement of
equality applies to the subjects of rights rather than to the
objects or victims of a crime. Justices Mano and Hozumi
Shigeto, both later participants in the Supreme Court
Mission, which I describe in Chapter 22, argued in courageous dissenting opinions in favor of invalidation of the
provisions, criticizing the majority for confusing law and
morality. In a concurring opinion, Justice Saito Yusuke
vehemently attacked the two dissenters and the original
judgment of the Fukuoka District Court, which had arrived
at the same result as they did. Saito called the minority
opinions "conceited notions of ingratitude, lacking in understanding . . . morality, and aimlessly chasing after innovations." He expressed himself with special bitterness
against Mano, writing: "I find it unbearable to read the rest
of the opinion for it develops an academically prostituted
theory that is a national disgrace, a theory based on self-
centered egoism under the beautiful name of democracy."

Because of these insulting remarks by the legally competent but hopelessly antireformist Saito, the patricide case
had important political repercussions. It came just at the
time when a Diet Committee held public hearings on the
proposed Contempt of Court Bill, which had been opposed
by lawyers and legal scholars as unconstitutional and open
to abuse by the judges. Chief Justice Tanaka informed me
that Professor Suehiro in one of these hearings characterized
it as strange that the Court, which made public a decision
so harmful to its dignity desired to be granted contempt
power.[16] This called the attention of the Diet Impeachment

[16] Contempt of court power was greatly needed in a period when
trials were frequently disturbed by uproarious radicals and rowdies.
The mild police power which the courts could use at that time did not
suffice to control them. Still, the enactment of a law conferring effective
contempt power upon the courts was repeatedly delayed because of
negative reaction, particularly from the lawyers. A Contempt of Court
Law was finally enacted by the Diet. We had been consulted, but the

Committee to Saito's derogatory opinion, and an investigation of his conduct was initiated. Tanaka and I agreed that Saito's aggressive behavior, while violating the unwritten laws of collegiality and tact, did not justify impeachment. The Diet Committee came to the same conclusion.

The majority's and Saito's traditional view on the patricide question did not prevail, however. By a decision of April 3, 1973, the Supreme Court reversed the precedent and declared the pertinent provision in the Criminal Code unconstitutional.[17]

There existed, in my opinion, a definite constitutional problem, which has recently plagued our own American courts, namely, the question of whether the death penalty provided in the Code violated the prohibition of "cruel punishments" in the Japanese Constitution—which, unlike the Bonn Constitution of Germany, does not explicitly ban that type of punishment. Since this subject matter is very close to my heart and has occupied my mind, I shall elaborate on it.

I am and always have been against the death penalty. When I was a judge in Berlin almost forty years ago, I joined in a public petition of German jurists for the abolition of capital punishment. It merely satisfies the demands for retribution and deterrence, although a comparison of

---

time had come when we left the initiative for legislation to the Japanese. The motivation of the lawyers' opposition became clear to me when, in March, 1951, a leader of the Federation of Bar Associations made the naive personal remark that the bar would have no objections to such a law if the lawyers were excepted from its application.

[17] The decision was reported in *Mainichi Daily News* of April 5, 1973. I welcomed it as a progressive step away from the Supreme Court's overcautious use of judicial review. I think, however, that the legal question of different treatment under the law escapes a simple answer. Differentiation is indeed, as Saito points out, sometimes unavoidable, as with regard to minors, women, and public officials. In connection with lese majesty, the assassination of President Kennedy has somewhat shaken my former conviction that the general sanctions of the criminal law sufficiently protect heads of state or monarchs, who are in constant danger of life.

capital crimes committed in American states that have
laws providing for capital punishment with those committed in other states that do not has shown that there is
no essential difference in the frequency of capital crime.
Thus, the deterrent effect may well be doubted.[18] The ir-
reversibility of the death sentence, once executed, appears
to me as a strong argument against it in light of the human
fallibilities of judges and of the forcible methods applied by
ambitious investigating agents, even in our country. Beyond
that, I feel that the guillotine and the gallows are remnants
of the Dark Ages, that the gas chamber and electric chair
are not much better, and that to subject a human being to
any of them violates the prohibition of "cruel punishments"
in both the American and Japanese constitutions. Finally,
the inequality of the application of the death penalty, which
is seldom imposed upon members of the upper classes, is
another argument against it. The difference in punishment
of rape dependent on the race of the defendant, as practiced
in the South, may illuminate this. It has been mainly because
of this inequality that the United States Supreme Court in
1972 decided that the death penalty in its present form, and
in the cases decided upon, constitutes cruel and unusual
punishment in violation of the American Constitution.[19]
I find the concurring opinion of Mr. Justice Brennan particularly illuminating. He points out that death remains the
only punishment that may involve the conscious infliction
of physical pain, and emphasizes the mental pain resulting
from the inevitably long wait between imposition of sentence and actual infliction of death. Unfortunately, as
Wilson, in his aforementioned article, observes, the Supreme
Court decision has not settled much, and has had an effect
opposite to what abolitionists had hoped, since a number of
states afterwards enacted laws with mandatory capital pun-

[18] James Q. Wilson, in a lucid article in the *New York Times Maga-
zine* of October 28, 1973, makes it clear that the deterrent effect of the
death penalty has not and probably cannot be proved.

[19] See *Furman* v. *Georgia*, June 27, 1972, 40 LW 4923.

ishment for specific felonies. This was supposed to eliminate inequality of treatment, but in leaving the judge no opportunity to consider the mitigating circumstances of the individual case, established the most objectionable inequity in the application of criminal law. It is to be hoped that a new decision of the Supreme Court will eliminate all ambiguities, but regardless of how it will decide, the trend is toward abolition not only in most other civilized countries but also in the United States. Here no death penalty has been executed during the last several years. Perhaps the conviction has gained ground that criminal offenses are caused by the sickness of society or of the offender's mind in many cases. The late Governor Winthrop Rockefeller's commutation of all death sentences in his State of Arkansas, fifteen in number, is symptomatic of the trend.[20] He was severely criticized for his clemency.

Since society must be protected from dangerous lawbreakers, parole should be excluded unless a thorough examination arrives at the conclusion that the prisoner is no longer a danger. Otherwise, he should not be released. I am aware of the objection that such a system would often lead to lifetime feeding of the most unworthy criminals. I do not think, however, that we should sacrifice humanitarianism on the altar of budgetary considerations.

Still, life is too complicated to stick unalterably to principles. To be completely honest, I must confess that I myself have not always been free of retaliatory emotions. When the Nazi leaders were hanged, it was the monstrosity of their crimes that made me feel, against principle, that the execution of most of them was the proper and the only possible thing to do, although it could not be a true atonement for the incredible tortures, humiliations, and cruel deaths of millions of their victims.[21]

[20] See *New York Times*, December 30, 1970.
[21] Since I had nothing to do with the trial of the Japanese war criminals, I refrain from comment on this controversial subject, except to say that in my view it would have been preferable to have them

In light of my abomination of the death penalty, the question will be asked why I did not endeavor to bring about abolition in the Criminal Code of Japan. I raised, indeed, no objection to its retention because I had arrived at the conclusion that the overwhelming majority of the Japanese were still convinced of the deterring effect of capital punishment, which some of them also regarded necessary for the retributory satisfaction of the victim or his relatives. Since among us Americans, too, the adherents were more numerous than the opponents, I felt that merely on the basis of my personal aversion, I had no right to press for an innovation for which, as I saw it, neither the Japanese nor our own nation was ripe at that time. Soon after the enactment of the Code, namely, on March 12, 1948, the grand bench of the Supreme Court of Japan rejected an appeal from a death sentence in a murder case by holding that the penalty imposed did not violate the constitutional prohibition of "cruel punishments."[22] The majority opinion emphasized that the threat of the death penalty may be a general preventive measure, its execution may be a means of cutting off at the root special social evils, and both may be used to protect society. The Court suggested that its approval of capital punishment means "giving supremacy to the concept of humanity as a whole rather than to the concept of humanity as individuals." Ultimately, the majority resorted again to the magic formula in the Constitution of public welfare, consideration of which, it held, limits the "right to life," as all other civil liberties, and requires the retention of the death penalty. Interestingly enough, in a concurrent opinion four associate justices, who consider "the feelings of the people decisive with regard to the question of cruelty

---

tried by a tribunal composed of an equal number of representatives of the victor, the vanquished, and of a neutral nation. I never liked the idea that the victors alone were judges of the acts of the defeated side's statesmen and generals.

22 For a translation into English, see Maki, *Court and Constitution in Japan*, pp. 156–164.

of punishments" appear to share my opinion that the eventual trend, and I may add the desirable trend, is toward abolition. While recognizing that the people still favor capital punishment, their feelings are described as subject to change. The judges foresee the elimination of the death penalty "as a nation's culture develops to a high degree and as a peaceful society is realized . . . and if a time is reached when it is not felt to be necessary for the public welfare to prevent crime by the menace of the death penalty."[23]

Japan had a variety of very severe penal sanctions against treason in time of war. The renunciation of war clause in the Constitution and its whole pacifist spirit led to their deletion. It was optimistically believed that there remained only a need for protection of the nation from treasonable acts in conspiracy with a foreign power that would force war upon Japan by aggression. Military service in such a power or otherwise aiding it militarily is made punishable by stiff penalties, including death. These provisions were considered necessary for the inalienable right of self-preservation, and therefore permissible under the Constitution.

The new idea of international cooperation anchored in the preamble to the Constitution required the disappearance of an odd provision in the old Code that seemed to reflect the previous racial superiority complex of the Japanese. It had made the Japanese Criminal Code applicable to every foreigner who committed certain offenses against a

[23] Opinion polls in 1956 and 1967 seem to confirm the fact that the feelings of the Japanese people at those times were still against abolition. In a 1956 poll by the Mainichi press, only 23.8 percent of the 2,904 persons polled favored abolition, while 59.3 percent declared themselves against it. In the same year a poll organized by the government resulted in an increase of the percentage of the antiabolitionists to 65 and in a decrease of the abolitionists to 18. In a 1967 poll by the government of 2,500 people, the vote against abolition rose to 71 percent, and that in favor of it declined to 16 percent. The data on the polls are taken from "Results and Problems of K. O. L. Research in Japan," a preliminary report by Chiba Masaji to the *Symposium of the International Research Committee on Sociology of Law in Noordwijk, Netherlands*, September 1972.

Japanese citizen outside of the Empire of Japan. A similar extension of Japanese law and jurisdiction, which resulted in constitutionally prohibited double jeopardy, was born out of a related attitude. It made it possible to prosecute and convict a person under Japanese law even though a final judgment for the same offense had been rendered abroad. As a matter of course, this article had to be and was abolished.

There exists an essential difference between Western and Japanese ideology with regard to truth. While we believe, at least in theory, that truthfulness is an overriding ethical command, the Japanese, if I may generalize, are inclined to the attitude that to be polite is more important and decent than to say the truth if and when the latter would hurt the other fellow. It is, therefore, not astonishing that the old Criminal Code, in its chapter on defamation and libel, protected the reputation of a person regardless of the truth of publicly alleged damaging facts about that person. Such allegation was a criminal offense, and truth was no defense. This made adverse criticism of established powers within the state dangerous, if not impossible, and flagrantly violated the constitutional guarantee of freedom of speech. That had to be changed without doing away with the protection of people from false accusations and other forms of calumny. The revised Code, while increasing the penalties for libel, to a considerable extent admits evidence of truth as defense. Allegations injurious to the reputation of another person are not punishable now if made in the public interest and primarily for the public benefit, *and* if the alleged facts are found true. Two examples in which the public interest and the motivation for the public benefit can be assumed are listed: first, facts concerning the commission of a criminal offense as long as no prosecution has been initiated; and second, facts injurious to the reputation of a public official or a candidate for public office. The first illustration serves to promote the detection of crimes by the law-enforcement agencies, and the second emphasizes the principle, indispensable in any free nation, according to which he who holds public office or runs for it must be exposed to public criticism, inasmuch as a higher degree of integrity is expected of him than of others.

Among the more technical revisions, I may mention one correcting undesirable aspects of the police state: we increased the penalties for abuse of power by public officials in the process of prosecution or police investigation. More severe punishment was provided for the guard who treats a convicted prisoner with violence and cruelty. In light of the third-degree methods that prevailed among Japanese police and prison personnel, this was deemed imperative. We did not overlook the problem involved in fighting these methods, which also exist in our own country, namely, the reluctance of the cruelly treated person to complain and the inclination of the higher authority to refrain from taking action against the guilty official.

Minor offenses had not been dealt with previously in the Criminal Code, but under an ordinance, and were tried by the police courts, which were now abolished. The new Constitution requires that penal provisions be enacted by Diet legislation unless explicit delegation is made to the cabinet. The Minor Offenses Law of May 1, 1948, replaces most of the regulations of the old ordinances by compiling a list of these insignificant offenses, carefully omitting those that could infringe on constitutional safeguards, such as freedom of assembly and speech.[24]

[24] Important amendments of the Commercial Code enacted in 1948 and 1950 were not handled in Government Section, but in the Economic and Scientific Section (ESS). They are, therefore, outside the scope of this report on the legal and judicial reforms in which my division was involved. Blakemore, and after him Steiner, participated as observers in the deliberations, in which the Anti-Trust and Cartels Division of ESS exercised domineering influence. Blakemore has described the procedure and substance of these revisions, together with Yazawa Makoto, a Japanese law professor, in a partly critical article: "Japanese Commercial Code Revisions Concerning Corporations," *American Journal of Comparative Law* 2 (January, 1953), 12-24.

◇◇◇

CHAPTER TEN

Procedural Codes and Miscellaneous

CIVIL PROCEDURE

The existing Code of Civil Procedure of 1890 leaned heavily on its German model of 1877. There were not many provisions in this law that clearly violated principles of the new Constitution. Although the constitutional requirement of a speedy and fair trial is restricted to criminal cases in the instrument, the changes in the Code, some of them purely technical, were also motivated by the desire to expedite the civil procedure and to relieve the courts from an excessive burden of work. The dominant role played by the single judge or the presiding judge of a collegiate court during the trial had manifold reasons. First, as we have seen, the training and prestige of lawyers had been inferior to those of judges. Pretrial procedures were unusual because the few lawyers who practiced in Japan had neither the time nor, often, the ability to examine witnesses—apart from the fact that such pretrial examination by the parties was regarded as unethical in light of the danger of coaching.

The public itself apparently looked at the lawyer less as one who acts within the framework of the process of achieving justice than as a private businessman whom the client had to pay. The judge, on the other hand, was respected and even trusted as bearer of governmental authority. No wonder that under such circumstances the forensic tradition we found in Japan was very like that in Germany (where the

bar had reached higher prestige): the judge wielded almost
complete power in conducting the trial, investigating, clarifying, taking evidence, and sentencing. He would always be
the first one to examine the parties and witnesses, and he
did it in an efficient and inquisitorial manner that many
Japanese jurists now admit to have been paternalistic.[1]
The parties could ask supplemental questions, but this did
not amount to much, since the thoroughness of the judge
had usually exhausted the subject matter. The other side
of the judge's domineering position was the overexertion
of the courts, which resulted in postponements, piecemeal
trials, piled-up case loads, and other forms of slow justice.
The absence of a jury in Japanese law meant that the judge
had the combined responsibilities of fact finding and sentencing, besides taking care of order in the court and conducting the trial.

Even the piecemeal trials have found their defenders. It
has been argued, for instance, that the passing of considerable time between the several trial terms helps the parties
better to understand each other's viewpoint, and also makes
them more apt to settle their conflicts. I feel, however, that
these arguments are rationalizations of the traditional Japanese reluctance to fight for one's rights in court, rather than
convincing justifications.

Behind the few changes brought about by the amendment of the Code, dated July 1, 1948, were two main considerations: first, to relieve the courts, and second, to democratize the procedure by weakening judicial paternalism.
We have already mentioned the limitation of appeals to
three instances in those petty cases that start in the summary courts.[2] The deletion of former Article 261, which
authorized the presiding judge to take evidence ex officio,
is now being interpreted as the most important innovation
introducing the adversary system into the civil procedure.
This change was certainly a step away from the inquisitorial

[1] See Von Mehren, *Law in Japan*, pp. 89, 95.
[2] See above, p. 103.

conduct of the trial. The spirit of "making the party win who should win" may be somewhat appealing, but independent evidence-taking by the judge in a civil procedure, which is, after all, a conflict between private parties, drives it to an extreme. This is the way we felt; and by deleting the article we also aimed at relieving the judge from a responsibility whose assumption added to his burden and slowed down the procedure.

Was the deletion of Article 261 really the signal for the introduction of the adversary system? In answering this question, we must consider some other provisions of the amended Code. A new Article 294 provides that a witness shall first be examined by the parties, and that the presiding judge may do so after the examination by the parties has been concluded. While this appears to place the primary responsibility for the conduct of the trial and the main initiative on the litigants, some other articles of the old Code that strengthen the position of the presiding judge have remained unaltered. Article 336 authorized him to examine the parties themselves under oath, on application or ex officio if he thinks it proper, and Article 259 conferred power on him to disallow the taking of evidence tendered by a party if he finds it unnecessary to do so. In light of such seemingly contradictory arrangements, it may be correct to say that the revision did not constitute a categorical introduction of the adversary system. It still leaves open the possibility that an energetic or highhanded judge may dominate the trial by inquisitorial methods, even though he can no longer take evidence ex officio and may examine witnesses only after the parties have done so.

What, then, did we reformers have in mind? It was probably to be expected that my associates strongly favored the adversary system, as prevailed in the United States. But even I who, thanks to my German background, had a certain sympathy for the judicial endeavor to discover the truth in the trial, was inclined to move away from the rigidly inquisitorial Japanese system, particularly in civil procedure;

I shall elaborate on my attitude toward the two systems in connection with the revision of the criminal procedure.

Both systems have their definite pros and cons. The Japanese societal and judicial tradition would have made the categorical introduction of the adversary system a hasty and unwise imposition. The revision was, therefore, designed to pave the way for an eventual adoption of the adversary system after a process of adaptation that could, possibly, last a long time. The enhanced prestige of the lawyers and their improved training, the disapproval by the young generation of jurists of judicial paternalism, and the increasing necessity of relieving the courts from excessive burdens of work—all that encouraged us in the belief that the civil procedure of Japan would move a significant step in the direction of an adversary system, but we did not anticipate a replica of the American practice. Here again, as in most of the legal and judicial reforms, the *leitmotif* has been to find what Judge Tanabe terms a "midway position" or "in a real sense a fusion of the Continental and Anglo-Saxon philosophies."[3]

As for the remaining changes in the Code, the penalties against noncooperating witnesses were increased in view of the bad habit of ignoring summonses. This was all the more necessary since the Japanese were not yet ready to adopt some form of contempt of court along American lines. The abolition of the waiver of appeals previously permitted in

[3] See Von Mehren, *Law in Japan,* p. 110. Tanabe's essay, "The Process of Litigation, an Experiment with the Adversary System," is the most thorough analysis written in English by a Japanese expert. The author shows the interesting fluctuations in the legal world of Japan between enthusiastic acceptance of the adversary system, rejection, and partial return to traditional attitudes. Notwithstanding a mild criticism of the reforms, he arrives at the conclusion that their basic themes are in the Japanese law to stay, and that while "we may not yet be out of the woods, progress in adjusting and adapting the changes to the peculiarities of our society will be steady." I was particularly delighted with Tanabe's emphasis on the middle-of-the-road approach as the road to future development. It is exactly what we had in mind when working on the revision of the law.

advance of the judgment perhaps came nearest to requiring an amendment under the Constitution, since it was looked upon as jeopardizing the guaranteed right of access to the courts. Sociologically interesting were the extensive immunities from the duty to testify in the old Code. They were based on concepts of loyalty and clan obligation, which not only the Occupation but also progressive groups among the Japanese regarded as incompatible with a democratic society. I refer particularly to the rights to refuse to testify against an employer and a relative within the sixth degree of blood. They were eliminated in the new Code to a considerable extent.

ADMINISTRATIVE LITIGATION

The eagerness of the reformers to change Japan from a police state to a government of law found its most sweeping expression in the Procedure for Administrative Litigation Law of June 25, 1948. We have already noted that the Administrative Court, with its limited jurisdiction, was abolished. Now the revolutionary principle was established that the legality—not the expediency or discretion—of any administrative act could be challenged in the regular courts, where the rules of civil procedure were to apply. This protection of the citizen from violation of the law by the executive branch goes beyond that granted in most Western states. Before he appeals to the court, he must, as a matter of course, exhaust the channels of administrative complaint, but even from this rule two exceptions were made: the court may dispense with it either if "heavy damages" are to be anticipated, or if the administrative office fails to make a decision on the complaint within three months.

The Japanese drafters of this remarkable law took care, however, in connection with injunctions against allegedly illegal administrative acts, that the proper functioning of the administration not be disturbed or paralyzed by judicial interference. Injunctions suspending the administrative action are admitted only under rather limited conditions; namely, if they are deemed urgently necessary to prevent irreparable damage. Even then no injunction should be made if the suspension of execution would be against the public interest. Moreover, a check by the executive over the judiciary was introduced, whose constitutionality appears doubtful in light of the principle of the new charter that the whole judicial power is vested in the courts. The law permits the prime minister to declare that an injunction is against the public interest. Such a declaration would prevent the injunction, although it would not stop the continuation of the main court procedure against the administrative disposition.

One should assume that this extraordinary veto power will be used by the prime minister only in cases of exceptional national importance if he does not want to make himself politically vulnerable. One instance in which he did use it was the Kyoto Students Case. The students of the Kyoto Prefectural Medical School had requested to be admitted to a conference of the faculty and upon refusal invaded the conference room, disobeyed the order to leave, and disturbed the proceedings. The president thereupon imposed on them the disciplinary punishment of expulsion. The Kyoto District Court, on their complaint, did not deny the legal authority of the president to punish his students, but held that in selecting one among several possible penalties, his discretion was limited by considerations of appropriateness "in accordance with the common sense of society." Within this limitation the court declared expulsion to be excessive and undeserved, and cancelled the disposition as illegal. While differently formulated, this theory comes close to that of the abuse of discretionary power applied by American courts. Since the ousted students had successfully requested the court to order a stay of their expulsion by an injunction, the prime minister decided that the occasion justified the use of his veto power. The high court reversed the judgment of the district court, and the Supreme Court in a decision of July 30, 1954, confirmed the verdict of the high court. Emphasis was laid upon the discretionary power of administrative agencies.[4]

CRIMINAL PROCEDURE

It has already been pointed out that the amendment of the Code of Criminal Procedure, enacted on July 10, 1948, and in effect since January 1, 1949, was the most complicated and time-consuming legal reform. This was the consequence of the rich catalogue of safeguards in the new Constitution for those entangled in criminal prosecution. Law-and-order champions of today may easily find them excessive, but for an Occupation resolved to introduce fundamental rights, it was necessary to provide the legal foundations for far-reaching rights in the very sphere where the individual's life and personal freedom are eminently involved.

Among the constitutional safeguards, I may mention the rule that no person shall be apprehended except upon warrant issued by a judicial officer that specifies the offense charged, unless the person is apprehended while committing the crime; the right to counsel; the right of all persons to be secure in their homes, papers, and effects against searches and seizures, except on judicial warrant or when apprehended while committing the offense; the absolute prohibition of the infliction of torture and cruel punishment; the right to a speedy and public trial by an impartial tribunal; the rule that no person shall be compelled to testify against himself, and that confessions made under compulsion, torture, or threat, or after prolonged detention shall not be admitted in evidence; moreover, the prohibition of conviction or punishment in cases where the only proof against the defendant is his own confession; the principle of *nulla poena sine lege* (no punishment may be inflicted unless provided by law); and exclusion of double jeopardy.

[4] See p. 328 below for further comment on this case.

All these safeguards have been implemented and further developed in minute detail in the four hundred articles of the Code. Many changes have been made in the interest of expedition and efficiency of the criminal process as well as of humanization, and antiquated features of the old law have been deleted. Within the limited space available only the most important innovations can be sketched.[5]

If we start with the investigative stage, when the public procurator or the so-called judicial police suspects the commission of a criminal offense and wants to arrest the suspect, he must now, as a rule, have a warrant of arrest from a judge. Formerly, he could himself issue one. The law provides, however, for two exceptions to the rule. The law enforcement official may, without having obtained a judicial warrant, carry out the arrest first, if a person is caught *in flagranti delicto* (while committing the offense); and second, when a serious crime is involved and a judicial warrant cannot be obtained beforehand because of the urgency of the situation. If the procurator or police officer wants to detain the suspect, he must, within prescribed time limits, obtain a judicial warrant of detention, something different from the warrant of arrest. This is, however, not necessary if the procurator has instituted public action (indictment) before expiration of the prescribed time, which in the original Code was not to exceed seventy-two hours after the arrest. The procurator must also bring public action within specific periods. Some of these time limits, established to protect the suspect from prolonged detention habitually practiced by the police, were subsequently extended, since the law enforcement agencies insisted that compliance with the short time requirements seriously hampered the fulfillment of their duty.

We Occupation lawyers would have welcomed a clear-cut division of responsibilities between the procuracy and the

---

[5] For a more detailed analysis, see R. B. Appleton's "Reforms in Japanese Criminal Procedure under Allied Occupation," *Washington Law Review* 24 (November 1949), 401–430.

police, leaving the detection and investigation of the offense
to the police and the indictment to the procurator. This
could not be achieved, however, since we had to recognize
the merits of the objections by the procurators to such an
arrangement. They argued that not only were the police
often unable to handle complicated cases—for instance, of
an economic nature—but also that they were exposed to
local influences more than the procurators, whether it be to
bossism and intimidation, or to corruption. Here again the
middle of the road was chosen: the Code confers on the
"judicial police officials" the primary responsibility to "investigate the offender and the evidence," but permits the
procurator to investigate the crime himself "if he deems
it necessary." In this case, but not otherwise, he retains a
certain power of instruction to the police, and may cause
them to assist him in the investigation. As far as I could
observe, the procurator, who has remained the sole agent
of indictment under the regime of the new Code, has continued to play his powerful and efficient role as investigator
of criminal offenses.

Release on bail in case of extended detention, formerly
completely a matter of judicial discretion, is now provided
as a right, except when specifically listed felonies are involved. I have always frowned on the bail system as pluto-
cratic and dangerous to society when habitual burglars
and muggers, seized while committing their offenses, benefit from it. For Japan, it was, however, preferable to excessively long detentions. During the whole procedure the
suspect also has the right to defense counsel. He must be
informed of this right, and if he is unable to retain a
lawyer, the court must appoint one for him. When in
detention, he may interview his defense counsel without
the presence of a guard or watchman, who previously had
been the inevitable witness in such conferences. At various
stages the suspect and accused must be given notification
of the charges against him and an opportunity to be heard.
He may, however, refuse to testify, and must also be told

of his right to remain silent. Some of this seems to fore-shadow certain controversial decisions rendered years later in the United States by the Warren Supreme Court.

A significant innovation was the abolition of the preliminary investigation well known to me from Germany, and also traditional in France. It was conducted by a judge, and the idea behind it was that the investigation of grave offenses would be more impartial in the hands of a magistrate than if conducted by the prosecutor. In practice, it seldom worked this way either in Germany or in Japan, since the investigating judge was usually as eager as the procurator to prove the guilt of the accused in what amounted to a secret preparatory trial hardly reconcilable with the constitutional demand of publicity of a criminal trial. The device has, indeed, been compared to the medieval inquisition. Its abolition did not meet much opposition from our Japanese conference partners.

Unless very minor offenses are charged, the trial must take place in the presence of the accused; service by publication was formerly possible, so that a man could be convicted without his knowledge. Under the old procedure the first information that the trial court or single judge received of the facts of a case consisted of the records and dossiers of the police and procurator. This inevitably influenced him in favor of the prosecution. The new law prohibits the submission of these papers. The evidence must be provided by testimony or documentary evidence in the presence of the parties and, apart from exceptional situations, in open court. As pointed out by Nagashima Atsushi, counselor in the Ministry of Justice,[6] this change in connection with what he terms transition to the adversary system has caused much difficulty to the defense counsel in preparing the case. Formerly he had been given an opportunity to see the pretrial evidence that the procurator had submitted to the court. Due to the thoroughness of police and procuratorial investigation methods, this gave him a

[6] Von Mehren, *Law in Japan*, p. 308.

pretty good factual picture of the case before the trial, and spared him the burden of examining witnesses himself in pretrial procedures. Now, if he does not want to appear unprepared before the court, he must take evidence on his own initiative, something the Japanese lawyers are not yet fully equipped to do. The pretrial investigative records will and must, according to a Supreme Court decision, be disclosed to him only insofar as the prosecution makes use of them in the trial. I believe that these difficulties are unavoidable in the evolution from an inquisitorial to at least a partially accusatorial criminal process.[7] Unless the Supreme Court reverses its view and concedes the right of defense counsel to inspect without limitation the pretrial evidence, the development to larger lawyers' offices may be the answer. The junior law partners could then be given the task of preparing the case before the trial. This would also improve the ability of the defense counsel to examine and cross-examine witnesses.

Public procurator and defense counsel are now conceived as equal parties in the procedure, which is symbolized in

[7] Chalmers Johnson, in *Conspiracy at Matsukawa*, analyzes the monstrous trial against radical railroad union members charged with having caused the overturning and derailment of a passenger train at Matsukawa on August 17, 1949. Since the Supreme Court remanded the case to the Sendai High Court, the parties had to undergo five trial procedures, one in the district court and two in each the high court and the Supreme Court. The final decision of the Supreme Court was rendered in September 1963. All defendants had been acquitted by the second high court verdict, which was greatly influenced by newly discovered pretrial evidence favorable to the defendants, allegedly suppressed before. Johnson, on p. 340, seems to agree with the view that "the American-inspired Code of Criminal Procedure had caused a twelve-year delay in bringing these materials to light." Apart from the consideration that criticism of the new Code should not be based on the experiences made in one most unusual trial, in which dangerously polarized political forces were confronting each other, the suppression of pretrial evidence could as well have happened under the previous system. The procurator or the police who wanted to withhold facts favorable to the accused could just have removed the pertinent parts from the records.

the trial by the seating arrangements. Previously, the procurator, sharing in the governmental authority, sat on an
elevated level together with the judges, while the counsel
had his place next to or near the defendant. Their positions
have now been symbolically equalized—to what extent in
actuality, is hard to verify.

With regard to the system of trial, the tradition and the
law were as inquisitorial and paternalistic as they were in
civil procedure. Here again, the presiding judge was the
sovereign master; he was the one who did the essential
examining of the defendant as well as of the witnesses.
Only when the parties had additional questions were they
allowed to ask them. Some of the Occupation lawyers
favored the complete adoption of the adversary system in
which the initiative lies with the defense counsel and the
prosecutor, while the judge towers over the parties as a
detached umpire. Both systems have their advantages as
well as disadvantages. In the Continental type, for which I
have retained a certain inclination with respect to criminal
procedure, the court, through the presiding judge, aims at
finding out the truth. He may bring to light facts for or
against the accused by taking ex officio additional evidence
that a less conscientious counsel or procurator has overlooked or intentionally omitted. On the other hand, the
presiding judge who conducts the taking of testimony is
always in danger of growing inquisitorial, particularly
if his concern for law and order overrides his consideration
for the rights of the accused. Hence, apart from the difference that the trial is public, similar doubts can be raised
as for preliminary investigations.

The adversary system avoids the danger that the judge
may become prejudiced by his direct involvement, but, as
far as I have observed, it has its own weaknesses, at least the
way it has developed in the United States. Comparisons are,
of course, precarious because the Japanese, unlike us, have
no jury. While in our courts the parties are assured of

having the opportunity of exhausting all means of proving the merit of their cause, their duel in the court has frequently degenerated to a kind of boxing match in which the stronger one prevails. In other words, especially in a jury trial, the greater efficiency, resourcefulness, and eloquence of the defense or the prosecution may—and too often does—influence the decision. While within the adversary system the cross-examination constitutes an effective means of finding the truth, the traditional reluctance of the American judge to interfere has also led to the bad habit of the parties intimidating and grilling the witnesses without being adequately restrained.

In view of these pros and cons, our "experiment with the adversary system" again was not a radical one but moved along the middle road. The revised Code shows traits distinctively adversary as well as inquisitorial. The strengthening of the parties' position, especially that of the defense counsel, and of their role in the trial belong to the former; and so does the replacement of the principle of free judicial evaluation of the evidence by binding rules of evidence, that is, the exclusion of hearsay and of confession made under specific circumstances. Still, traditional elements of the presiding judge's power are evident in provisions such as Article 297, which authorizes the court to determine and change the scope, order, and method of the examination of evidence after hearing the opinion and suggestions of the litigants. According to subsequent rules of the Supreme Court, the presiding judge usually starts the examination of witnesses and is followed by the parties. This order may be changed. The parties may, however, now examine and cross-examine the witnesses by way of right. Several detailed provisions, some in the Code and others in Supreme Court rules, intensify their opportunity to challenge evidence.

The effect of all this is that the character of the criminal trial will never be the same again. In what direction the pendulum will move, however, I am not in a position to predict. It is even risky to speculate where it has moved to now, since the conduct of the trial depends so much upon the attitude and temperament of the presiding judge.[8]

Among the new rules of evidence the constitutionally anchored prohibition of punishment or conviction of any person if the only proof against him is his own confession is of particular significance. One must remember that, as pointed out before, the procurator had often obtained a confession from the accused which he presented to the court before the trial, and also that the defense counsel in such cases advised the accused to stick to the confession and then merely pleaded for clemency. Before the new Code was enacted, the Supreme Court had decided that the constitutional guarantee did not apply to a confession in open court, where the behavior of the defendant could be observed. The Court may have had in mind an analogy to the American plea of guilty. Still, we believed, and most of our Japanese colleagues agreed, that the constitutional prohibition should not be interpreted in a restrictive sense. It was always possible that an accused had been threatened by the police or his guards with beatings or other forms of torture in case he denied his guilt in court. It is now generally suspected that Van der Lubbe, the accused in the famous *Reichstag* fire trial during the Nazi period in Germany, was doped before he entered the courtroom. For this reason

---

[8] While Nagashima characterizes the change from inquisitorial to accusatorial criminal procedure in Japan as clear and steady, and even believes that the road will be opened, eventually, to the introduction of the jury trial (see Von Mehren, *Law in Japan*, p. 321), he must admit that according to some schools of thought the fundamental character of Japanese criminal procedure, even under the new Code, may in light of the continued active role of the presiding judge be deemed inquisitorial, in the sense that it is fundamentally different from the Anglo-American accusatorial procedure (*ibid.*, p. 316). This will probably remain true as long as the generation of judges trained and experienced in the Continental type of law constitutes an essential segment of the Japanese judiciary. After all, Nagashima's observations were made ten years ago.

the Supreme Court view was explicitly refuted by the new Code, which excluded confession as the only evidence supporting a conviction, regardless of whether or not it was made in open court.

Witnesses may also refuse to answer any question that tends to incriminate themselves. The privileges in the old Code permitting employees and relatives refusal to testify have, however, been reduced in the same manner and for the same reason as in the revision of the civil procedure.

The important simplification of the appeal system has already been treated in connection with the Court Organization Law. It consisted mainly in the change of the nature of the *koso* appeal and in the reduction of the instances from four to three. A constitutional question arose concerning the right of the state to appeal from a judgment of acquittal or for the purpose of having the penalty of the defendant increased. To some of our lawyers it appeared doubtful whether it did not violate the prohibition of double jeopardy or, as the Japanese prefer to call it, ne bis in idem. American precedents are hardly applicable, since they link the question with the jury system, which does not exist in Japan. While in the United States the established rule is that double jeopardy begins with the swearing in of the jurors, the Continental European and Japanese view is that no double jeopardy is involved in the appeal by the state, since the criminal process ends only with the final judgment, in other words continues as one and the same in all instances. I find great merit in this argument, and we did not think it wise to impose on the Japanese different legal conceptions. Moreover, even in our country, where only Vermont and Connecticut permit an appeal by the state, the advantages of such a system are being recognized to an increasing extent.[9] I also had political reasons why I preferred to have it retained in Japan, where it could be a weapon against favoritism showed a powerful boss by an

[9] See Appleton, "Reforms in Japanese Criminal Procedure," p. 426, note 169.

intimidated or otherwise influenced local court or single judge. The Supreme Court of Japan, by a decision of September 27, 1950, upheld the constitutionality of the prosecutor's appeal.[10]

There was no doubt, however, that some remedies in the old Code against a final judgment conflicted with the exclusion of double jeopardy. I refer to the Extraordinary Appeal by the Procurator General in case it was discovered after the judgment had become final that the trial or the decision had violated the law. Another such remedy open to the defendant as well as to the prosecutor was the reopening of the procedure (saishin) after the judgment had become final. The old law listed specific cases in which it was available, mainly bribery of a judge or other miscarriage of justice, perjury committed by a witness in the trial, or discovery of the forgery of a document used in the trial. There was no justification for deleting these extraordinary means of challenging a final judgment against which the possibilities of regular appeals had been exhausted, since they were useful and even necessary. It was clear, however, that to use them to the disadvantage of the defendant would constitute double jeopardy. Such a use was, therefore, excluded by the revision of the Code.

Whoever sticks to the idea that finding the truth is the ultimate purpose of trial may regret that the courts are prevented from changing their verdict from acquittal to conviction because of new after-trial discoveries of a quite exceptional nature clearly proving the guilt of the defendant. I was not completely free from such feeling, inasmuch as I never had doubted the wisdom of the same provisions in the German Code of Criminal Procedure. However, not only were we bound by the constitutional prohibition of double jeopardy, but we concluded that there must come a time after the end of the trial when the defendant is free of further uncertainty about his fate and free from additional harassment by the state.

[10] See Maki, *Courts and Law in Japan*, pp. 219–227 for a translation.

Looking, in conclusion, at this all-important reform, one has only to remember which significant elements of American law have *not* been adopted by the new Japanese Code to realize that the Americanization was rather selective. We did not impose a jury system, neither the grand jury nor the petty one, although the latter is the darling of Anglo-Saxon people. A petty jury system, patterned again on the German model, existed in Japan from 1923 to 1943, but never enjoyed much popularity during its short lifetime. Apparently, the majority of Japanese did not think too highly of the judicial competence of "the people." The reluctance to entrust to a jury the decision over their fate as defendants also indicates the general confidence in the professional judge, who, strangely enough, generally rendered more lenient verdicts than the jury.[11] Actually, the Japanese jury system was even a watered-down edition of the German. The verdict did not bind the court. If the judges did not like it, they could rescind it and have the case retried. Since no appeal as to the factual evidence was allowed and the decision of the jury could be challenged by the parties only on legal grounds in the Supreme Court (*Daishinin*), it is understandable that in light of their past experiences our Japanese counterparts did not favor another jury experiment. My own view is that the jury system, as practiced in the United States, has its merits in criminal cases, which can frequently be decided by mere common sense, but that the same is not true of civil cases, which all too often involve extremely complex legal problems transcending the horizon of the average citizen. The jury serves as a beneficial counterpoise to the doctrinaire American objectivism in criminal law and courts. Such counterpoise is certainly less needed in Japan. I also believe that the grand jury system, which shifts the responsibility for indictment from the government prosecutor to the people, has

11 According to Abe Haruo (see Von Mehren, *Law in Japan*, p. 336), it was reported that 98 percent of the accused waived their right to a jury trial.

proved its validity in our country. But we did not feel that we ought to adopt, against the opposition of the Japanese, institutions historically grown, after all, on a very different soil.

Neither did we urge the Japanese to follow the American pattern of pleading guilty or innocent, because we were afraid that the public procurator's customary predilection of obtaining a confession before taking public action, combined with the tendency of the Japanese people to avoid trial, would result in pleas of guilty by numerous innocent defendants. I personally was also afraid that such an innovation would soon be accompanied by plea bargaining and promises of immunity to codefendants and witnesses, as practiced in the United States. While these institutions have their advantages for those involved, the prosecutor, and the court, I have always considered them as violating the principle of equality before the law and as basically unethical. One ought not to bargain with justice.

It may be argued, however, as our Anglo-Saxon lawyers did, that we did not go far enough in Americanizing the Japanese law, insofar as it protects the defendant in the trial to a perhaps excessive degree. I have in mind his right to lie. While in our country a defendant, if he does not prefer to remain silent, must testify as a witness under oath, the Japanese defendant never becomes a witness and may defend himself as ever he likes without the risk of perjuring himself. I do not think, however, that this "permissiveness" is actually too dangerous, from the point of view of seeking the truth. Though not risking perjury if he lies, the defendant risks the loss of his credibility when the lie is discovered; and lies are usually short-lived. Moreover, the American transformation of defendant to sworn witness puts him into a precarious dilemma: if he remains silent, this will inevitably strengthen the suspicion that he is guilty; if, however, he decides to testify, his motivation to defend himself will, considering the frailty of human nature, continuously tempt him to deviate from the truth. He would then have added the prospect of a prosecution for perjury to his present tribulation.

These three important illustrations of restraint in Americanization on the part of the Occupation lawyers may suffice for our purpose, but they are not the only instances in which a change of the Code along American lines was considered unwise. What we have, then, as the product of the revision is sometimes characterized as a "hybrid" law,[12] a term easily understood as having a negative connotation. I prefer to write about a "synthesis" of the American and Japanese systems.[13] One may, indeed, ask: is not the culture of most nations, including their law, a combination of indigenous customs and imported concepts? Has not the Japanese law always been hybrid and adaptable to foreign influences, first Chinese and later continental European?[14] If the imported goods satisfy a need—in other words, if the adopting nation is ripe for the innovation—the import will have staying power, regardless of whether or not the adoption was fully voluntary. The great codification of the law during the Meiji period, which survived half a century, was also born out of a considerable degree of international pressures, especially the strong desire of the Meiji rulers to get rid of the humiliating extraterritorial judicial rights of big powers by modernization of the Japanese law.[15]

12 For instance, by Nagashima in Von Mehren, *Law in Japan*, p. 298, and by Professor Dando.

13 See my article in *Contemporary Japan*, p. 5. A similar idea has been expressed by Dan Fenno Henderson in *The Constitution of Japan, Its First Twenty Years*, p. xiii. He writes that "the post-war blend of concrete case law and synoptic civil analysis may produce a juristic method drawn from the best of both worlds," and he feels that "the Japanese jurists seem to be evolving a useful middle way in recent years."

14 "During every age imported culture became the flesh and blood of Japanese civilization. A positive attitude toward new ways of doing things has always been the driving force between Japanese developments." Cited from *Japan Quarterly* 20 (January-March 1973), 12, "Youth at the Prow."

15 Marius B. Jansen writes: "The modernization process was itself to a large degree the product of foreign policy." See *Political Development in Modern Japan*, p. 150.

Apart from the basic codes covered above, numerous other enactments completed the legal and judicial reforms. Without elaborating on them, I might list and very briefly explain the more important ones among them.

HABEAS CORPUS ACT

This law implemented the constitutional guarantee that no person shall be deprived of life or liberty, except according to procedure established by law. Here again, the Government Section was careful not to put pressure on the Japanese to adopt something resembling the American writ. The Japanese themselves took the initiative, and after thorough preparation in which the judiciary, the executive branch, the legislature, and the bar had a hand, while my division was available for advice, a Habeas Corpus Act was finally introduced as a member bill into the Diet, and was enacted on July 30, 1948. General MacArthur was particularly delighted with this piece of legislation, since his father had introduced a Habeas Corpus Act in the Philippines.[16]

JUVENILE LAW

In connection with the Court Organization Law, we have already mentioned the much-needed creation of the family court, whose Juvenile Division replaced poorly coordinated nonjudiciary agencies. It deals mainly with juvenile delinquents, whose maximum age is set high, at twenty years. The court has available a wide scope of dispositions, but may not impose a more severe penalty than thirty days' detention, the mildest type of imprisonment, or a fine. Transfer to a public procurator by the juvenile court is provided only when the offense is a serious one and committed by a person sixteen years or older. If the procurator

[16] For a more detailed analysis, see *Political Reorientation*, pp. 232–233.

takes public action, the case will be tried in the regular court. The proceedings in the juvenile court are not public; they need not necessarily even take place in the courthouse; and they are characterized by a lack of formality and a more congenial atmosphere than in an adult court. Decisions may range from an oral admonition by the judge to the commitment to a reformatory and limited criminal punishment. This enactment was primarily handled in the G–2 Section, but coordinated with my division.[17]

STATE REDRESS LAW

This statute, enacted on October 27, 1947, implemented the constitutional guarantee that "every person may sue for redress as provided by law from the state or a public entity, in case he has suffered damage through illegal act of any public official." The Japanese law and judicial decisions based on it seemed to us ambiguous, since they vacillated between the Continental system, which holds the state responsible for the acts of its servants and the Anglo-Saxon, which makes the latter personally liable for damage caused by them. It would have made no sense to insist on the adoption of the Anglo-Saxon system, which originated in the conception that the "king can do no wrong." From the point of view of the protection of the individual, I have always regarded the Continental system as preferable. The State Redress Law provides for the obligation of the state or public entity in question to compensate any person for any damage inflicted intentionally or by negligence by their public official if and when his act has been illegal. That excludes merely unwise or otherwise improper official actions. The official who has caused the damage must reimburse the state or public entity if he has performed the illegal act intentionally or by gross negligence. The law grants the right to claim redress to an alien only if reci-

[17] Much credit is to be given for the drafting of this law and related legislation to Dr. Burdett G. Lewis, chief prison administrator of that section.

procity is guaranteed by his country. This limitation has been challenged as possibly in conflict with the Constitution, which confers the relief upon "any person," and not merely on Japanese citizens. The Supreme Court has apparently had no opportunity to decide the question.

CRIMINAL INDEMNITY LAW

This law liberalizes and modernizes an existing law, and thus intensifies to a large extent the constitutional guarantee according to which any person, in case he is acquitted after having been arrested or detained, may sue the state for redress. The rate of indemnity has been increased considerably from the pitiable former maximum of 5 yen per day in prison to an amount ranging from 200 to 400 yen. Additional more generous provisions for indemnity to relatives in case of an execution of the death sentence and for the loss of confiscated articles, as well as for the payment of interest when a fine has been imposed, make this statute one of the most progressive indemnity laws now in existence.

AMNESTY LAW

Acts of grace within the framework of the administration of justice were formerly the exclusive prerogative of the Emperor. Now, the Constitution lists in Article 73, among the functions of the cabinet, decisions on general amnesty, commutation of punishment, reprieve, and restoration of rights. The coming into force of the new charter was a welcome occasion for the exercise of clemency. The Amnesty Law enacted by the ninety-second Diet was made effective on May 3, 1947. The preliminaries leading to this enactment and its main contents are described in Chapter 11.

PETITION LAW

This law, enacted on March 13, 1947, implements the very explicit guarantee in Article 16 of the Constitution, according to which "every person shall have the right of peaceful petition for the redress of damage, for the removal of public officials, for the enactment, repeal or amendment of laws, ordinances, or regulations and for other matters; nor shall any person be in any way discriminated against for sponsoring such a petition." This provision is self-explanatory, and the law sets forth detailed prescriptions implementing its broad principles. As a supplement to the freedom of expression, the right to petition is basic to a democracy where sovereignty rests with the people; but it had actually existed in Japan since time immemorial in some form or other, as in many Oriental nations. The Petition Law does not require an answer to the petitioner by the authority, but restricts itself to the vague prescription that "the petition . . . shall be received and disposed of in sincerity by the governmental or public office." Making an answer mandatory would in any case have imposed intolerable burdens on the governmental bureaucracy. Thus, the right of petition remains necessarily an incomplete one, but for the government it facilitates the discovery of inequities and other weaknesses of law and administrative practice.

NATIONALITY LAW

The existing Nationality Law was characterized by the attitude engendered by the house system and the resulting superior position of the male. It made the nationality of the wife dependent upon that of the husband. Thus, when an alien woman married a Japanese, she became automatically a Japanese citizen. Likewise, any change in or loss of his nationality affected her status. This arrangement was irreconcilable with the new constitutional ban of discrimination on account of sex. The essentially amended law, enacted in 1950, recognizes the independent status of the wife, regardless of whether acquisition, change, or renunciation of nationality is involved. While naturalization is now required of a foreign woman who marries a Japanese if she wants to become a Japanese national, the law makes a simplified form of naturalization possible. Similarly, the previous rule that a child shares the nationality of its parents has been abolished as contrary to the dignity of the individual, which the Constitution emphasizes. That excludes the automatic effect upon minor children of acquisition, change, and renunciation of nationality by parents. Moreover, recognition or adoption no longer has the consequence that the child shares the nationality of its parents. Interestingly enough, the law prohibits discrimination against naturalized citizens and excludes subversive elements from naturalization.

This ends the description of the most important legislation implementing the Constitution. If the preceding analysis proves anything, it is the moderation with which Anglo-Saxon concepts were introduced into this Continental type of law. This confirms my previous assertion that the essential character of the Japanese system has remained unchanged. Our very moderation, in my view, explains the amazing fact that apart from some organizational revisions, no significant changes or abolitions of the laws here covered have been legislated within the more than twenty-three years since the Japanese nation resumed its sovereignty after the Occupation.

◇◇◇

CHAPTER ELEVEN

A Diary for a Short Period

I would like to give a few specific examples of my activities, which were of a great variety. Unfortunately, I have no notes, apart from occasional calendar remarks, because I did not keep a diary. There is, however, one important exception. Between July 1946 and February 1947, the time I worked alone without the help of associates, I dictated short personal activity reports to my secretary. In the following, I shall cite or summarize some of these notes—more or less in telegraphic style—and add a comment if it appears necessary for understanding. This will allow, so to speak, a look into my workshop.[1] It should be kept in mind that these notes cover an early period, during which the new Constitution was not yet enforced, and the implementing reform legislation still in the planning stage. It nevertheless appeared advisable to arrange the notes to come after the previous chapters in which I made systematic analysis of the legal and judicial reforms, in order to facilitate understanding them.

[1] Ralph Braibanti, in *Political and Administrative Development,* Center for Commonwealth Studies pub. no. 36 (Durham, N.C.: Duke University Press, 1969), p. 86, n. 182, regrets the absence of a separate, coherent description or analysis of the technique of inducing development in Japan during the seven-and-a-half-year occupation. My notes, though sketchy, may at least offer some insight into that technique, which must have been used by other occupationnaires as well. Since the first names of the contacts frequently do not appear in the notes, I may be forgiven for sometimes omitting them here.

1 9 4 6

JULY 22. Meeting with the representatives of Diplomatic Section, Judge Advocate, and Legal Section on problem of criminal and civil jurisdiction over civilians attached to the Occupation, particularly dependents. Arrangement considered desirable. Application of Japanese or possibly American law (District of Columbia law) in Japanese courts versus extraterritoriality discussed.

JULY 24. Assisted in the drafting of the purge directive.
[*Comment*: The assistance was restricted to the legal terminology. I had nothing to do with the policy. I therefore refrain from discussing the merits of choosing as criteria individual conduct or the holding of positions and membership in certain organizations. SCAP chose mainly the purge according to categories, considered by many the more objective and democratic method. It is also the administratively easier and more practicable one. As in other fields, the effort of the Occupation to bring about a change in the ruling classes by doing away with ultranationalist and militarist organizations and individuals was an ambitious one. It is regrettable that the system of indirect occupation through the Japanese government resulted in leaving, as a rule, the execution of the purge in Japanese hands. The difficulty of controlling its fairness, as well as the genuine cooperation of those charged with it, is obvious. I had some criticism on the inclusion of all officers of the Japanese army and navy in the purge, since making military service a career does not necessarily reveal a militarist mind. I also had serious doubt regarding the wisdom of extending the purge to relatives within the third degree by blood, marriage, or adoption. Hans H. Baerwald, a junior member of Government Section, who worked in the Purge Division, in his well-balanced analysis of the purge, rightly emphasizes the inconsistency between our efforts to make the

traditional family system disappear in the Civil Code with
the implied recognition of the strength of this system.][2]

JULY 29. Complaints of citizens of Fukuoka prefecture
against the judicial administration.

JULY 30. Discussion with Professor Kawashima Takeyoshi
on family law.

Dinner in the Ministry of Justice with Minister Kimura,
Tokutaro, Vice Minister Tanimura, and members of ministerial committees.

AUGUST 13. New assignment: Look for precedents in the
election laws of other countries for regulations establishing
restrictions on small political parties to have their members
run as candidates in primary elections, and for compulsion
of one-man parties to have their candidate run on the
ticket of recognized major parties. How is it in the United
States, in France, Germany, Switzerland?

Meeting with Lt. Weed, Okuno Kenichi, Naito, Ministry
of Justice, and Professor Kawashima. They told us that they
were *personally* all in favor of the complete abolition of the
old family system and that the reform of the inheritance
law is also worked out with statutory inheritance rights for
the wife.

When I was alone with Naito, I warned him that SCAP
followed the case of lese majesty with utmost attention;
that we think the decision should no longer be delayed; and
that it is considered doubtful whether the prosecution is not
in violation of the SCAP Directive of October 4, 1945,
subject: Removal of Restrictions on Political, Civil, and
Religious Liberties.

[*Comment*: There was still pending the so-called placard
case of lese majesty in a Tokyo court. I referred to this in
my remark to Naito.]

2 See Hans H. Baerwald, *The Purge of Japanese Leaders under the
Occupation*, University of California Publications in Political Science
(Berkeley and Los Angeles: University of California Press, 1959), VIII,
74.

AUGUST 15. Evening: President Hosono, Kawashima, and Beate Sirota were my guests in Dai Ichi Hotel, discussing problems of judicial administration.

[*Comment*: Beate Sirota, now Mrs. Joseph Gordon, was an able analyst in Government Section. She also had a European background and participated in the meeting because she was a long-time resident of Japan, and spoke and understood Japanese very well.]

AUGUST 16. Representatives of the Ministry of Justice were advised that arrest and detentions made by public procurators and police ought to be checked by a judge within forty-eight hours.

AUGUST 19. Meeting with representatives of G–2, Counter Intelligence Section (CIS), Legal Section, and ESS on enforcement of compliance with SCAP Directives and on the creation of a central machinery in GHQ. ESS favors entrusting the Japanese government and courts with this task, but G–2 and I were opposed to that idea.

[*Comment*: I felt that this was definitely an authoritative measure to be reserved to the Occupation and that the transfer of the function to the Japanese would only add another embarrassing assignment to their execution of the purge.]

AUGUST 20. Meeting with Kades and Hussey on question of whether prostitution ought to be made a criminal offense, a proposal advanced by Hussey and mostly motivated by concern over the health of Occupation personnel, which rapidly had become a favorite customer of the institution. I objected to the idea, since I did not believe that the threat of punishment would stop or reduce prostitution, which would only go underground. I also felt that to impose puritan morality on this oriental nation was beyond the objectives of the Occupation and may even expose us to some ridicule. We should, however, intensify our measures for the protection of our men from venereal diseases and severely act against forced prostitution.

[*Comment*: The last remark refers to such cases as the sale by a farmer of his young daughter to a brothel owner in order to be able to pay his debts. The girl, who had to serve for years in a condition frequently characterized as slavery, usually accepted her fate as the fulfillment of her filial obligation. The Japanese government had already, on January 21, 1946, been directed by SCAPIN 642 to "abrogate and annul all enactments which directly or indirectly authorized or permitted the existence of licensed prostitution in Japan, and to nullify all contracts and agreements which had for their object the binding or committing, directly or indirectly, of any woman to the practice of prostitution."[3] While prostitution had not been made a crime, prostitutes were, indeed, regularly subject to medical checks. Long after the Occupation had ended, the Prostitution Prevention Law, Law 118 of 1956, prohibited the maintenance of houses of prostitution, but even then the act of prostitution itself was not made a criminal offense.][4]

SEPTEMBER 10.   Meeting with representatives of the Ministry of Justice and Central Liaison Office (CLO) on the Penal Code. I told them that the retention of the provisions concerning crimes against the Imperial House would be inconsistent with the changed political situation and in conflict with the SCAP Directive of October 4, 1945.

SEPTEMBER 11.   Continuation of discussion on lese majesty. Nakano read a statement made by the Provisional Legislative Investigating Committee about the reasons why the Committee did not favor any changes in the provisions concerning crimes against the Imperial House.

SEPTEMBER 13.   Assignment to write, for future use, a staff study and a draft of a directive for the Japanese government for the abolition of the lese majesty provisions, abrogation of the sentence of the district court in the placard case, and release of all prisoners who served sentences for lese majesty.

[3] See *Political Reorientation* I, pp. 195–196.
[4] Von Mehren, *Law in Japan*, p. 281.

[*Comment*: The respect of the governmental leaders and bureaucrats for the imperial institution, on the one hand, and SCAP's adamant insistence on doing away with the privileged protection of the members of the Imperial House on the other hand, were at the point of developing to a dramatic conflict. This interlude, during which the otherwise cooperative Japanese showed definite resistance, was the psychologically most precarious experience of my activity in the headquarters. MacArthur, despite his friendly feelings for the person of the Emperor, apparently saw in this privileged protection a remnant of the archaic myths to which he attributed much of past ultranationalism and militarism.]

SEPTEMBER 17. Professor Tanaka and Judge Tanaka of the Administrative Court discussed with me the reform of administrative litigation. They informed me that a general clause will be introduced admitting judicial review of all administrative acts.

SEPTEMBER 18. Naito and Hattori, Liaison Section of the Ministry of Justice, delivered the ministerial report on lese majesty. They declared that chief of the Criminal Affairs Bureau, Sato Tosuke, and Takahashi, Section chief in this bureau, were responsible for the report, which also states that no persons convicted of lese majesty are in prison at the present time.

OCTOBER 4. Meeting with Osabe, K., public procurator for the Supreme Court and Akiyama, H., public procurator in the Criminal Affairs Bureau of the Ministry of Justice, on the complaint of farmers in Odawara about the rigidity of sentences imposed on them for nondelivery of barley and the prevention of legitimate farmers' meetings by the police. They informed me that out of 1,548 offenders 70 had been prosecuted and 38 sentenced by the Odawara local court. Penal servitude ranging from ten months to two years and fines up to 2,500 yen had been imposed, but the penal servitude sentences were suspended. As to the meeting, a regulation of the military government exists according to which public meetings must be reported twenty-four hours in advance of the meeting. The applicants did not comply with this regulation and therefore, the meetings could not be allowed.

The two officials also discussed with me the salaries of judges and public procurators, which were utterly inadequate.

[Comment: Similar regulations regarding public meetings were issued by Japanese local ordinances, for instance in Tokyo, and were subsequently examined with regard to their constitutionality in several instances by the Supreme Court.]

OCTOBER 11. Officials of the Ministry of Justice submitted a comprehensive project for a generous amnesty, which is to come into force the day when the Constitution is effective. It provides for a general amnesty for certain offenses, particularly political, military, and economic ones. It includes lese majesty. General amnesty has the automatic effect that the case is dropped and, if a verdict has been rendered, it becomes extinct; furthermore, special amnesty may be granted on individual application; provision will also be made for general commutation (automatic reduction of penalties already enforced), special commutation, and special rehabilitation. I expressed satisfaction with the spirit behind the project.

OCTOBER 15. Meeting with Harold, Labor Division of ESS, Ishikawa, professor of admiralty and labor law, Professor Dando, and graduate students of the Tokyo Imperial University on the question of whether and to what extent the Labor Relations Committee could exercise quasi-judicial functions and enforce its decisions. Interesting discussions on the nature of that agency.

OCTOBER 17. Submitted memorandum on the amnesty plan.

OCTOBER 18. After a labor union leader of the *Mainichi* newspaper complained to me about the arrest of union members in connection with the newspaper strike, I arranged a meeting with Tanakawa, chief of the Police Affairs Bureau of the Home Ministry. He will submit a report covering all facts of the arrest.

OCTOBER 21. According to press reports, Minister of State Dr. Kanamori Tokujiro, the main government spokesman in the debate of the Diet on the Constitution, is being considered for the position of chief justice of the new Supreme Court. Together with Peake, I was assigned the task to examine whether he possesses the qualifications for that important office.

Meeting with Ministry of Justice on crime statistics.

[*Comment*: The appointment of Kanamori did not materialize.]

OCTOBER 23. Informal conversation, together with Peake, with Miyagi Minoru of the *Daishinin* on questions related to the appointment of judges to the new Supreme Court. Miyagi pointed out that no safeguards existed for the positions of the members of the present Supreme Court. The cabinet would actually be free to remove all of them and appoint others to the new highest tribunal. He described the career of President Hosono, praised his courage and independent character, and told the following story. During the war, when Hosono was president of the Appellate Court in Hiroshima, Premier Tojo Hideki had a conference with a judge of that court, emphasized the national emergency and gave instructions camouflaged as "advice." Thereupon, Hosono protested in writing to Tojo, criticizing him for interfering with the independence of the judiciary. Later on, Hosono himself appeared and joined in the conversation. He expects the Minister of Justice to remove all present Supreme Court judges and replace them with individuals who can be trusted not to make trouble for the executive branch of the government.

[*Comment*: Hosono's pessimism was not justified. Three judges of the old Supreme Court were taken over into the new one, and six who had at one time been judges of the old Supreme Court were subsequently appointed to the bench of the new court. While I regretted that Hosono and Nemoto were not among them, I would not have considered it proper for the Occupation to sponsor any individual for the appointment. We could have rejected a candidate whom we regarded as undesirable, but we should not show any favoritism.]

OCTOBER 24. Conference with Ito, his lawyers, and friends. Ito, a former newspaper editor and leader of a religious pacifist group, claims to have planned the assassination of Premier Tojo, but asserts that he was arrested before he could carry out his intention. He is still in detention, not on the charge of attempted murder, but for fraud because he received six million yen from his friends in order to prepare the assassination plot. The case will be examined. Possibly, it may fall under the amnesty.

The required report of Tanakawa, police chief of the Home Ministry, was submitted on the arrest of the union members of the *Mainichi*. All persons have been released in the meantime. We found out, however, that the warrant of arrest was not issued by a judge but by a public procurator. The minister of justice will report about the reasons for this procedure.

OCTOBER 25. Meeting with General Harrison, deputy chief of staff; report on activities.

Conference with Peake, Bisson, and Lt. Col. Colbert, Colette, and Becker of Labor Division, ESS, on forced labor in the industry of Hokkaido and in textile plants. Study on that question submitted.

OCTOBER 28. Meeting with officials of the Ministry of Justice and of the CLO. They were told that the Supreme Commander highly commends the intention of the Japanese government to grant a generous amnesty in connection with the enactment of the new Constitution. Two reservations were made, however: a) violations of SCAP directives and offenses against the Occupation must be excluded; b) the same applies to offenses against election laws, insofar as committed during the Occupation.

Certain complicated problems were discussed, e.g., mixed offenses and economic offenses.

[*Comment*: exception b) above was subsequently dropped, after Prime Minister Yoshida requested it in a personal letter to SCAP (see *Political Reorientation* II, 669).]

OCTOBER 29. In cooperation with Peake, worked on memorandum for Chief, Government Section, concerning the composition of the Supreme Court under the new Constitution. The danger exists, indeed, that the Ministry of Justice will use the forthcoming shift in the personnel of the court for the appointment to the bench of men who might be expected to be subservient to the ministerial bureaucracy. Therefore, we considered it necessary to subject appointments to the Supreme Court to SCAP approval.

NOVEMBER 1. Meeting with representatives of the Cabinet Bureau of Legislation on the Administrative Litigation Law. They requested a more detailed description of the procedure to be followed in administrative appeal, of the method of conducting hearings, and of the meaning of the term of "question of legality." They were uncertain how far the courts were to review the action of an administrative agency.

NOVEMBER 4. Representatives of the Cabinet Bureau of Legislation were informed that SCAP did not approve the inclusion of disciplinary offenses in the amnesty.

NOVEMBER 5–12. Wrote paper on comparative analysis of the Constitution.[5]

---

[5] See Chapter 10.

NOVEMBER 22. Meeting with Ministry of Justice officials, who were told that SCAP would insist on the budget of the courts being prepared by the Supreme Court and not by the Ministry of Justice.

NOVEMBER 26. Discussion with Tilton on police reorganization. Division Chiefs meeting on Cabinet Law and Imperial Household Law.

NOVEMBER 27. Meeting with Ministry of Justice officials. Told Naito that SCAP wants Japanese government to request his approval of the appointments to the bench of the new Supreme Court.

NOVEMBER 29. Meeting with judges of the Supreme Court on Court Organization Law. I told them that the new Supreme Court would, in my opinion, not be able to fulfill its part because it would be overburdened. They should either increase the number of the judges or reduce the functions of the Court or, better, both. I made several suggestions, such as rigid restrictions to questions of constitutionality, introduction of a minimal value of appeal in pecuniary matters, and making the high court the court of last resort in cases when the suit or trial starts in the summary court.

[*Comment*: While the number of judges of the Supreme Court was not increased but remained at fifteen, my last advice concerning the high court functioning as court of last instance in petty cases was accepted in the final codification of civil procedure.]

DECEMBER 2. Meeting on same problem with Okuno, Ministry of Justice, and Judge Nemoto. Apart from the suggestions for the relief of the Supreme Court, I raised the question of introducing something like the American writ of certiorari, which would make it possible for the Court to refuse acceptance of a case. There was also a discussion of the question of whether the Supreme Court should be the only one to decide on constitutional question or whether this power should also be entrusted to the lower courts.

[*Comment*: The latter alternative materialized.]

DECEMBER 3. Memorandum on the placard case of lese majesty. I criticized the judgment of the 5th Section of the Tokyo District Court of November 2, 1946, because the accused Matsushima was not sentenced for lese majesty, obviously in evasion of the controversial issue, but for libel of the Emperor under the general provisions of the Penal Code. The Court circumvented the legal requirement of a complaint from the injured person by holding that the complaint of the Emperor was replaced by the public action of the procurator, thus making this specific libel an offense demanding public prosecution. This construction is legally objectionable.

DECEMBER 4. During the discussions on the Court Organization Law, I objected to the proposal that judges should not be members of political parties because such prohibition would be a restriction of their civil rights guaranteed in the Constitution. The whole question of political activities of judges was discussed. Furthermore, I doubted the constitutionality of a provision that judges could be punished through a disciplinary procedure with suspension from office up to one year, since the Constitution requires *impeachment by an Impeachment Court of the Diet for removal*.

DECEMBER 10. Colonel Kades and I met with Vice Minister of Justice, Tanimura Tadaichiro; chief of the Criminal Affairs Bureau, Sato Tosuke; and other officials of the ministry on lese majesty. Kades, referring to the statement of General MacArthur in connection with the dropping of the prosecution in four lese majesty cases, emphasized that this statement permitted only one conclusion, namely, that the lese majesty provisions of the Penal Code had become obsolete. The same conclusion was reached, he said, in the decision of the Tokyo District Criminal Court, which sentenced the accused not for lese majesty but for insult of the Emperor according to the general provisions of the law. The Japanese representatives were, therefore, advised that we expect the abolition of Articles 74 through 76. Libel and insult against the Emperor and other members of the Imperial House must in the future be punished in accordance with the general provisions of the law. The concession was made, however, that the Emperor should not be compelled to comply personally with the requirement that an insulted person must lodge a complaint with the court. No objection would be raised to a provision authorizing the prime minister or the minister of justice to act on behalf of the Emperor with regard to such a complaint.

DECEMBER 19. Kades and I met Tanimura and Sato on the same subject. They pointed out that the Japanese government wants to resolve the question of lese majesty in such a way that in case the Emperor is insulted or slandered, the offender should be prosecuted ex officio without any complaint. Kades vigorously rejected this suggestion as another version of lese majesty.

DECEMBER 20. General Whitney, Colonel Kades, and I received Minister of Justice Kimura, Sato, Yamoto, and Akatari. Whitney announced that the Supreme Commander desired the immediate abolition of chapter one of the Penal Code. He repeated the directions given by Kades the day before, among them that the Emperor, when lodging a complaint, might be represented by the prime minister or the minister of justice but not by the public procurator.

[Comment: The issue of the privileged protection of the Emperor and other members of the Imperial House had come to a dramatic climax. How important it was to SCAP is proved by Whitney's personal intervention, the only one in the revision of the codes of law. The issue was, however, just as important to the Japanese from their point of view of traditional reverence for the imperial system. While they were reluctantly willing to accept the abolition of the insult and libel provisions in view of the concession made by SCAP with regard to the complaint, they loathed the idea of doing away with Articles 73 and 75 of the Code relating to "acts of violence against the person of the Sovereign" and his family. My impression was that the conservative cabinet did not want such an irreverent action to be taken by the Diet or any other Japanese governmental agency without being forced by the higher power of SCAP. What followed, therefore, was the letter of Prime Minister Yoshida to General MacArthur of December 27, 1946 (*Political Reorientation* II, 679).]

DECEMBER 24. Met with officials of the Home Ministry, together with Major Jack P. Napier, Korean Division, on the Alien Registration Law, which affects large numbers of Koreans. I expressed the opinion that the bill, in providing for the exclusive power of the prefectural governor to determine on the deportation of an alien violates the new Constitution. An appeal from the decision of the governor to the district court should be introduced.

DECEMBER 26. Memorandum for the Chief, Government Section, concerning the establishment of the offices of 600 assistant procurators. I suggested that we approve it because of the urgent need of the procurators for help (one for more than 100,000 people) and because my initial apprehension that the new offices may develop to a Japanese FBI did not appear justified. The new commissioners, as they may be called more correctly, do not constitute an agency of their own, and there is no interrelationship between them, since each official is exclusively the helper of the procurator to whom he is attached and subordinated.

DECEMBER 30. Pursuant to Yoshida's letter on lese majesty, I did research on the question of legal protection of the president of the United States and the king of England against bodily harm.

1 9 4 7

JANUARY 2. Worked on the draft of the legal part of an answer by MacArthur to Yoshida's letter regarding lese majesty.

[*Comment*: The letter was finally sent on February 25, 1947, after repeated editorial changes.[6] Thus, the Japanese government, which could hardly have expected the prime minister's action to change MacArthur's mind, got what it wanted, a directive from SCAP in writing, this time in the form of a "Dear Mr. Prime Minister" letter.]

JANUARY 14. Discussion on the question of salaries of judges and the budget of 1947 and 1948 with Ministry of Justice officials. The minister made all efforts to have them increased, but did not succeed because of the objections of the finance minister. We agreed that the budget estimate did not prevent enactment of the salary law providing higher salaries.

JANUARY 16. Memorandum for the Chief, Government Section, on the Petition Law. Suggested, among other proposals, that a provision be included corresponding to Article 16 of the Constitution, that no person shall be in any way discriminated against for submitting or sponsoring a petition.

[*Comment*: A corresponding safeguard has been included in Article 6 of the Petition Law.]

Ministry of Justice representatives submitted the final draft of the Public Procurators Law in Japanese, as prepared in the Bureau of Legislation. I objected to the provision that a procurator loses his position automatically when he is punished with imprisonment. On request of the Purge Division, I also stated that I do not consider favorably the general exclusion of purged judges and procurators from the legal profession.

6 See *Political Reorientation* II, 680.

JANUARY 21. Meeting with Toh, Central Liaison Office, on the Petition Law. Speaking for the Bureau of Legislation, he asked whether we had any objection to replacing the term "illegal" by "improper" in the original Article 6 of the bill. It provides that no petitioner has the right to force an interview by threat, violence, or any other illegal means.

JANUARY 22. I advised Mr. Toh, in answer to his question, that the suggested change was undesirable because it would give the bureaucracy too much discretion. It was, however, left to the Japanese government to omit this article completely, since it was unnecessary.

[Comment: In the final law this provision was, indeed, omitted.]

Meeting with Kurimoto, Ministry of Justice, and Hirota, Central Liaison Office, who asked for our approval to apply special amnesty to the cases of sixty-nine officers of naval air units who had disobeyed the cease-fire order in 1945 and were sentenced for disobedience, conspiracy, desertion, threatening of and injury to superiors. The offenses are not covered by the general amnesty from which conspiracy is excluded. The only specifications we made were offenses against the Occupation, which did not yet exist when the offenses of the officers were committed.

JANUARY 23. In memorandum for the Chief, Government Section, suggested that SCAP show generosity and leave the decision in the amnesty case of the officers to the Japanese government.

JANUARY 24. Meeting, together with Grajdanzev and Bisson, with Hardie and Williams, Natural Resources Section, on questions of succession into agricultural farmland in light of the inheritance provisions of the new Civil Code. The problem is to avoid a further division of farms which are, as a result of the land reform, already extremely small.

JANUARY 28. Meeting of the Section with newspaper publishers and editors from the United States: Roy Howard, president of the Scripps-Howard newspapers; Carroll Binder, editor of editorial page of the Minneapolis Tribune; Sevellon Brown, publisher of the Providence Journal; Erwin Canham, editor of the Christian Science Monitor; Wayne Coy, assistant publisher of the Washington Post; E. Z. Dimitman, executive editor of the Chicago Sun; Ralph J. Donaldson, chief editorialist of the Cleveland Plain Dealer; and Thor Smith, assistant publisher of the San Francisco Call-Bulletin.

General Whitney gave a long information talk on the various activities of Government Section. He also criticized the attitudes of certain Tokyo press correspondents and of sections of the American press toward the Occupation. The meeting took the whole day.

[*Comment*: This is another illustration of the headquarters' sensitivity to criticism.]

FEBRUARY 3. Representatives of the Ministry of Justice reported that the cabinet has serious objections to the distribution of power between the public procurators and the police, as provided for in the Public Procurators Office bill. They want to retain the power of command of public procurators over the police and do not like the new arrangement, according to which procurators may only request assistance from those in charge of criminal investigation. This would, in the opinion of the cabinet, increase the independence and power of the police with regard to investigations. The public, because of the experiences of the past, dislikes the police and would react unfavorably. I answered that the real reason for the public dislike was not connected with the investigating activities of the police as such, but with their practices of arbitrary arraignments and detentions as well as third-degree methods. What the cabinet really wanted was to keep a purely national police with all its judicial police officers under the jurisdiction of the Ministry of Justice, which would, through the procurators, control the whole police force down to the last village cop. This would have been contrary to the policy of decentralization of the police followed by SCAP. I advised them to either submit the bill in its present form to the Diet or wait for the reorganization of the police.

FEBRUARY 4. Discussion with Tilton on the status of the reorganization of the police. After contacting Kades, we decided to urge Public Safety Branch, CID, to hasten their presentation of the reorganization project. Tilton's telephone conversation with CIS' Colonel Pulliam revealed that they are in favor of retaining a strong national police, and do not like to have anything changed in the police organization for the time being. A check sheet will be sent to CID pointing out the necessity of quick action with regard to the police reorganization.

[Comment: Government Section's decentralization policy was reflected in the Police Law. The reorganization of the police, not the responsibility of my division, was ideologically sound, but may have been somewhat unrealistic. The country is too small, and the financial resources of local entities are too inadequate to allow every small town to have its own police administration. I was, therefore, not surprised to see that this became one of the first areas where the clock was subsequently turned back.]

FEBRUARY 5. MacArthur announced that a new general election to the House of Representatives would take place soon after the present session of the Diet.

[Comment: This happened shortly after MacArthur was forced by the machinations of radical union leaders to prohibit the threatened general strike. Justified dissatisfaction of labor with the austere wage policy of the Yoshida government during an inflation made their threat attractive to the moderate sections of the unions. SCAP's call for new elections proved that his prohibition of the general strike did not represent a pat on the back of the government, but was motivated by his fear of a resulting economic chaos.]

FEBRUARY 6. Inspection of Fuchu prison with Dr. Lewis, CID, and Dr. Hayao Torao. We conversed with the prison director, Warden K. Kayasu. I was impressed by some good features of this prison, which is one of the largest and most modern in Japan.

FEBRUARY 7. Officials of the Ministry of Justice and of the CLO were informed that the decision on special amnesty for the sixty-nine officers will be left to the Japanese government. Mr. Nakano asked, furthermore, for instructions in the case of the assassination attempt against Baron Hiranuma, minister of the interior, by an ultranationalist in 1941. Due to the political implication of the offense, the Ministry of Justice does not want to grant special amnesty without the approval of SCAP. I advised him that the ministry submit an official report to Government Section.

Here ends my diary. These notes show that I meddled in many things, and sometimes by way of more or less mandatory "advice." It must be kept in mind, however, that these initial contacts took place in the early period of the Occupation when both the crusading spirit of us reformers and the confusion of the Japanese were at their height. The subject of discussion was less often connected with the legal and judicial reforms, regarding which the positions taken were of a preliminary nature, than with specific issues on which the Japanese wanted to know the policy of headquarters. Consistent with the principle of indirect military government, we had to work through the medium of a tradition-minded leadership and bureaucracy, about whose enthusiasm with respect to our reforms we did not have much illusion. Nevertheless, it can be seen that when I resorted to authoritative instruction, I was usually either directed to do so, or constitutional questions, such as violations of civil rights, were involved. The diary antedated the truly free exchange of ideas between members of the Occupation and representatives of the Japanese official and legal world that resulted in the revision of the basic codes.

CHAPTER TWELVE

A Socialist-Led Cabinet

The April 1947 election to the lower House gave the Socialist party a plurality and resulted in the premiership of the Christian labor leader Katayama Tetsu. My hope that this change would promote Occupation objectives, since we would from now on have to deal with a more sincerely cooperative administration, materialized to a considerable extent, as far as my own jurisdiction was concerned.

The new minister of justice, who, after the reorganization of the ministry and the police became the first attorney general, was Suzuki Yoshio. While he initially impressed me as a rather reticent, if not cool, personality, there eventually developed between us a gratifying understanding and an awareness that basically in our ideologies we had much in common. MacArthur, when commenting in his press release of May 24, 1947, on the selection of Katayama as prime minister, regarded the choice as demonstrating the "middle-of-the-road course" of Japanese internal politics. This qualification applied, at least at that time, however, only to the moderate or right wing of the Socialist party— and the party, unfortunately, was badly split. Its left wing, though not communist, represented the militant radical purists who advocated socialization of the economy and were opposed to the compromises required of a party in a coalition government with two other parties of a more rightist, "bourgeois" coloration. Suzuki, a former lawyer and intellectual, belonged to the moderates, who politically (though not economically) resembled the liberal wing of our Democratic party. I saw again a parallel with the Weimar Social Democrats. In both cases Allied occupationnaires— in Germany after World War I and in Japan after World War II—frequently out of ignorance of the true nature of the so-called socialists, were deterred by the mere label of socialism from establishing closer contacts with the parties best able to appreciate Western democracy. Instead, they found it more pleasant to meet the well-mannered and smooth members of the predominantly conservative upper class of the occupied societies.

I have sometimes wondered whether, if the Occupation had relied on a specific progressive political group, we would not have avoided many of the difficulties of having to deal with a Japanese administration that, while giving lip service to us, was in its inner heart lukewarm to the idea of democratization. As it was, Japan had new highly advanced laws that, notwithstanding the purge, were applied and executed by a reluctant leadership and, essentially, the old bureaucracy. Reliance on and positive support of one specific party would in all probability have led to different election results, and given the supported party a permanent plurality, if not an absolute majority. This, however, would have been a precarious alternative. The Socialist party, which at least during the revolutionary period of the Occupation could have been the choice, was badly inexperienced in administrative matters. While Katayama himself was a man of great integrity and good will, many of the Socialist party bosses were as corrupt as some of those of the conservative parties, and quite a few were as reactionary. The party's dependence on the predominant, powerful labor organization, the General Council of Industrial Unions (Sohyo), impaired the freedom of its policy determination. Reliance on any political group would, moreover, have exposed SCAP to the charge of favoritism. Nevertheless, this problem is of a more subtle nature. The solution might have been not to support any existing party, but to build up something new, a group led by dependable, thoroughly tested individuals. They could have been found. I do not overlook the danger, however, that such a group would have been labeled by many Japanese as quislings or puppets of the Occupation.

These are the crucial alternatives with which occupations are faced, and one cannot criticize MacArthur for having ruled through the government that came to power by way of the democratic process which he sponsored so energetically. Whether, under the prevailing circumstances, elections truly expressed the free will of the people or continued to be influenced by long-time dependencies and by the very support or nonsupport from SCAP, may well be doubted. Still, there was no better way, and the government resulting from those elections was, except for the brief interruption by the Katayama and Ashida eras, the conservative cabinet of clever Yoshida Shigeru. Sincerity requires, however, the admission that support of and cooperation with his party and government by SCAP was not exclusively due to respect for the democratic process. After the dynamic period of democratization had passed and the principal concerns of the Occupation were dictated by the polarization between the free and the communist worlds, as well as by the need for the economic rehabilitation of Japan,[1] preference for the conservatives over the socialists, who still adhered to Marxism, was clearly in line with general United States policies.

Yoshida had a clean record as an opponent of the expansionist policies of the militarists, and considered himself a liberal, but he still remained the tradition-bound Japanese of the upper classes. In his memoirs he is critical of the zeal of the reformers, whom he either suspects as leftists or characterizes as "idealists" in contrast to practical "realists," such as Generals Charles A. Willoughby, who disliked the purge and the decentralization of the police, and Robert Eichelberger, chief of the Eighth Army.[2] Nevertheless, he

[1] For more elaboration on these developments, see Chapters 16 and 17.

[2] See Yoshida, *Memoirs*, p. 55.

tried with considerable success to be "a good loser." I, for
one, and several of my colleagues in the Government Section, did not completely trust him; we felt instinctively
some passive resistance to our reformatory policies. Those
who are skeptical regarding these policies find it, however,
advantageous that the continuity of an unenthusiastic
government somewhat slowed down the traumatic tempo
of social and political changes. Yoshida's memoirs have
revealed that he was personally more open-minded and
positive towards the Occupation than I would have expected. Apart from his admiration for General MacArthur,
he recognized the inevitability of a new Constitution. There
is no doubt that his conservatism was of a more liberal
brand than that of some of the premiers after him, such as
Kishi. Of course, he seriously criticized certain aspects of the
Occupation, and some of his comments on the purge, and
the educational and the police reforms are not without merit.
His disapproval of the "excesses" was in part based on his
deep-seated fear of communism, which he shared with many
Americans during the period of his regime, and which
developed into the paramount bond between it and SCAP.
My own ideas on the danger of communism in Japan will
be offered in Chapters 16 and 17.

There is this similarity with the Weimar precedent, that
the socialists in both cases were forced by their dependence
on coalition with other parties to compromise and abandon
their mild program of socialization when they were in
power. The ill-fated conflict of the Katayama cabinet with
the coal mine operators is an illustration. To be middle-of-
the-road may prove wisdom, but it is not the most effective
means of achieving political success. Between the devil of
their left wing brothers, who wanted more radical changes,
and the blue sea of their coalition partners who wanted
less, hurt by defections and corruption scandals, the Katayama cabinet was politically doomed, and the short-lived
Ashida cabinet, in which the socialists remained as partners,
was not more fortunate.

During their tenure the cooperation of the ministerial bureaucracy in my special field had, indeed, a more sincere quality because the attorney general, unlike some of his predecessors and successors, was in sincere agreement with our reforms, most of which were enacted at the time of his membership in the cabinet. When we told Suzuki that in the attorney general's office of the United States there existed a civil liberties unit, he enthusiastically adopted the idea and established such a bureau in his ministry. This again led to a substructure of regional civil liberties commissioners. I have subsequently characterized the coming into existence of such an organization as a milestone in Japan's history of human freedom. It emphasized, I said, the obligation of a free democratic government not only to refrain from infringing on the people's rights, but affirmatively to safeguard and promote them.[3]

After Suzuki's death I summarized his many accomplishments for the democratization of his nation in a letter of condolence, dated February 13, 1964, to his widow.[4] I pointed out, among other things, that even before he was a member of the Katayama and Ashida cabinets, I had admired his enlightened position as member of the House of Representatives during the Diet deliberations of the new Constitution. In the discussion of the question of sovereignty most speakers ambiguously evaded the real issue, I wrote, but Suzuki made it absolutely clear that under the new charter sovereignty should and would rest no longer with the Emperor, but with the people. He observed that the affection of the Japanese people for the Imperial House had nothing to do with power, but was purely "moralistic and emotional." This ideological background of the first top law officer under the new Constitution confirmed my confidence that he not only played the game, but believed in the necessity of the reforms in which he so willingly cooperated.

[3] See *Nippon Times* of March 18, 1951.
[4] The letter has been included in a biography of Suzuki in the Japanese language.

◇◇

CHAPTER THIRTEEN

Japan's Civil Liberties Union
and Eleanor Roosevelt

Since the principal goal of our legal reforms was the strengthening of individualism and fundamental rights, the promotion of civil liberties inescapably became an essential part of our responsibilities. We were in the fortunate situation of benefiting from a long American tradition of individual freedoms, although the period of Occupation saw the attacks by Senator Joseph McCarthy against them. Steiner and I probably knew how to appreciate this tradition resulting from a revered Constitution more deeply than the native-born American, since, thanks to our European background, we remembered the nightmare that the destruction of all individual rights by a ruthless dictatorship meant. Whatever the fascists and the communists may argue to the contrary, there must be a well-defined area of civil rights that the citizen may defend against established authority. Not that we were unaware of the necessity of drawing the line between rights and egoistic self-interest, which the state is entitled to repress; but in balancing the powers of the government with the people's rights in Japan, we found that the latter definitely weighed too lightly. Hence, while in other countries the proper thing might have been to fight excessive individualism or "permissiveness," and stress the demands of the community, in Japan, with its past history of suppression of rights, the task for us appeared to lie in the emphasis on strengthening them. General MacArthur certainly indicated that he shared this view, when he invited Roger Baldwin to establish a Japanese Civil Liberties Union. By assigning Blakemore and me to assist Baldwin, he must have recognized the close connection between our reform work and fundamental human rights.

With our assistance, Baldwin helped progressive Japanese to set up the Japanese counterpart of the American Civil Liberties Union. It was born on November 23, 1947. Its first director was a levelheaded lawyer, Unno Shinkishi, a socialist of the moderate brand, whom the Occupation had used before in a semiofficial position. It was a good beginning, and I sometimes attended the meetings of the new institution, lectured to the participants, and engaged in discussions with them. In the foundation meeting, the Union stressed that "the various evils which have oppressed the Japanese people for the past several centuries cannot be wiped out so easily," and that to root out these evils is not only an inalienable right of the Japanese people but also their sacred responsibility. This, the declaration continues, "also means contribution to the peace of mankind and participation in international society."[1] The founders then solemnly swore "to promote democratization of the Japanese people by securing fundamental human rights and contribute to the peace of all mankind, conducting all-out struggles against all infringements upon freedom and civil liberties by feudalistic, bureaucratic, and all other undemocratic systems and elements."

I may summarize additional parts of the declaration, using the English of the paper:

Principles and Tendencies which the Union opposes:
(1) Mysticism;

[1] Quoted from a paper of the Union, which also contains much detailed information on its tendencies and activities during the years following the foundation.

(2) Feudalism—superstition, irrational tendency, ter-
roristic and barbarous trend, predominance of man over
woman, dictatorship of the family head;

(3) Bureaucratization—despotic dictatorship, police
state, secrecy;

(4) Deformed Capitalism—Unreasonable profits inim-
ical to social welfare, cheap labor, tenant farmer system.

The Union lists six categories of activities with innumerable examples, namely: (1) Disposal of issues relating to the
abuse of official position by civil service employees. Examples: use of violence and torture by police during investigation; illegal detention cases; arrogance of young tax
official; police misuse during a strike. (2) Issues concerning
racketeer organizations; for instance, the case of Uwajima
city, Ehime prefecture, where racketeers assailed villagers,
which resulted in three deaths and two severe wounds. (3)
Publicity of General Views; here the Union mentions its
participation in the conferences on the revision of the Code
of Criminal Procedure. It has published a book with explanations of the new Code, and at the time of reporting
had sold six thousand copies. Lectures were held on the
Civil Code, the Labor Standard Law, and for the purpose of
promoting a Habeas Corpus Act. (4) Others; examples are
several cases of defense of people involved in legal and
social difficulties. (5) Lecture Meetings; examples show
that they were held in many places throughout the country.
(6) Cooperation with International Organizations; specifically mentioned are participation in the International
League of Man, an advisory body of the United Nations,
and the close contact with the American Civil Liberties
Union, whose honorary member is the Japanese Union. In
connection with the Judd bill for the abolition of the Exclusion Act of Japanese Emigrants, a correspondence took
place between Baldwin and the Japanese Union, which had
urged promoting of the bill.

There is no doubt but that the Japanese Union worked

indefatigably and effectively in its fight along these lines. At the end of the Occupation the organization drifted toward pacifism and opposition to nuclear testing and rearmament. It became more politicized. Just as the Socialist party, after its failure to remain in power, grew more radical leftist, so did the Union. To be sure, its pacifist posture and opposition to rearmament conformed with a strict interpretation of Article 9 of the Constitution, and was shared not only by the leftist parties but also by many intellectuals of the academic world and by common people. But the Korean conflict, among other things, had shifted United States and Occupation policy away from the stance of a Japan without armed forces, a stance by then recognized as unrealistic. The Union, following the lead of the leftist parties, favored neutralism in international relations and understanding with the communist nations. This contrast in positions gave it an anti-American flavor, and my contacts with them grew less frequent.

In the spring of 1952, Eleanor Roosevelt visited Japan, and on that occasion I received an invitation to a meeting with the Union. Unno sent me a very friendly letter, telling me that Mrs. Roosevelt had agreed to talk to the Union, reminding me that I was one of the founders of the organization, and urging me to attend the meeting. I felt that if the widow of a president of the United States was willing to honor the Japan Union with her presence, I should accept the invitation.

When the day of the meeting came, Eleanor appeared with her daughter-in-law, Elliot's wife Minerva. The two ladies, George Koshi (a lawyer in my division, whose mastery of Japanese was extremely useful), and I were the only Americans among a group of fifty-odd Japanese, many of them young men. I observed a great number of students, and if I had known at that time anything of the Students for a Democratic Society in our country, I might have compared these participants to our type of young academic militants. The guest gave a gracious little lecture and was afterwards bombarded with embarrassing questions. Among other things, she was asked why the United States, which talks so much of humanity, threw the atomic bomb on Hiroshima and Nagasaki, killing and maiming more than a hundred thousand innocent civilians. Mrs. Roosevelt held her ground beautifully, and while her listeners in all probability did not agree with her, they were impressed by her intelligent eloquence and charm. She tried hard to justify the atomic attacks, but I doubted that in her inner heart she considered them defensible.[2] From time to time she asked me for information on the new Japanese Constitution. It was an unforgettable experience for me personally to meet this great and warmhearted woman.

[2] This doubt must be revoked in light of Mrs. Roosevelt's explicit statement quoted in the subsequently published book by Joseph P. Lash, *Eleanor: The Years Alone* (New York: Norton, 1972), p. 225. In connection with her inspection of Hiroshima, she remarked: "Hiroshima was a moving experience. I know we were justified in dropping the bomb but you can't help feeling sorry when you see suffering." She rationalized the use of the bomb as she had done in the meeting with the Union, by saying that "It is the causes of war which bring about such things as Hiroshima and we must try to eliminate these causes because if there is another Pearl Harbor, there will undoubtedly be another Hiroshima."

◇◇

CHAPTER FOURTEEN

Happy Reunion

Finally, after fifteen months of separation, my family joined me. My wife arrived at the end of May 1947 in the company of our daughter Ellen, who had graduated from high school the summer before. In preparation for their coming, I had to resolve the housing problem. Several requisitioned houses had been offered to me. I had an aversion to living in the newly constructed army development of Washington Heights, but was also reluctant to take one of those private homes from which the Japanese owner or tenant had been expelled; the consideration that if I did not move into one of them another occupationnaire would, did not overcome my hesitation. Therefore, I was glad when I found a charming, typically Japanese house belonging to a family that had moved into a second house they also owned in the immediate neighborhood. That made my decision easier. The house was located in Setagaya-ku. It had a large parlor, the only Western-style room; the other rooms were Japanese, tatami-covered, with movable paper windows facing a most beautiful garden with exotic trees and a goldfish pond. There was a front porch, on top of which flourished a purple wisteria flowing from a hundred-year-old tree beside the house. I was enchanted and so were my two women.

Here I experienced again my wife's great sensitivity, and her compassionate soul. She was, of course, more than one year behind me in her first impressions of Tokyo, and

therefore went through some of the emotions of horror at
the consequences of the war and of pity for the misery of
the people, which I had felt when arriving in Japan. The
tragedy of the situation lies in the necessity of getting
accustomed to all this if you want to live and work, and
by and by you must somehow neutralize those feelings to
some extent. This is human nature, although the tempo of
adjustment is different depending upon the individual
character.

Charlotte was, however, far from resigning herself to a
passive attitude of pitying, but helped as much as she
could those plagued by misfortune or confusion. Soon she
discovered in our street an orphanage in which boys and
girls were cared for under minimum postwar accommodations. They had lost their parents during the war. They
particularly lacked the most necessary clothing. Throughout our years in Tokyo, Charlotte did whatever she could
to improve their lamentable condition. She provided the
children with all kinds of garments from a school in Oklahoma, whose principal was a friend of ours. He persuaded
his pupils to discard some of their dresses, suits, shoes, etc.
Since the orphanage had no bathing facilities, Charlotte
financed the construction of a large bathtub and steel boiler.
On special occasions she treated the children with large
quantities of doughnuts.

Subsequently, Charlotte taught languages at a college
and also frequently gave lectures at various universities in
Tokyo. Her guidance of women's groups will be the subject
of Chapter 15.

When my family joined me, the United States had already
started to provide the Japanese people with large amounts
of food, thus saving them from threatened starvation. They
will never forget this completely, and from the very beginning they appreciated the fact that the Occupation took
care of its own food. Still, the tremendous contrasts between
American and Japanese living conditions remained a potential source of bitterness in a long occupation. It was like

5. Charlotte distributing clothes for her orphanage.

two different worlds: here the bombed-out Japanese in primitive, makeshift abodes, lacking the necessities of life, especially clothing, being dependent on a minimum of food calories, without proper heating and transportation, not to speak of pleasure and fun; and there the occupationnaires, living in the best well-heated houses that the war had left intact, dining and wining abundantly in their elegant officers' clubs or fully staffed mess halls, having commissaries available in which all kinds of merchandise could be purchased, driving around in jeeps and later in sedans, and, while vacationing, having a good time in the most fashionable requisitioned hotels in the mountains or at the seashore. While the privileged life of the members of the victorious nation could be rationalized by the argument that service in a country far away from home had to be made attractive to recruit qualified men and women, I could not help feeling uneasy about this situation during the first years, when poverty and calamity still prevailed in Japan. I therefore sympathized with the shock my wife suffered at her arrival.

Because of the arrival of my family I was granted two weeks' leave, and we could get out of Tokyo into the magnificent countryside. I drove Charlotte and Ellen to the famous Fujiya Hotel in mountainous Miyanoshita by way of Kamakura, where we admired the bronze statue of the Amida Buddha with the mysteriously detached wise and kind expression on his face. We enjoyed the stay in the hotel and our various excursions along the narrow Long Trail Pass to Hakone Lake and Atami.

The vacation passed all too fast, and we moved into our Japanese dream house. Envious critics of the Occupation will certainly apply to us the oft-repeated slogan: "they never had it so good." Here we were in a lovely house with a cook, a housemaid, and a houseboy, who also served as chauffeur and stoker. Well, my answer is that first of all, after more than a year of living in a little cubbyhole of a hotel room, separated from my family, and embroiled in hard work, I could now claim a certain amount of comfort.

Second, however, while I would never have hired three domestic servants on my own initiative, we were encouraged for charitable reasons to accept a number of young Japanese men and women as help. To serve in an American home meant having shelter, warmth, and food at a time when there was a gruesome shortage of all of these. The unwise regulation prohibiting American householders from sharing their meals with their Japanese domestics could not possibly be and never was obeyed or enforced. Finally, one must consider the strict division of labor customary in Japan. The cook, following a hierarchical pattern, was the senior lording it over the two others, and she would never have been willing to clean a room, while the housemaid would not fire the stove. The two girls, who were both fairly well educated, cheerful, and enthusiastic about anything beautiful—whether nature, music, or art—were soon treated as part of our family. The first houseboy we had was not too intelligent. When he drove the car, he never knew how to find the place to which we wanted to go, but did not admit his ignorance. He thought that if he did, he would lose face.

It did not take us long to befriend the houseowner and neighbor, Mr. Hirayama and his family, consisting of his wife, one son, and three daughters. On Thanksgiving Day we had them all for dinner. It was in connection with this family that we could observe the weakening of the traditional system, according to which marriages were arranged by the parents of the potential bride and bridegroom through a go-between, as well as the developing emancipation of women. The son, who worked in a bank, fell in love with a girl employee there and married her. The young couple moved into the house of the husband's parents and the new wife had to do all the hard work in the household. One could see, and certainly the son did, that the bride was not happy. And behold what happened: against all precedents, the newly married couple moved out of the paternal home!

About two years later old Hirayama, a friendly man, died

of cancer. The family planned a big funeral ceremony in the Buddhist rite. It was summer, and since they did not have sufficient space in their smaller house, we offered the widow the opportunity to have the rites in our home. She gratefully accepted the offer, and soon afterwards the body of the *pater familias* was carried into one of our *tatami* rooms in an open casket and placed high on a shelf directly under the ceiling. It was a strange feeling for us to live for a few days with a dead body in the house. We were, of course, invited to the funeral, and were astonished to see how many people, seated in the garden, participated. A Buddhist priest officiated, and it was a solemn and impressive affair. Gifts of food were offered by the guests and nicely arranged next to the body for the long journey into a better world or into nirvana.

This may well be the proper occasion to emphasize that the pioneers of democracy in the Occupation, contrary to some criticism, respected, with the exception of a few ignorant fools, the Japanese culture, and that nothing was farther from their minds than the attempt to destroy or interfere with the beautiful aspects of Japanese building and garden architecture, with the very special fine arts, and with pure literature. To be sure, some isolated stupid mistakes were made of intruding into this sphere—for instance, interruptions of the classical Noh plays on the pretext that fighting between feudal knights shown in the performances reflected militarism. But what the serious reformers attacked had little to do with culture. While our ambitious endeavor had to be accompanied with some iconoclasm, quite a few occupationnaires yielded to the exotic charm of the country. They could not find the way back to the United States after the end of the Occupation, and probably never will, and I do not mean only those who married Japanese women. Most of us who returned treasured the memory of the Japanese period of our lives, and retained our deep interest in things Japanese. Some even became experts in cultural aspects of Japan.

CHAPTER FIFTEEN

Charlotte and Women's Emancipation

The Occupation-sponsored emancipation of Japanese women had shown progress after the legislation abolishing the house system. The crucial test of its success was, however, the actual use the women made of their legally won rights. We knew that it would take time until the new ideas would fully and willingly be integrated into Japan's society. We had good allies in Japan, and the best ones were the educated Japanese women. Among the most enthusiastic ones were the few Japanese female lawyers. I had regular meetings with them in which we discussed their problems and dwelt on the interpretation of the new law. I remember particularly Miss Watanabe Michiko as an eager feminist. She subsequently joined the Civil Liberties Division of the Attorney General's Office. In September 1950, the female lawyers formed the Women Lawyers' Bar Association. I also want to mention Miss Shiraishi Tsugi, the intelligent editor of the *Nippon* (later *Japan*) *Times*, who in her column courageously called for women's rights.

Against expectation, the women made intensive use of these rights in the political field from the start. In the first post-Occupation elections to the Diet, their participation in the voting was nearly equal to that of the men, and thirty-eight female members were elected to the Lower House on April 10, 1946, among them the pioneer feminist, Mrs. Kato Shizue, former Baroness Ishimoto. Although the percentage of women on the active as well as on the passive

side of voting declined in subsequent elections, the first
enthusiastic reaction to their enfranchisement granted at
the very beginning of the Occupation by SCAP directive
and anchored in the Constitution proves that Japan's society
was ripe for a change in the status of her women. The
practical problem now was to open their eyes to what they
had won. Here I wish to describe an interesting attempt in
this direction, in which Charlotte played a guiding role.

It was during the Katayama premiership that Attorney
General Suzuki encouraged his wife and two adult daughters, Ayako and Yuriko, to seek contacts with American
women, who already had invited Japanese women to meetings in the Chapel Center of GHQ. This contact started a
series of lectures. There were, among others, exchanges of
ideas between leading members of the Japanese YWCA and
Americans. More regular meetings in the Research Institute
of the Attorney General's Office followed. In most of them
the American participants elaborated on the contributions
to society of women in the United States. My wife looked at
many faces worn out by the strain of the postwar suffering,
when she was invited to this group to talk about child
psychology. Before the war the women had been resigned
to conditions as they were, but now they realized to what
misery this resignation had brought them and were willing
to work on the betterment of their status. Charlotte wanted
the Japanese to find out for themselves where their most
urgent needs existed and what remedies they could afford.
Therefore, she had the idea of inviting a small group of
Japanese women to our house in order to do some preliminary study together. She selected persons who could
speak some English and had enough time to engage in
research and to learn to give lectures in Japanese to a larger
group. The lecturing in Japanese was an important point
for my wife, who wanted to be in the background herself
and give the Japanese women the feeling that they were the
ones who had the responsibility and did the work. This
small nucleus proudly called itself "the research group."

They chose the subjects and were helped to find the material. Two or three members volunteered to be discussion leaders and had to be prepared to speak to the larger group. This was a new form of training and experience for them. In some instances they asked an expert in a specific field, a Japanese woman doctor or social worker, to do the lecturing. For the benefit of the listeners, charts and summaries as well as lists of "do" and "don't" were distributed. I have seen, for example, a fine colored chart of their country's fruits and vegetables containing important vitamins.

Everybody, regardless of social status or creed, could attend the meetings of the larger, fast-growing group, now called "New Japan Mothers' Group." Charlotte rented for these meetings the seventh floor of the large Nomura Bank building on certain afternoons. In September 1948, in an interview with a representative of the *Mainichi*, she emphasized the purpose of the meetings, which was mainly for the women to encourage and comfort each other by discussion and work on problems of family relations, child psychology, education, and civic duties.[1] I think it was the arrangement whereby Japanese women themselves carried the ball that made this organization a success of amazing duration. It lasted more than ten years, until we left Japan at the end of 1959, and in the course of time a true friendship had developed between Charlotte and the women. Even afterwards the members of the group have continued to meet regularly.

Charlotte was fully aware of the tremendous difficulties in home life, multiplied by the destruction of the war, and by inflation and unemployment following it. While in the United States the housewife enjoyed all kinds of modern conveniences, from gas and electric heating to refrigerators and washing machines, her Japanese counterparts had still to toil within a most primitive home economy. One day I came home earlier than usual and found the women's group on our terrace, where several *hibachis* (charcoal

[1] See *Mainichi*, September 12, 1948.

burners) over charcoal fires were lined up. The United States had sent corn meal as a relief gift, but it seemed useless to the Japanese housewife. Charlotte wanted to show them what good meals, such as soup, griddlecakes, or dumplings, they could prepare from it. After they had tasted this food, recipes were written down and distributed.

One prominent Japanese woman speaker fittingly pointed out that if all handicaps could be alleviated, the Japanese women would be able to cut themselves off from the vicious circle—"the lack of desire for self-improvement; a kind of mental inertia; and the lack of social interest and the resulting inactivity in this realm." In light of such contrast between the women of America and Japan it would have been absurd to suggest remedies along the line: why don't you do it as we do in the United States? Their situation had to be improved within the framework of what was possible at that time in Japan and with the means available to them. Charlotte's main role was one of organization and inspiration. She often guided the group in the selection of subjects, but left the preparation of the lectures and the lecturing itself to the Japanese, who spoke in their mother language. Only in the question and answer period did she express her opinions through an interpreter.

The research group met once weekly, and the larger mothers' group every third Friday of the month. The number of participants in the larger mothers' group naturally varied. Usually around fifty women attended the meetings. Once, when the Asaka palace was available, a much larger group of almost one hundred appeared. After the Nomura Bank building could no longer be used, the women assembled in our house.

A report and analysis of the activities of this organization during more than ten years would easily fill another book. Here I must restrict myself to a few illustrations. Since this was a mothers' group, many lectures covered children's feeding, training, and education. The bringing up of a baby, the child of different ages, and the adolescents with their specific problems were explained and discussed. It was continuously emphasized that on the proper rearing of the children depended the future of the nation. As a matter of course, coeducation as well as sex education played an important part in the program. The Japanese custom of married children living with their parents led to the discussion of the psychological problems of this togetherness. Household chores were a natural subject in these meetings where wives were in the majority. Different ways of saving time in shopping and cooking were proposed. The guidance went, however, beyond motherhood and housewifely concerns. There was general agreement that if the women were to improve their social status and grow to be equal marriage partners, they had to broaden their intellectual horizon and their interest in governmental and political affairs. Thus the new Constitution was studied, and its Bill of Rights compared with the Universal Declaration of Human Rights, the function of the family court was explained, and the Supreme Court visited and observed in action, an experience the women had never had before. Charlotte took her group to her orphanage when the clothing from Oklahoma arrived. This was intended as an illustration of how aid to the stepchildren of society could be practiced.

In a meeting on the subject of coeducation, several high school and college students asked for permission to participate in the debate. They were so fascinated by the free exchange of ideas that they desired to attend other meetings. Because the mothers felt, however, that the presence of the male youngsters could sometimes be embarrassing during the discussion of feminine problems, Charlotte established a separate student group. It consisted of students of colleges and high schools of both sexes, a somewhat unusual combination for such discussion meetings. The initial shyness in communicating with one another and in talking to an audience was soon overcome, and the meetings grew to very lively affairs to which the young people looked forward with anticipation. The subjects on the program were of a much more sophisticated nature than those dealt with in the mothers' group, and of great variety. Education played an important part here, too. The students examined the questions of whether its aim ought to be the training of the intellect or the cultivation of the character, and how the new Constitution had affected education. The debates covered the meaning of freedom of religion and the impact of the constitutional principles on the family system. One day was devoted to an analysis of the character of the Japanese people. The speakers delivered reports on books which they had read. In the list of the authors treated I discovered Plato, Max Weber, Dostoyevski, and Norman Mailer. "Love" was not neglected among the topics, nor the propriety of dating. A young girl, daughter of an artist, spoke about expressionism and cubism in art. Another speaker described the *kabuki* play as an impressive piece of traditional Japanese culture. A lively discussion ensued on the advantages and disadvantages of modern mass communication.

I think that the success of these meetings was mainly due to the fact that Charlotte had nothing to do with the Occupation, never acted in the role of a superior mentor, and always tried to understand the young men and women as a mature friend. When she left Tokyo, each of the student participants expressed their gratitude and appreciation in writing. Two of these farewell notes deserve to be quoted because they complement each other, although they seem to be contradictory. One reads:

> I don't know the word of thanks for you. We've had a very good time and enjoyed every minute of the meetings for a long time. You are the true Japanese in the true sense of the word and a good ambassador. . . . See you again in Japan or America.

The other message reads:

> Thank you very much for your kindness. We can know the real American, so I think. I hope you will tell

others the real Japan and Japanese. I feel I could get
something important from you.

The definition of Charlotte as "the true Japanese" may
have had different psychological motivations: it may just
mean that her understanding of the nation and its people
was exceptional for an American, but it may also reveal an
emotional desire for identity between student and guide,
perhaps with the subconscious thought that since Charlotte
appealed so strongly to the group, she must be a Japanese,
ideologically speaking.

Charlotte looks back with deep satisfaction at her work
with the Japanese women and students. The enthusiastic
response she received encourages her in the hope that,
within the limited scope of her efforts, she may in the
difficult postwar period have contributed to better understanding of new ways and ideas.

CHAPTER SIXTEEN

Labor Problems and Communism

I have mentioned before the prohibition of the general strike scheduled by the labor union leaders for February 1, 1947. Those were exciting days for all of us, and we had mixed feelings. On the one hand, we were concerned over the infiltration of radical leftist and communist elements into the union movement, which the Occupation had created and promoted. On the other hand, we admitted that their complaints about starvation wages during an inflationary period were justified in light of a long passivity of the government. The would-be strikers were not merely motivated by economic needs, however, but also politically, by the expectation that a general strike would mean the overthrow of the Yoshida government. Still, the "MacArthur Constitution" guaranteed in Article 28 the right of workers to "act collectively," and we could well understand SCAP's reluctance to interfere by direct prohibitive action. We were afraid that the reactionary Japanese forces would interpret any such interference as their victory and as the twilight of the Occupation.

A sinister political boss who served these forces had sent his hatchetmen to one of the strike leaders, Kikunami Katsui, chairman of the General Council of Industrial Unions (Sohyo). They threatened him with violence, and actually injured him. MacArthur must have felt deeply the gravity of the dilemma, as his statement of January 31, 1947,

calling off the general strike, shows.[1] He emphasized his reluctance to intervene and the necessity to do so in order to
avoid the catastrophic consequences of a general strike, but
added that he did not otherwise intend to restrict the
freedom of action heretofore given labor in the achievement
of legitimate objectives, or in any way "to compromise or
influence the basic issues involved."

It is interesting to note what Japanese involved in that
labor offensive had to say about it some thirteen years later,
long after the nation had resumed its independence. Dr.
Ayusawa Iwao, who was secretary general of the Central
Labor Relations Board in 1946 and professor at the International Christian University in 1959, observed correctly
that "in those days the Occupation authorities were en-
grossed with the task of accomplishing its two missions: the
eradication of Japanese militarism and the democratization
of the country," and that "the promotion of labor movements suited their mission." He also confirms the fact that
"the Occupation authorities were extremely reserved about
interfering with the labor unions." He concludes that the
abortive February 1 general strike threat was one of the
peaks as well as a turning point of the labor movement in
Japan.[2] Kikunami, who, after the drama of January 31,
joined the Communist party, somehow antedates the turning point to the "People's Rally to Get Rice" on May 19,
1946, in front of the imperial palace. A day later MacArthur
cautioned the Japanese people that the growing tendency
towards mass violence and physical intimidation, under organized leadership, presented a grave menace to the future
development of Japan.[3] Kikunami recognizes that "in the
beginning, it was the aim of the Occupation forces to aid
and foster 'democratic' forces among the people," but he
adds that "with the appearance of friction between the

1 *Political Reorientation* II, 762.
2 *Asahi Shimbun*, quoted in *Asahi Evening News* of August 21, 1959.
3 *Political Reorientation* II, 750.

United States and the USSR and of revolutionary trends in
Japan, the Occupation authorities turned around and supported the reactionary conservative forces. . . . The Occupation's aim was to use the conservatives to control the
'democratic forces' which had become unruly. This policy
was fully exposed when . . . general strike were [sic] ordered
banned."[4]

I consider these post-Occupation comments important for
several reasons. At first, the question may be raised: were
the radical strike conspirators really shortsighted enough
to believe that SCAP would tolerate a general strike under
the prevailing economic conditions, and thus were they
ready to do irreparable harm to the Japanese nation; or did
they deliberately force MacArthur's hand, possibly upon
orders from the Kremlin, because they felt it to be of paramount significance to destroy his prestige as friend of the
working classes? I favored the second alternative.

The events of the fateful incident touches, moreover, on
a frequently heard disparagement of the general, as epito-
mized by Ayusawa's remark that "the Occupation forces of
those days were not aware of the existence of 'two worlds' or
of the 'threat of communism.'" American writers have
taken up a similar theme by stating that the Occupation,
while understanding the international danger of communism, inadvertently helped communism in Japan to
thrive and to assume a leading role in the labor movement
without being aware that some of its leaders were guided
by Moscow. Harry Emerson Wildes gives, indeed, striking
examples of SCAP tolerance toward leftist radicalism in the
first period of the Occupation, and expresses the belief that
the naive and inexperienced occupationnaires were duped
at that time by the softspoken communist leader Nosaka
Sanzo, who professed democracy and evolution.[5]

George Kennan blames the Occupation policy as po-
tentially paving the way to communism, although he

---

[4] *Asahi Shimbun*, quoted in *Asahi Evening News* of August 20, 1959.
[5] *Typhoon in Tokyo*, chap. 25.

recognizes that SCAP's directives were the reflection of international agreements, the altering of which represented formidable problems.[6] He voices disapproval of what he terms "the evangelical liberalism" by which the Occupation policies were "ostensibly" governed and, I may add, men like myself were inspired. He also frowns on the other attitudes that pervaded the wartime policies of the Allied powers, namely, "love for pretentious generality, self-righteous punitive enthusiasm, pro-Soviet illusions, and the unreal hopes for great power collaboration in the postwar period." I regret that this prominent diplomat and scholar, whom I admire and whose brilliantly unconventional observations with regard to other countries have often impressed me, resorted to a one-sided evaluation of the Occupation reforms without giving credit to their merits. His description of Allied, including American, policies by which SCAP was bound is simultaneously the explanation for the initial toleration of communism in Japan. It seems to me that much of the criticism of this toleration is not based on the situation as it existed at the time of the events under scrutiny, but influenced by subsequent developments and insights.

Americans do not like today to be reminded of the fact that Soviet Russia was our ally in the war, when Hitler was enemy number one, and that our immediate postwar policies were to a large extent compromise solutions in which Stalin had a heavy hand. When the Occupation started, the Truman Doctrine had not yet been announced, it was before Berlin, and before Joseph McCarthy. Of course, there were early flashes of disappointment among those who, like President Roosevelt, had for some time lived in the illusion of a postwar harmony between the big powers, but the cold war was only in its initial stage. If anybody was free, however, from illusions regarding the power behind the iron curtain, it was General MacArthur.

[6] See George F. Kennan, *Memoirs: 1925–1950* (Boston: Atlantic-Little, Brown, 1967). pp. 372–388.

He has been severely criticized for evading the Far Eastern
Commission in connection with the Constitution, and for
preventing Russian interference by neutralizing the Allied
Council for Japan. Furthermore, the nonformation of a
Soviet zone of occupation on the main Japanese islands,
which avoided the troubles resulting from the different
arrangement in Germany and Korea, can to a large extent
be attributed to MacArthur's influence. According to certain critics, he was even convinced of a communist conspiracy against him.[7]

I shall never believe that this man, of all people, would
not have seen the potential link between the Japanese
communists and the Kremlin. Clear evidence that he actually did is supplied by President Truman himself, not
exactly an enthusiastic defender of the controversial general. Truman reports in his memoirs on a visit to Japan by
Edwin Locke, Jr., whom he had sent on an economic
mission to China. Locke wrote to the president as early as
October 1945: "General MacArthur gave considerable
emphasis to the influence of Russia on Japanese affairs,
expressing concern over 'underground Communist agitation' in Japan. Many of the so-called liberal elements of
Japan are Communistic, he stated, and in his opinion,
Japanese Communism is dominated from Moscow."[8] I do
not exclude the possibility that individual SCAP officials
may have been deluded, to begin with, by the belief that
they were dealing with a genuine Japanese nationalist
movement that supported the Occupation policies. I did not
know any in important positions who himself was a communist. But MacArthur could not possibly say publicly
what he had told Mr. Locke without provoking an international incident. This is also the reason that he usually

[7] See Richard H. Rovere and Arthur Schlesinger, Jr., *The MacArthur
Controversy* (New York: Farrar, Straus and Giroux, 1965), p. 272.

[8] See *Memoirs* of Harry S Truman (Garden City, N.Y.: Doubleday,
1955), I, 519.

did not explicitly refer to communist activities, but rather to "radicalism" or "extreme movements."

Seen from within Japan, the problem was even more delicate. The members of the Communist party were the only Japanese group which without exception had fought all those forces the Occupation was directed to eliminate: the war lords, feudalism, *zaibatsu* capitalism, and so on. They had suffered exile, long imprisonment, and even worse for their resistance, and for some time after their return and release from jail they were hailed by many Japanese as heroes and martyrs. From the strict point of view of our mission, they were the least vulnerable elements of Japan society. Thus, shocking as this may appear to a great many readers today, in light of the priority of SCAP's democratizing mission they were regarded as somewhat mistrusted allies against a common enemy, as long as they supported the objectives of the Occupation and did not show themselves unruly. Did not the United States government do the same when allying itself with Stalin against Hitler?

The turning point had to come sooner or later, however. To put it on the date of the "Give Us Rice" demonstrations or of the canceled general strike might be too early. The latter event was certainly a disappointment for SCAP in relation to the attitude of labor, but his call for new elections and his welcome of the Katayama government proved that this did not mean a lessening of his reformatory zeal in general, but that he was still willing to give a progressive regime a chance. In my own field I did not experience any retrogressive tendency at this time, and when I first discovered it sometime in the summer of 1948, the legal and judicial reforms were completed or near completion.[9] The

[9] Robert Ward, in *Political Development in Modern Japan*, p. 503, puts the time when emphasis on and priority of democratization diminished "from late 1947 onward." While this earlier date is probably irrefutable with respect to SCAP's disappointment with the actions

result of the April 1946 elections satisfied me that those who voted for the Communist party were only a small fraction of the population, which overwhelmingly favored the conservative candidates. I was concerned over the leadership in the labor unions, although I suspected that the red and pink infiltration had been somewhat exaggerated,[10] and over the radicalization of the teaching profession and of large segments of the student community. Nevertheless, I was convinced that a policy of repression, a replica of what the Japanese rulers had done before us, would create the worst possible credibility gap for the Occupation. It would have benefited the forces of yesterday, who would exploit such difference between theory and practice as evidence that our democratization policy was unreasonable and impracticable. What else could have been expected after the disastrous failure of the former rulers but a definite trend toward the left? Add to this the fact that economic misery always generates extremism, and the conclusion may be justified that patience and a wait-and-see attitude was, indeed, the wisest course of action. None of us could imagine a communist revolution during the Occupation; and even if the plan of ending it much earlier had materialized, the presence of United States forces would have been likely to continue, as they did under the Security Treaty of 1951, and prevent a communist takeover. More

of labor, a point also made by Ward: the start of diminishing democratization is hard to fix. I think that for some time the headquarters' policy was a balancing of democratization with security objectives. As reported before, the committee in which we prepared the important revision of the Code of Criminal Procedure in lengthy conferences with the Japanese met in spring 1948, and although our innovations were quite liberal and have been criticized by law enforcement officials as overemphasizing the rights of the accused and defendant, there was never any interference by the front office. Edwin O. Reischauer in *Japan, the Story of a Nation* (New York: Knopf, 1970), p. 233, observes that by the autumn of 1948 a great shift of emphasis from reform to economic recovery was evident in the Occupation.

[10] Yoshida, in his *Memoirs*, pp. 223–224, maintains that the majority of Japan's workers has no sympathy with the aims of the extremists.

importantly, we did not see sufficient indications that the
bulk of the Japanese people would have tolerated or supported it. To be sure, most of them favored harmonious
relations and trade with the outside communist world, but
that did not mean that there was a powerful desire to have
a communist regime established in Japan.

Harvard Professor Edwin O. Reischauer, former ambassador to Japan, the most experienced and knowledgeable American expert on the political and social aspects of
contemporary Japan, apparently did not share Kennan's
view that an early end of the Occupation would have led
to a takeover by communist forces. He thought that it
lasted about twice as long as it should have.[11] I am inclined
to agree with him also, since in my view the long duration
of the Occupation had the effect that this enterprise, which
started with so much élan, became somewhat anticlimactic.
The "uncertain and unsatisfactory transition" of Japan's
society in 1947, which Kennan deplores, was inevitable
unless the occupant refrained from any attempt of political
transformation and restricted himself to demilitarization.
Then the danger of a radical leftist upheaval would have
been real. As a matter of fact, the domestic atmosphere
improved considerably once the United States had begun
to send large shipments of food to Japan for the starving
population.

I find Kennan's argument unconvincing that the Occupation reforms, such as land reform, the purge, and trust
busting, promoted the cause of communism because the
communists had also advocated them. I had always looked
at them as effective instruments for taking the wind out of
the sails of communist propaganda. This is most of all true
of the land reform, which improved the wretched condition
of those who farmed the land. To be sure, it was radical and
therefore has caused misgivings to orthodox believers in the
sanctity of private property, inasmuch as it amounted pretty

[11] See Edwin O. Reischauer, *The United States and Japan*, 3rd ed.
(Cambridge: Harvard University Press, 1965), p. 287.

much to confiscation. But the revolutionary impulse to do
away with the unjust bondage of the peasant was stronger
in MacArthur's early proconsulate than were traditional
American legal considerations. The principle of inviola-
bility of "the right to own or hold property" is also
anchored in the new Constitution of Japan, and under the
circumstances one could very well doubt the constitutionality of the land reform. The affected landowners challenged it in the courts, mainly on the ground that what
they received as payment for the land they had to give up
was not "just compensation," as required by the Constitution in case private property is taken "for public use." The
plaintiffs lost in all three instances (district, high, and
Supreme Court). The date of the judgment of the Supreme
Court on the land reform was December 23, 1953.[12] The
Court was therefore not under pressure from SCAP, since
the Occupation had ended almost two years before, but
Maki is absolutely right in his comment that the opinions
in the case "bring out clearly the tremendous significance—
legal, political, and economic—of the land reform and,
perhaps indirectly, at least indicate the impossibility of
making a narrowly legal interpretation of the key phrase
'just compensation' in the present case." This was a pragmatic decision, similar to those in other countries recognizing the legality of a successful revolution. The political
and financial consequences of an invalidation of the completed land reform or its method of compensation would
have been most disturbing, if not chaotic.

What I felt as an anticlimax, beginning sometime in the
middle of 1948, was brought on by a variety of complex
factors. Not that the democratization was ever completely
discarded as an Occupation objective, but one cannot keep
alive an "evangelical" reform spirit for too long a period.
There was also the developing priority of Japan's economic
recovery, often incompatible with revolutionary surgery,
such as the purge and the deconcentration of economic

[12] Maki, *Court and Constitution in Japan*, pp. 228ff.

power. The failure of the Katayama cabinet and the corruption scandals evolving during the Ashida regime contributed to a shift in SCAP's support to the politically stable right. More decisively, however, the cold war had increased in severity, national security was suddenly the overruling concern, and this led to some decline of the efforts toward democratization.

By and by the metamorphosis of Japan from a defeated enemy and ward to the needed and most important ally in the Far East took shape. The January 1949 elections to the Lower House resulted in a seemingly dangerous polarization, with the conservatives receiving the absolute majority, and the communists obtaining thirty-five seats, or almost ten percent of the votes. The success of the Yoshida liberals finds its explanation in the disgust of many middle-of-the-road voters with the quarrels and corruption of the preceding regimes. The advance of the Communist party did not necessarily mean that all those who favored it were communists, inasmuch as the local elections to prefectural and municipal offices at the same time showed quite different and more conservative trends. In the national sphere, the procommunist vote was also a vote of nonconfidence against the Occupation and against the other parties that had carried out its will. The austerity policy directed by SCAP in the interests of economic reconstruction naturally met the opposition of a great number of those affected, who might otherwise not have supported the communists. And without doubt, the Nosaka policy of depicting his party as "lovable" and as "party with a heart" contributed to the communist success.[13]

MacArthur's shift of attitude in July 1948 toward labor unions, in connection with the rights of public service workers, caused dissatisfaction among the rank and file of labor. It was, in part, the result of serious disturbances by

[13] For details on the Communist party of Japan, see Robert Scalapino, *The Japanese Communist Movement, 1920–1966* (Berkeley and Los Angeles: University of California Press, pp. 79ff.).

railway workers. A dramatic dispute between James S. Killen, head of the Labor Division of ESS, and Blaine Hoover, chief of Government Section's Civil Service Division, had preceded SCAP's decision. Not only the right of civil servants proper to organize, bargain collectively, and strike was involved, but also the question whether and to what extent certain other workers employed by the government should enjoy these rights. The importance of the issue can be seen in the fact that almost three million workers were affected. They included large numbers of manual workers in the government-run railways as well as in the state monopolies. The products thus monopolized were tobacco, salt, crude camphor, and camphor oil. Killen advocated the cause of labor, while Hoover urged restrictive action, as far as all public employees and workers were concerned. This dispute within headquarters was one of the rare occasions in which MacArthur left his phoneless chamber and presided over a conference on the division chief level. The two division chiefs, of course, argued their case in the presence of their Section chiefs, Generals Whitney and William F. Marquat, respectively. Hoover, a man of authoritative dignity, conservative in outlook, and very sure of himself, was probably more General MacArthur's cup of tea than the former American union official, Killen, whose deep conviction that SCAP should not abandon or lessen his pro-labor policy was voiced with courage and ability, but at a time when the Occupation had reason to feel disappointed by the conduct of labor. Anyway, Hoover won his case. Civil servants proper were even prohibited from genuine unionization and from collective bargaining, and were deprived of the right to strike, while the railway and monopoly workers retained the right to organize and to bargain collectively, but were not allowed to strike, either. Killen, unwilling to carry out a policy with which he disagreed, resigned.

It was this decision by SCAP that indicated to the Japanese again that the trend had changed. While I have always held that civil servants who exercised governmental functions, and workers in essential enterprises, such as transportation and communication, should have no right to strike, I felt somewhat doubtful whether the workers in the monopoly industries, which were newly organized in a public corporation, should have been deprived of that right, since they were merely engaged in the type of labor usually performed in private business.

◇◇

CHAPTER SEVENTEEN

National Security versus Pacifism

When the cold war reached its climax in the Korean conflict, the Occupation was in a vulnerable position. It had instilled a pacifist spirit in the bulk of the Japanese nation, a spirit anchored in the famous Article 9 of the Constitution, which MacArthur had so avidly endorsed, if not inspired.[1] After Korea dispelled all illusions of a peaceful coexistence with the communist world, which had been tremendously enlarged by the emergence of Red China, this constitutional provision—and even more, the psychological disarmament of Japan—stood in the way of alleviating her defenseless condition. We who had disarmed the defeated enemy now desired to see the potential ally rearmed; we also wanted to relieve the United States from

[1] The question of whether the general inspired the inclusion of the war renunciation clause in the Constitution or merely endorsed it has remained controversial. To be sure, at first sight the unique ban looks very much like a product of MacArthur's imaginative mind, but he has repeatedly gone on record that the idea originated with a proposal made to him by Prime Minister Shidehara to demonstrate to the world the conversion of his nation to a model pacifist spirit. MacArthur, according to his version, avidly welcomed it and personally drafted the text of the clause. Shidehara's successor, Yoshida (see his *Memoirs*, p. 137), and other particularly conservative, Japanese remained skeptical about this story, inasmuch as Shidehara in a cabinet meeting allegedly indicated that it was MacArthur who suggested the provision. Subsequently, however, Shidehara reversed himself. According to Takayanagi, Shidehara had feared that Article 9 would be rejected by the cabinet if he admitted his authorship (see *The Constitution of Japan, the First Twenty Years*, p. 87).

the burden of maintaining its protective military umbrella. The wording of Article 9 suggests to the unprejudiced reader that Japan is prohibited from maintaining armed forces even for defensive purposes, and this was the initial understanding both of MacArthur and of the government spokesman in the Diet, Kanamori. Nevertheless, an ambiguous amendment proposed by Ashida, and the consideration that the right of self-defense of a nation is inalienable and cannot be abridged even by a Constitution, opened the legal way to a modest rearmament, disguised at first, after the outbreak of the Korean conflict, under the name of Police Reserve, more properly termed Self-Defense Forces. The Supreme Court of Japan, ruling not on the constitutionality of the Self-Defense Forces,[2] but on that of stationing of United States forces in Japan under the Security Treaty, held in December 1959 in the Sunakawa case that Article 9 "does not in the least negate the inherent right of self-defense of this country as a sovereign state." According to the Court, the principle of peace cannot be identified with defenselessness and nonresistance, but Japan can take the measures necessary for the preservation of its existence, peace, and security.[3]

Still, the Japanese have resented pressure on our part to speed up their rearmament. Ironically enough, the leftist parties, otherwise so critical of the Occupation, resist any change of Article 9 of the "MacArthur Constitution," a change the United States would welcome, and have up to

[2] In 1973 Fukushima Shigeo, as judge of the District Court of Sapporo, Hokkaido, declared the Japanese Self-Defense Forces unconstitutional (see *New York Times* of September 8, 1973). This decision was rendered in a case in which the constitutionality of the construction of a missile base was challenged. The case had started with the disciplinary events described in note 16 of Chapter 8. For a recent analysis of the decision see Robert L. Seymour, "Japan's Self-defense: The Naganuma Case and Its Implications," in *Pacific Affairs* 47 (Winter 1974/75), 421ff.

[3] See the article by the author, "The Sunakawa Case, Its Legal and Political Implications," in *Political Science Quarterly* 76 (June 1961), 247.

now been in a position to prevent it, since the conservative advocates of a revision did not and do not have the required two-thirds majority in the Diet. Even they are not over-eager to bring the provision of the charter into accord with reality, since the small size of the defense budget of the government has handsomely contributed to the fantastic surge of the Japanese economy. Rearmament has remained a politically touchy issue. The volte-face in American policy may have been necessary in view of the changed world picture, but this is hard to explain to idealistic youngsters who had wholeheartedly accepted the pacifism we preached, and now felt that we abandoned high principle in favor of expediency. This produced anti-Americanism among students and intellectuals.

The irrational appeal that Marxist theory—not necessarily in its Soviet form—has traditionally had for Japanese scholars and students also intensified the criticism by these groups of the SCAP-authorized repression of communists and fellow travelers in government positions by the Yoshida cabinet in 1949. At this time the purge, which had aimed at the removal of militarists and ultranationalists, was applied to the communists. After June 1950, the purge of leftists was extended to the press and to private industry. These measures, in connection with the beginning of rehabilitating the rightists, indicated to many Japanese a "reverse course" of Occupation policy. Still, the unpopularity of these policies could be attributed not so much to the purge of communist leaders, into which the Occupation had been virtually forced, as to complaints that the conservative government had used the opportunity to remove from influence a number of people who were strongly liberal, moderately socialist, or otherwise nonconformist.

The communists, after their election success in January 1949, had already lost much of their hold, not only because of the betterment of the economic situation, but also as a result of their own stupidity and recklessness. Their agitation bred violence and crime. As a reaction to the SCAP-directed retrenchment program of the government, acts of sabotage had been committed. For instance, the director general of the Japanese National Railways, Shimoyama Sadanori, was brutally murdered in July 1949, and his body found across the tracks in Tokyo. Moreover, trains were derailed and several people were killed. One of these incidents was the monstrous Matsukawa case mentioned before, which started on August 17, 1949, when a passenger train was derailed and overturned. Although these crimes have remained a mystery and all defendants in the Matsukawa case were acquitted after fourteen years, the fact that they happened after twenty-five percent of the railway workers were affected by dismissals had turned the suspicion against radical labor leaders.

The communist *Akahata* (Red Flag) resorted to a sordid type of vilification of Occupation personnel and to attacks of United States "imperialism." Trying to give a racial and nationalist flavor to Japanese communism, it described SCAP as the alien enemy of the Japanese people and as the restorer of the hated police state. Whoever was deceived by this type of unexpected patriotism must, however, have discovered the dependence of the Japanese communist movement upon Soviet Russia when, in January 1950, the "soft" Nosaka line was censored by the Comintern as being irreconcilable with Marxism-Leninism, and when, after a brief interval, Nosaka gave up his "deviationism." This obvious subservience to the Soviet master did the communists even more harm than their advocacy of the abolition of the Emperor. In May 1950, communist-inspired demonstrators physically assailed American military personnel. MacArthur lost his patience and started his vigorous purge of the communists, which was extended when, after the Korean war, they openly voiced support for the North Koreans.

Even in August 1950, MacArthur expressed the optimistic view that communist infiltration into Japanese life was in no sense a threat, as communist ideas did not appeal to the

Japanese but, more importantly, because it had the Russian label. The Japanese, he said, both feared and hated the Russians.[4] This statement was, in my view, too much of a generalization; while true of the majority of the Japanese people, it did not take into account that the emergence of Soviet Russia as a superpower impressed certain elements of Japan's society. This was to become even more true with regard to Red China, which, apart from cultural ties, was still largely looked upon as the Asian brother. Political ideologies played a lesser role with the Japanese. In the case of Russia there were, however, additional reasons for resentment. Many Japanese considered the last-minute entrance of Soviet Russia into the war on the Allied side as the breach of a treaty. Her long failure to release the Japanese prisoners of war, and the conduct of the selected group of brainwashed prisoners who were released and returned to Japan from Russia made bad blood. Finally, there was the territorial conflict over the Southern Kurile Islands. MacArthur's remark to Harriman, like his above statement to Locke, makes it clear that he saw "the Russian label" on Japanese communism. It appears all the more puzzling that, according to Rovere and Schlesinger, he had told G. Ward Price, a British journalist, in March 1949 that he did not think the Japanese communists had any direct link with Moscow.[5] Surely, he must have known of the close contact of the Japanese red leaders with the Soviet liaison office in Tokyo. I cannot guess what tactical reasons, if any, motivated him to express a view he did not hold.

As for the May demonstrations and violence against our military personnel, it was staged, and did not indicate a widespread wave of anti-Americanism. This was the first such attack; the second happened on May Day 1952, when the same elements celebrated the end of the Occupation and the resumption of independence for Japan by a riot on the palace ground, in which automobiles of Americans were

[4] See Truman, *Memoirs* II, 350.
[5] See *The MacArthur Controversy*, p. 91, note.

burned. The shocked reaction of the Japanese people to this kind of violence was evident in the October 1952 election to the House of Representatives, in which the Communist party did not obtain a single seat. During all our years in Japan my wife and I felt perfectly safe in the streets of Tokyo, even by night, something I could never say of New York City.

◇◇

CHAPTER EIGHTEEN

Press Conferences and Public Speeches

In connection with my concern for the civil liberties guaranteed in the new Constitution, I inadvertently became publicly involved in the communist problem. On May 7, 1950, the Japan Civil Liberties Union held its annual convention and invited me to deliver a speech. Influenced by the recent communist excesses, I emphasized that there exists in the field of citizens' freedom a dilemma, since certain minority elements "use the tools of democracy to destroy it." Thinking of the Weimar Republic, I said that there are precedents in history of excessive toleration of the enemies of free institutions leading to the downfall of all freedom. "Japan, too," I continued, "has at the present time her gravediggers who undermine the new foundations of a free society. On the other hand, the defense against them should never degenerate into a general limitation of the freedom of expression and other fundamental human rights. Only when discussion and dissent are allowed can the free society visualized by the Constitution prevail. Much wisdom will be required to draw the accurate line between the legitimate exercise of civil rights and criminal activities. Moreover," I remarked, "there is always the danger that overeager law enforcement officials are unable or unwilling to distinguish between those gravediggers and progressive-minded reformers who make use of their right of legitimate criticism of the government."

This was the gist of my lecture, the ABC's of liberalism in its effort to resolve the eternal dilemma by steering a course between the two horns. It was prepared completely on my own initiative, and my purpose was merely to warn the Civil Liberties Union of leftist radicalism, which, I foresaw, was a potential danger to some of its members. Perhaps because of the usual restraint in public utterances of a political nature by most occupationnaires, who cautiously left this business to the virtuoso in the field, MacArthur, this harmless talk developed into a journalistic sensation. It was given full first-page coverage in Japanese papers, often with my picture, and was widely interpreted as a trial balloon in preparation for an intensified SCAP purge of communists. I liked best the headline of the *Tokyo Shimbun* of May 7, 1950: " 'Protect Freedom by Overcoming Dilemma,' Emphasizes Section Chief [*sic*] Oppler." Even the *New York Times* noted the event under the headline: "Tokyo Red Ban Defended. Japanese Civil Liberties Group Hears MacArthur's Legal Expert." The most detailed report was sent by Howard Handelman, Far Eastern director of the International News Service.

Public speaking had by this time become one of my routine activities. Headquarters made ample use of press conferences, in which the official in charge of the subject of discussion faced Japanese and Allied journalists. His presentation was followed by a question period, which I soon began to enjoy. I held my first press conference in April 1947, on the reform of criminal procedure. In May, I talked about the importance of the forthcoming appointment of the justices of the Supreme Court in view of their new tasks. In December 1947, the subject was the Penal Code and the abolition of lese majesty. In the same month, I explained the dissolution of the Ministry of Justice and the creation of the Attorney General's Office. In August 1948, I stated that publicity and popularization of the recent legal and judicial reforms are a prerequisite for the development

of Japan into a free society, and I appealed to the press to
help in enlightening the people, inasmuch as jurists are
probably least able to simplify these matters. In July 1950,
I explained the new Nationality Law.

This does not exhaust the list of press conferences, to
which must be added those of my associates. I can only say
that we were struggling hard for the conquest of the soul
of the Japanese people. The largest audience I had was in
the summer of 1947, when I talked to almost two thousand
blue-collar workers in Osaka about the rights of the citizen
involved in a criminal trial under the new Code. I also
addressed the general public in a large meeting at the town
of Urawa on the first anniversary of the United Nations'
Universal Declaration of Human Rights. It was sponsored
by the Civil Liberties Bureau of the Attorney General's
Office. There I compared the new constitutional guarantees
of Japan to the Declaration, and pointed out that, although
Japan was not yet a member of the United Nations, her
Constitution lived up to the demands of the world document.

Even in 1951, I continued imperturbably as knight of
civil liberties. In March, I talked before a large number of
people in the Kyobashi Auditorium at a meeting sponsored
by the attorney general's Legal Affairs Bureau. Here again
my effort was to balance antireaction with anticommunism.
Perhaps my views were a product of my past experiences in
Nazi Germany, just as Mr. Kennan's international policy
views resulted from his close contact with and intimate
knowledge of the Soviet system. While always aware of the
communist danger, I never lost sight of the other one, the
resurgence of the old sinister rightist forces. At times when
justified indignation against radicalism of the left was at its
peak, that danger appeared to me considerable. I stated in
my speech that while war was raging on Japan's doorsteps,
the existence of a small but factious group in her midst, the
communists, who were allied to the cause of foreign imperialism, was no longer a mere civil liberties problem. It

6. Clipping of *Tokyo Times,* March 19, 1951, covering the author's civil liberties speech.

threatened the integrity of the state and the security of the nation as a whole, I said. They exploited the privileges of democracy for their purposes, but once in power, they would follow the pattern of their masters and annihilate all individual freedom. Fortunately, I continued, the Japanese people were becoming increasingly conscious of this danger and had already acted against it but, using a Chinese proverb, I said: in watching for the tiger at the front door, don't forget the wolf at the back door! I then warned the people against the reestablishment of the old police state under the guise of patriotism and anticommunism. Communism in the long run can be fought only by ideas. Democracy must be able to pass the test of emergency without adopting the methods of the very system it wants to beat. I cited the courageous words of United States Attorney General McGrath to make it clear that our own country faced the same dilemma. It was just the time of the "spectacular demagoguery" of Joseph McCarthy.[1] McGrath had expressed concern about the sins committed in the name of loyalty by those who would smear any opposition with the label of communism, and who would penalize unorthodox thought or nonconformist writing. He remarked that "in destroying the fabric of our democracy, they play directly into the hands of the Kremlin agents."

Some readers may look at all this talk as a tiring repetition of the often-heard sermon of liberalism, but others may find that twenty years later, when the target was "radical liberalism" in addition to communism, it had remained perfectly applicable even in our own country.

I have dwelt on my speeches in some detail because I wanted to show that even after the cold war had become hot, the libertarian voice was not silenced within MacArthur's Occupation. In the propagation of civil liberties Kurt

[1] A term used by Samuel Eliot Morrison in *The Oxford History of the American People* (New York: Oxford University Press, 1965), p. 1074.

Steiner played an important part. His public speeches were very impressive.

The response of the Japanese listeners was positive, if not enthusiastic.[2] More importantly, they understood fully what we wanted to bring home to them. I believe this disproves the assertion of some critics that to the Japanese, who were brought up with the idea that devotion to Emperor, state, and family is the paramount ethical demand, emphasis upon individual rights did not mean anything or must have been even repugnant. This is another oversimplification.

[2] My speech was covered in most Japanese papers, and by the *Nippon Times* of March 18, 1951, in toto.

◇◇◇

CHAPTER NINETEEN

Old and New Tasks in the Legal Section

In the spring of 1948 General Whitney believed, as he stated in the history of his Section, that the primary mission of my Court and Law Division had been accomplished. In his desire to reduce his greatly expanded Section to a small rump organization, he recommended that my whole division, its "residual functions," and its personnel be transferred to the Legal Section.[1] The transfer took place on May 31, 1948, and my associates and I left Government Section en bloc. I was not very happy about this change, although I knew that it was not motivated by the wish to get rid of me. I regretted leaving the SCAP unit where the action had been, and I feared that my future activity in the Legal Section would no longer be an exciting participation in policy making. As it actually turned out, the more dynamic period of the Government Section had largely come to an end at the time of the transfer; my work in the Legal Section was challenging enough; and I enjoyed even greater independence there than in Government Section. The necessity of having to change bosses is always unpleasant if one is getting along perfectly well with his present superiors. Most of my colleagues in the Government Section had become good friends, particularly Kades, Williams, and Hauge, and, although we sometimes differed in our views,

[1] See *Political Reorientation* II, 792.

we were in gratifying agreement to disagree. My departure was sweetened by my receiving the Award for Meritorious Civilian Service from General MacArthur.

The chief of the Legal Section was Colonel Alva Carpenter, who probably owed this position to MacArthur's loyalty to the "Bataan Crowd," friends and admirers from his Philippine days. During the Occupation, Carpenter resigned from the army and became a civilian. A tall, good looking, and dignified man, he was reserved and a good listener. At first I thought that this reserve stemmed from excessive pride, but after knowing him better, I had to correct this impression and found that a certain shyness might be at the root of it. While not brilliant, he was a man of great integrity with a strong sense of justice and fairness. His outstanding virtue consisted of his ability and willingness to delegate responsibilities, and he was lucky enough to have as the head of the Law Division of his Section an efficient and resourceful lawyer, Jules Bassin, who exercised a dominating influence when I joined the Section. After the Occupation he became the legal attaché of the American embassy in Tokyo.

Bassin must have had mixed feelings when another division with different personnel, tasks, attitudes, and loyalties was suddenly added to the Section. I had reason to believe that he would have liked nothing better than to integrate me and my associates into his division. That was, of course, not the idea of Whitney, and after I hinted my suspicion to him, he immediately called up Carpenter. When I introduced myself to the latter, he reassured me that we would remain intact as a separate division within the Legal Section, on an equal level with Bassin's Law Division. We thereupon changed our name into Legislation and Justice Division. As it turned out, the separation between the two divisions was easily workable in view of their clearly different assignments: we were in charge of supervising Japanese law and justice, and the Law Division advised SCAP on all other legal matters, particularly United States law and international law not connected with Japanese legislation. There were two other divisions in the Legal Section, which handled the prosecution and trial, respectively, before military tribunals of so-called minor war criminals charged with atrocities in war, who were not defendants in the International War Crime Tribunal.[2] Hence, there were no jurisdictional disputes between the other division chiefs and me, and once Bassin had accustomed himself to our existence, harmony and mutual respect developed between Colonel Carpenter's lieutenants, both of whom enjoyed a unique freedom of interference from him and from the higher-up superiors.

The staff of my division was enlarged in the Legal Section by the transfer of several lawyers from Bassin's division. Some of them were fine additions, others did not compare with the nucleus I brought with me from Government Section. At any rate, suddenly I found myself leading a division of fourteen lawyers.

If I ever had the illusion that the work load would decrease after the transfer, I was greatly mistaken. Not only did we have enough to do with our "residual functions," but we ourselves continuously created new ones.

CHECK ON LEGISLATION

Among the "residual functions" was to check, from the legal and constitutional point of view, on proposed Diet legislation. According to SCAP directives, all important bills had to be cleared by headquarters, and this was the responsibility of the Government Section which, of course, had to coordinate the matter with the interested SCAP Section or Sections. As long as I was in Government Section, Dr. Justin Williams, who headed the division in charge of

[2] While I am not in a position to judge the performance of the chiefs of these two divisions, Hagen impressed me as a particularly able jurist, who also supported our training program described below.

the Diet with great astuteness, just transmitted the bill to my division with a request for comment or recommendations. Now a check sheet had to be sent from the Government Section to the Legal Section, which were organizationally on an equal level, containing such a request, and the answer prepared in my division had to be returned formally, after having been signed by the Section chief. In other words, what previously was an intra-Section affair had become an inter-Section matter, and in case of disagreement, an inter-Section dispute. This checking function was, quantitatively, a tremendous job for us. Fortunately, I could distribute it among my many associates, while I picked out for myself those bills in which I took a particular interest. Much of it was just routine, and when the Occupation was approaching its end, we relaxed controls, in conformity with the general trend.

There were certain requirements, however, on which we insisted until the very end, and the Government Section, naturally interested in a smooth relationship with the Diet, was not always happy about our orthodox adherence to principles. I may give two illustrations of what we considered necessary under the rule of due process of law. One requirement was that a public hearing must be provided before any administrative action adversely affecting a person; the other was that against any such action appeal to the courts must be explicitly admitted. As for the scope of our review, a weekly summary covering the period from February 26 to March 3, 1951, indicates that we checked on thirty-two bills and, even in that late part of the Occupation, found three objectionable. Needless to say, we were occasionally overruled by the Government Section, which was primarily looking at intended legislation from a political rather than legal point of view. It is important to note that headquarters' policy of relaxing controls over Japanese legislation had already started in the spring of 1949. At that time, we observed that the Government Section approved the submission of several bills to the Diet, although serious objections to them had been raised by the Legal Section.

Our complaint about this slighting led to a conference on April 29 with General Whitney, his Deputy, Mr. Rizzo, and Dr. Williams. The Legal Section was represented by Appleton and myself.[3] Whitney pointed out that the Supreme Commander had decided to bring about an essential shift in Occupation policy from direction to advice and educational guidance. Although certain controls in the economic field had to be tightened in connection with the Nine-Point Economic Stabilization Program, Occupation controls should be relaxed with regard to political issues, particularly in the field of legislation. Unless flagrant violations of Occupation objectives or the Constitution were involved, therefore, headquarters would in the future not object to the passing of bills into law. The Legal Section should, however, continue its reviewing activity, which the general characterized as essential and valuable. Our task would be to discuss our objections with the members of the committees in charge of the various bills. This direct contact with the legislators themselves in an advisory role would certainly have a wholesome educational effect, and would be preferable to the previous procedure of having arguments with the ministerial officials.

I replied that this procedure was agreeable to us, and that even in the past we had carried out our reviewing assignment by persuasion rather than direction, which the general acknowledged. The problem, I pointed out, was that other Sections, which were only concerned with their specific narrow purposes, continued to direct the Japanese government as to how they had to write their laws. Whitney

[3] See my Memorandum for the Record of May 14, 1949, Subject: Conference in GS on Legislative Review Procedure, SCAP Legislation and Justice Division, Legal Section, Chronological File, Box 1522, National Records Center, Suitland, Maryland (cited hereafter as Legal Section Chronological File).

remarked that this would be discontinued, though not by formal regulations. Mr. Appleton and I strongly emphasized that this practice, as well as the inclination of the Japanese government to submit voluminous and complicated bills to the Diet at the very last minute, had made it humanly impossible for us and the attorney general to examine proposed legislation conscientiously. In this situation the Diet was forced, we stated, to be a rubber stamp. Appleton suggested that in the next session of the Diet a deadline be fixed for the submission of bills so that sufficient time would be left to consider them. General Whitney did not favor any formal action on the part of GHQ, but expressed optimism that the Diet would take care of the situation on its own initiative.

I voiced concern over the increasing tendency of the Japanese government to regiment every phase of the economic and professional life of the people, and Appleton, by way of illustration, described some bills pending in the Diet. He had held a conference on one of them with the pertinent committee of the House of Councillors, and seriously criticized several features of the bill. The members of the committee had fully shared his views, but were hesitant to demand an amendment, since they had been told that the cabinet order hitherto regulating the matter expired in two days. Appleton had advised them that the Diet, as highest organ of state power, should not allow the executive branch to put pressure on its legislative functions. General Whitney expressed great satisfaction that the upper House had actually followed this advice, even though this would bring about a delay in the enactment of the law.

ADVICE AND SUPPORT

The relations of my division to Japan's legal world had grown extremely friendly. Judges, lawyers, ministerial officials, procurators, and even Diet members sought our advice on the revised codes and freely discussed their prob-

lems with us, frequently requesting our help.[4] We had, so
to speak, open house, and it may not be presumptuous to
believe that the Japanese trusted me, and that at least I
did not suffer from a credibility gap in their eyes. This was
certainly also true of most of my associates. The judicial
branch of the Japanese government, in particular, considered us as true friends of the judges, and I was amused
when I was once told by one of them that they had labeled
me the mother of the Supreme Court, in view of my fight
for the independence of the judiciary from the executive. I
replied that I was only the midwife.

While my own relations to the first chief justice of that
court, Mibuchi Tadahiko, were of a more official nature, a
true friendship developed between me and Tanaka Kotaro,
who succeeded him in March 1950. This happened after I
traveled with him and five other judges for seven weeks to
and throughout the United States on one of the GARIOA
(Government and Relief in Occupied Areas) Exchange of
Persons Program. It has been said, and I think it is true,
that traveling together is a good test of a human relationship. After a journey has lasted for some time, one either
dislikes the other fellow thoroughly, or the mutual rapport
has proved harmonious, and not only temporarily. In our
case, the latter occurred in spite of the great differences
between us in background and *Weltanschauung.* I shall
later report on this so-called Supreme Court Mission in
detail.[5]

Here I may give two illustrations of how the judiciary

4 My division organized continuous efforts to cope with the backlog
of cases in the courts, which made a speedy justice impossible. A
Memorandum for the Record of October 23, 1950, Subject: Action by
L & J Division During Period 17 September to 23 October 1950 Concerning Expedition of Trials, prepared by Appleton and Otto in my
absence (Legal Section Chronological File, Box 1500), proves the tremendous extent of interaction and coordination in the mutual effort
to improve the situation, which, however, was to a considerable degree
caused by the inadequate conditions under which the courts had to
work. These conditions will be described in greater detail in Chapter 20.
5 See Chapter 22.

sought and obtained our help. In September 1951, the Supreme Court got in touch with us on behalf of Ishiwara Takeo, former judge of Kyoto District Court, who had been dismissed by a SCAP directive in December 1945 because he had rendered an excessively mild judgment in a criminal case connected with an offense of grave concern to the Occupation. While this dictatorial type of action, which occurred before I joined headquarters, might perhaps be explicable in the first months of the Occupation, I subsequently made every effort to discourage interference in the judicial process. I maintained that it is preferable to tolerate an occasional judgment that appears disgraceful to us than to disturb the independence of the judiciary, which we were so proud of having introduced. This is another of the many dilemmas with which an Occupation is faced. Anyway, the Supreme Court wanted to explore whether, in light of the political situation after the signing of the Peace Treaty, and of the depurge, from which the judge did not benefit, his rehabilitation might be considered by SCAP. After having obtained the approval of the Section chief, I took the matter up with the Government Section, and the result was that by another SCAP directive the dismissal of Judge Ishiwara was rescinded.

The second illustration shows that the Supreme Court sometimes even sought our help against its own administration. They reported to us that there was a tendency among the Japanese government to abolish the Inquest of Prosecution system, and requested that Legal Section give support to the Supreme Court in its fight to preserve it.[6]

INTERFERENCE IN JUDICIAL AFFAIRS AND IN A DISCIPLINARY DRAMA

Few principles are without exceptions, and I felt, for different reasons, compelled in two instances to intervene in judicial affairs. The first was connected with the purge and

[6] See Chapter 8, n. 28.

with two decisions of the Tokyo High Court acquitting the
defendants, namely, a) Shigemasa Matsuoka and Ono; and
b) the purged minister of agriculture and forestry, Hirano
Rikizo. The charge against Ono had been bribery, while
the others were accused of having engaged in political activities in violation of the purge ordinance. The acquittal
of all of them showed a definite whitewashing tendency on
the part of the court. Its interpretation of "political activities," as well as the reasons why it did not arrive at a conviction of bribery, were of a very narrow nature and contrary to common sense. The Government Section, being in
charge of the purge, became seriously aroused; and the
Legal Section, including myself, joined in severe criticism
of the judgments. They were, indeed, dangerous precedents
threatening to undermine the whole building of the Occu-
pation-imposed purge, which was aimed primarily at de-
priving its objects of political influence. I was, therefore,
not astonished when General Whitney called me in and
made it clear to me in a lengthy conference that some action
by SCAP was required. He first played with the idea of
rescinding the judgments of the court and transferring the
two cases to an Occupation court, or even of taking disciplinary action against the judges, but finally approved my
suggestion that I take the matter up with the newly appointed chief justice of the Supreme Court, Tanaka Kotaro.

What I did then was a command performance, and constituted an obvious interference in a pending judicial procedure. The arrangement according to which these cases
so closely tied to Occupation objectives were tried in Japanese courts often created a delicate twilight situation, since
the Occupation could not allow the purge to be jeopardized
by such a court. I sometimes thought that theoretically it
might have been more appropriate to take the whole area
of the purge away from the jurisdiction of the Japanese
courts, although I was aware that the practicality of such an
arrangement was questionable. Anyway, in entrusting them
with decisions on violations of the purge ordinance, we

could expect a lack of objectivity on the part of some judges, who, like many other Japanese, wholeheartedly disliked the purge. While I had mixed feelings, I regarded the approach to Tanaka, though a deviation from principle, as a wiser solution to the dilemma than the harsh measures first considered by Whitney.

In the conference of June 9, 1950[7] I told the chief justice of headquarters' reaction, and requested that the Supreme Court go into a particularly thorough check of the judgments of the Tokyo High Court. Speaking as friend of Japan's judges and promoter of their independence, I remarked that although this contact of a more personal nature might be branded as interference, the harm that would result from a confirmation of the decisions by the Supreme Court would be more serious, and might bring about a true crisis in the relationship between the Occupation and the Japanese judiciary.

Tanaka accepted my statements with understanding and his usual cordiality. He expressed awareness of the political importance of the issues involved, without, however, committing himself, and volunteered the observation that judges of the lower courts sometimes interpret the law in a very narrow way instead of taking into account the spirit and intention behind it. He merely promised to study the cases, keeping in mind the real purpose of the purge ordinance.

I used the occasion to take up again as the second subject of our conversation the so-called Misjudgment Case Involving the Four Judges of the Supreme Court. I did this on my own initiative, although with the approval of Colonel Carpenter, who had previously discussed this matter with Tanaka's predecessor, Chief Justice Mibuchi, and the secretary general of the Supreme Court, Homma, in my presence. Now my deep concern was exactly the independence of the judiciary. I have told part of the story

[7] The meeting is covered in my Memorandum for the Record of June 19, 1950, Legal Section Chronological File, Box 1501.

before.[8] The four justices, among them Kuriyama, sitting
as a petty bench, had overlooked one of the innumerable
procedural rules of their Court in a murder trial. Due to
this mistake, the bench decided to remand the case to the
high court, while otherwise the appeal of the defendant
would have been rejected at once. Since a reopening of the
procedure because of an obvious mistake is not permitted
under Japanese law, the harm done was a delay, but not
more than that. What in other nations probably would have
evoked an indulgent smile with an acknowledgment that
even judges occasionally err, produced an amazing indignation among most of the colleagues of the four judges, other
jurists, the press, and the general public. Demands for their
removal from office or at least serious disciplinary punishment were heard. I was shocked to learn that the Judicial
Assembly of the Supreme Court had urged them to resign
"voluntarily," advice which they fortunately did not follow.

The next step was the submission of the case by the
Judicial Assembly to the Diet Impeachment Committee,
which, however, refrained from impeachment—not without
having deplored the "grave nature of the judges' neglect of
duties." I had been informed that the majority of the
Supreme Court members thereupon had voted in favor
of disciplinary punishment, which they had previously
thought inadequate. It was at this point and before the
actual disciplinary verdict that I had my conference with
Chief Justice Tanaka. I wanted to convince him that the
reopening of the case would unfavorably affect the prestige
and dignity of the Supreme Court. Judicial independence,
I argued, included the protection of the individual judge
from undue interference by the president of his court and
by his own brethren, as well as the right to make an occasional mistake without having to fear removal or disciplinary punishment. I referred to the impeachment procedure
against Justice Samuel Chase of the United States Supreme
Court, the outcome of which in scholarly opinion had a

8 See my article in *Contemporary Japan* 21, 34–36.

very definite effect on the history of the American judiciary and therefore of the United States. Likewise, the manner in which the Japanese Supreme Court handled the present case might very well have considerable influence upon the future of Japan's judiciary. In light of the multitude of new laws and rules in a period of sweeping reforms, I characterized the mistake of the judges as particularly excusable and maintained that legally it was not subject to disciplinary punishment which, in my opinion, was aimed only against serious violations of official duty and misconduct.

Chief Justice Tanaka answered that, generally speaking, he fully agreed with me, and that he, too, could never understand the excitement caused by this "insignificant matter." When he became chief justice, he had felt that because of the almost unanimous agreement regarding the gravity of the mistake, he was expected to initiate action against the four judges—against whom much personal animosity also existed. Tanaka therefore had to resubmit the case to the Judicial Assembly, which in its overwhelming majority favored disciplinary punishment. Even the three judges who voted against it did so for reasons different from those I had advanced. Tanaka therefore held the imposition of a reprimand or small fine to be inevitable. This led me to observe that I could not imagine judges of the United States Supreme Court continuing in office after having undergone such a disciplinary punishment. The four judges might likewise feel their reputations so much affected that they would retire. This, however, would be highly detrimental to the continuity and prestige of the highest tribunal.

Tanaka emphasized the pressure to which he had been subject from the presidents of the lower courts, who apprehended that if no action would be taken in this case they could no longer impose disciplinary punishment when their judges made a mistake. I answered that even judges of lower courts should not be punished for making an occasional mistake. I characterized the public opinion according to which the dignity and the prestige of the Supreme Court required some sanction against the erring judges as feudal, because it seemed to imply that judges of the Supreme Court are not human beings allowed to err, but infallible gods.

During the whole conversation, I wondered why the chief justice, though personally agreeing with me, had not voted against disciplinary action. When I voiced regret that he had not publicly declared the case closed, he replied to my astonishment that if he had vigorously fought the view of the majority and voted against it, he would have been overruled and compelled to resign. Upon my question of whether he really thought that the president of a court, when overruled, must resign, he said that this was certainly not his opinion in general, but in this specific case, which had assumed such political and personal importance, his resignation would probably have been unavoidable.

This ended our conversation. I found it psychologically difficult to understand Tanaka's attitude, although I appreciated the sensitive position of a newly appointed chief justice who, in the process of voting on an important issue, stands completely alone with his opinion. The reluctance to put himself into such a position was obviously related to the fear of losing face so strongly developed among Japanese. We had met a similar attitude in Tanaka's predecessor, Mibuchi, in a meeting also connected with the Hirano purge. This was a conference on March 2, 1948,[9] that Kades held with him, and in which Major Napier and I participated. On that occasion, we urged Mibuchi to initiate action in the Impeachment Committee against one of his associate justices, Shono Riichi. The latter, at a social party, allegedly accused the highly respected chief of the Screening Committee, Dr. Makino Eiichi, of having voted for Hirano's purge after being bribed, the implication being that he had received money from the Occupation. Mibuchi consistently

[9] See Minutes of Conference Concerning the Accusations against Judge Shono of the Supreme Court, Legal Section Chronological File, Box 1522.

refused to comply as long as he did not have full evidence that Shono had committed this libel. Without going into any detail on this unsuccessful intervention—the problem was eventually resolved by Shono's resignation from the bench—I want to note the parallel to Tanaka's reluctance. Mibuchi maintained that he "would take responsibility and resign as a judge" if his request for the impeachment of Shono were rejected.

To return to the disciplinary tragicomedy, this was again an instance in which the Occupation not only used persuasion rather than fiat, but also abstained from authoritative action after its attempt at persuasion had failed. The Judicial Assembly imposed a fine of 10,000 yen on the four judges. Tanaka, in a mild dissent from the majority, voted for a reprimand, together with two associate justices. All four judges responded to the punishment with their immediate resignations.

Apart from my general view on this strange affair, I regretted this also because I knew the affected judges personally and had a good opinion of them, particularly of Kuriyama. In my mood of fierce disapproval and deep concern over the Japanese judiciary, whose independence now appeared threatened from within, I decided to act without consulting any superior. In what capacity I did so was doubtful. It was a strange mixture between the personal advice of a friend and the "instruction" of a representative of headquarters, of which latter capacity I could not possibly divest myself completely. It was about ten o'clock in the evening when I learned of the resignations. I drove to the house of Justice Kuriyama and found him in understandable excitement. Still, he was level-headed enough to agree with me when I pointed out how ridiculous this whole tempest in the teapot was. Fortunately, he had a fine sense of humor, and while he was correctly restrained in his own comments, he probably enjoyed my jokes about the affair, the significance of which I emphatically minimized. I also said that the resignation of the four judges would mean a grave loss for the young Supreme Court, and concluded by urging Kuriyama: "You must immediately withdraw your resignation and persuade the other three to do the same." He did not at once make up his mind, but requested some time to think it over and to discuss the matter with his fellow sufferers. I was delighted when, on the next day, he informed me that he as well as the three other judges had followed my advice. There was no important public criticism of the continuation on the bench of the disciplined judges. The storm had subsided, the matter was no longer sensational, but I felt that the withdrawal of the resignations greatly benefited the Court, and the observation of their judicial activities afterwards has confirmed that conviction. Several years later Kuriyama was honored by an appointment to succeed Tanaka as associate justice of the Hague International Court.

CRIMINAL JUSTICE IN ACTION

American lawyers were sometimes tempted to interfere in the administration of justice because of the different attitudes of Japanese criminal judges. Since there was neither a probation nor a jury system in Japan, the judge performed, before arriving at a decision on the penalty, some of the work that in the United States usually is done by the probation officer after the verdict. Subjective, humane, and psychological considerations, therefore, play a much greater role in Japanese decision making than in our country. The courts look at the whole personality of the defendant, his past conduct as a citizen, as a child, parent, or spouse, and go deeply into his motivation for the offense with which he is charged. Consequently, much use is made of suspended sentences, particularly when the crime is one of passion or desperation, and when there is no danger of its repetition.

As long as prisons are merely instruments of retaliation, and the convict, after having served his term, is returned to society hateful and corrupt, instead of reformed, this sys-

tem has its definite merits. It had, of course, its basis in the
complete freedom of evaluation (in German, *freie Beweis-
würdigung*), that the Japanese judges used to enjoy. In the
United States, to be sure, it is more difficult to arrive at a
conviction by the jury in a criminal trial, not only because
the jury is inclined to consider subjective factors, but also
because of the elaborate rules of evidence, the most elementary of which we introduced in Japan. But once the
defendant has been found guilty, an uneven, often rigid,
justice falls on him, because the laws of our states, which
wield the usual criminal jurisdiction, provide different penalties for the same offense. These penalties are not fully
served in most instances, however, since the prisoner may be
released by parole before his term has expired. The minimum he has to serve is usually one third of the penalty.

I wish to give one illustration of a criminal case in which
the Japanese court went far—and many of my American
readers may think too far—in its compassion for a woman
who had committed an objectively most horrible act. She
had been abandoned by her husband, who no longer supported her and their three small children. She apparently
did not receive welfare payments, and she was not able to
work. She was suffering from depressions, and her condition was one of despair. Hence, she decided to end her own
and the children's misery. She served some sweet food for
the children, mixed it with rat poison, of which she kept
some for her own suicide. The three children died, but she
herself survived. Although she was not considered insane,
the district court, taking into consideration the desperate
psychological condition of the defendant at the time when
she committed the crime, imposed a suspended sentence of
three years for manslaughter. All the objectivists among
American lawyers were horrified by the benign treatment of
a mother who had poisoned her three children, and I was
repeatedly urged to suggest action by SCAP to invalidate
the judgment. Several others even recommended removal of
the judges who rendered it. I understood, but did not share

their indignation. It was one of those borderline cases in which it is not easy to take a definite position. One can very well feel that in view of the terrible effect of the offense, the punishment did not take into account its gravity and that the judges gave undue and excessive consideration to subjective aspects. On the other hand, the judges may, from a purely humane point of view, not have been far from the truth by concluding that it would make no sense to put this woman behind prison walls. She was hardly a threat to society, since she could not repeat her offense, nor was she likely to commit a similar one. The judges may have thought that she killed her children because she was obsessed at the moment of her action by the idea that it was best for them to be relieved from the sufferings of their lives forever. One may also argue, of course, that such considerations belong in the sphere of ethics rather than law. In the last analysis it boils down to the question of the true purpose of punishment, which occupied us in connection with the death penalty.

Since our concern over the administration of justice had become widely known among the Japanese, we were flooded with applications from private individuals involved in a civil or criminal procedure. We usually referred them to the bar associations or, if they charged a violation of their civil rights, to the Civil Liberties Commission of the attorney general, and, if we did not expect any action from this side, even to the Civil Liberties Union. I remember only one case in which an unsuccessful attempt of bribery was made.

There were, inevitably, instances in which the continuation of the worst features of the police state induced us to watch over the investigations by Japanese authorities. Once we received reliable information that a man had been sentenced to death for murder after he had been forced to confess through torture by the police. A thorough investigation confirmed the use of third-degree methods, and resulted in severe disciplinary action against the guilty officers; this did not save the convict, since the death sentence was based on a great deal of additional evidence.

CHECKING ON THE POLICE

We were less reluctant to interfere in activities of the police, who were sometimes unable or unwilling to understand the budding idea that the common man has certain rights inviolable even by law enforcement officers. Unfortunate incidents of decent girls being subjected to humiliating medical examinations have been blamed on the American military police. Although at the beginning of the Occupation the military police, in the process of rounding up prostitutes to protect our men from venereal diseases, made regrettable and occasionally unpardonable mistakes, in the later years this function was left to the Japanese police. In a specific case I found out why, nevertheless, the Occupation was still held responsible for such mistakes. An American sergeant and a Japanese girl appeared in my office. They both made an excellent impression. They told me that they had dated and that on their way to a restaurant the girl was arrested by Japanese policemen, while two MPs were standing by. When the sergeant protested that his friend was a decent girl, the Japanese policemen answered that they suspected as prostitute any girl running around with an American soldier. The sergeant could not prevent the arrest, since also his appeal to the accompanying MPs was unsuccessful. They said that this was a matter in the jurisdiction of the Japanese police, and that they accompanied the policemen only to protect them, if necessary, from GIs who were with the girls. According to the report of the girl, the police treated her rudely, asking her questions, such as how much money she received for her "business," as if she were a prostitute. The interrogating officer said to her that, if she was not married to the sergeant, she was presumed to be a prostitute. The girl was finally told that, if she was caught again, she would be fined, I checked with the provost marshal, Colonel Robert T. Chaplin, a man whom I found unusually understanding and cooperative, and learned that no Occupation authority had ordered a raid on prostitutes. Although police affairs were in the jurisdiction of G–2, the Legal Section requested an investigation of the case. As was to be expected, the police officers involved denied any improper treatment of the girl. We could only hope that our interference would serve as a warning against repetition of this type of police conduct.

The police, on the other hand, had their own misgivings about the Occupation. They resembled complaints by law enforcement agencies in the United States about the far-reaching protection granted an arrested person in decisions of the Warren Supreme Court. Similarly, the Japanese police criticized the safeguards granted the offender in the new Constitution and the Code of Criminal Procedure as making their work difficult and resulting in an increase of criminality. What the Japanese police particularly minded was the treatment of police records in the new Code of Criminal Procedure.[10] I suggested to the official of G–2 in charge of police investigation that we sit together with police officers of different rank and explain to them the reasons for the legal innovations. He gladly accepted this suggestion, and we had several interesting meetings in which the police officers freely raised their practical problems with us.

TRAINING OF JUDGES

We had long realized that postreform explanations and training was as imperative as the discussion had been before decisions were made on the reforms. The Japanese legal world saw itself suddenly faced with a large body of completely new and, in part, revolutionary laws or fundamental

10 See Chapter 10.

changes of the existing codes. In other fields, for which we were not responsible, new statutes were also enacted. I need only to refer to the economic legislation, following the advice of Joseph M. Dodge; the tax innovations suggested by Professor Carl S. Shoup; and the new approaches to education, public health, and welfare. This time of transition required fast adjustment, particularly by judges and lawyers, who were often at a loss as to how to apply the new provisions. When, in 1951, the end of the Occupation could be expected soon, we suggested to the Supreme Court the establishment of a judges' training institute designed to offer the judges of the inferior courts lectures and discussions on the revised law. Successively, groups of judges from all places throughout the country traveled to Tokyo, where in the institute they transformed themselves into students. Every judge was to attend this school, and underwent a two-week course. Teachers were, apart from Supreme Court justices or secretariat officials and other Japanese jurists, the members of my division. Blakemore had already left us, but McCormick, Meyers, Monagan, and Appleton contributed to the success of this important enterprise, and I myself addressed the judges regularly. I usually welcomed every incoming group and explained to them the purpose of the course as well as the background of the reforms. Subsequently, similar institutes were established for public procurators, and the bar associations, on their own initiative, followed suit.

Once a month the members of my division met all fifteen Supreme Court justices in conference in their building. There questions of mutual concern were raised and discussed in a friendly atmosphere, in which we were no longer in the role of occupationnaires, but rather met the judges as colleagues on fully equal terms. They frequently inquired into the way the United States handled similar problems. The question arose, for instance, whether relief from the excessive case load should be provided by limiting the jurisdiction of the Court to constitutional questions.

There was a period in which communist defendants ob-
noxiously disturbed court procedures by misconduct, by
offending the judges, and by making political propaganda
speeches, while a partly sympathetic audience loudly ap-
plauded. An effective system of contempt of court had not
been developed at that time, and the judges were interested
in the American practice. Subsequently, a Contempt of
Court Law was enacted. Perhaps the personal relationships
that grew out of this type of communication, which enabled us to have a pretty good impression of each of the
fifteen men on the bench, was as important as the exchange
of ideas.

VIPS VISIT THE SUPREME COURT

Always eager to see the prestige of Japan's Supreme Court
strengthened, I was delighted that American VIPs frequently paid it a visit. There appeared first the popular
"Veep," Alben Barkley, with his new bride, a charming and
elegant lady, his second wife. His cheerful and easygoing
manners were in amusing contrast to the formal and almost
ceremonial posture of the assembled justices. While they at
first showed surprise at the informality of the second highest
official of the United States, he soon won them over by his
wit and sense of humor. Japanese men, once they have
overcome their initial stiffness, like nothing better than a
good laugh, and Barkley gave them ample opportunity to
indulge in this pleasure. While walking through the halls
of the Court building, his wife had misplaced her valuable
fur stole. Jokingly, he expressed shock that such a thing
could happen in a Supreme Court, of all places. The em-
barrassed justices recovered fast when the stole was found.
Of course, Barkley's inborn gaiety was heightened to a
radiant mood when he traveled with his new and obviously
delightful life companion.

More serious visitors were Governor Thomas E. Dewey
of New York, Governor Earl Warren of California, and Dr.

Philip Jessup, the eminent scholar of international law, once ambassador-at-large at the United Nations, and subsequently judge of the Hague International Court of Justice. Warren, who arrived in August 1951, was most thoroughgoing in his inspection and inquiries, as if he had a foreboding that one day he would be the Chief Justice of the United States Supreme Court, which to a considerable extent had been the model for its Japanese counterpart.

CHAPTER TWENTY

A Visit to Military Government Units[1]

With the shifting of the Occupation's concern from national legislation to the actual administration of justice, we realized increasingly that the Tokyo-bound SCAP functions of observing and advising had to be broadened to cover the remaining part of the country. That made the task of the eight military government regions and of the prefectural teams even more important.[2] This substructure of the Occupation was under the command of the Eighth Army. Having been eager for a long time, but virtually unable to get away from my Tokyo desk and make contact with the legal officers in these units, I welcomed the occasion to do so—and simultaneously to see more of Japan—when, in 1949, the Civil Transportation Section requested the participation of the Legal Section in an inspection tour designed to promote workable administrative procedures for the national and local road transportation.

Monagan and I represented Legal Section on the tour.

[1] This chapter is based on and closely follows my Memorandum to the Chief, Legal Section, of February 11, 1949, Subject: Official Travel from 10 January 49 to 22 January 49. (SCAP, Legislation and Justice Division, Legal Section, General Alphabetical File, 1946–52, Box 1495, folder marked: Gen. Field Trips. General Records Center, Suitland, Maryland, cited hereafter as Legal Section Alphabetical File.)

[2] The term military government is misleading. There was no military government proper in Japan, and the regional and prefectural officers had no policy-making powers, but merely the task of advising, observing, and reporting. Subsequently the more appropriate term "civil affairs" replaced "military government."

The division of assignments was made in the following way: Monagan accompanied the officials of SCAP's Civil Transportation Section and the Japanese Transportation Ministry representatives on their inspections and conferences, and advised them on questions of administrative law and procedure. I did not take part in this activity, but made contact with the military government teams and regions at the various places we passed, particularly the legal and government officers, and conferred with the local Japanese judges and procurators. The very fact that we stayed at so many different places gave me an excellent overall impression of the atmosphere in which the military government officers in the field worked. I learned a good deal about their attitudes and the problems they faced. On the other hand, I was able to inform them of GHQ policies, and to advise them on the interpretation of the new reform legislation. I was also usually welcomed by the commanding officers of the units, and I occasionally discussed the civil rights programs with the information officer.

Our travel route took us not only to places on the main island of Honshu that we had not known, but even to the island of Shikoku. Our first stop was Niigata; Kyoto, a city I loved, followed. In Matsue, on the Japan Sea, I honored the memory of Lafcadio Hearn, who was so charmed by the land and nation that he became a Japanese citizen. In Fukuoka I visited the high court, and conferred for several hours with its judges. After that I attended a criminal trial in the same court. The next stop was Hiroshima, where I was continuously reminded of the deadly fireball of August 1945, the first step toward mankind's neurosis of fear of extinction, and where I was never without a feeling of uneasiness and compassion. I took a car to the interesting port city of Kure in order to meet the officers of that region, but the next morning I visited the Hiroshima High Court before the train left for Uno. From there we took a ferry boat to the island of Shikoku and arrived in Takamatsu. Two days later I was in Osaka. In both places I had long conversations with the judges and procurators of the respective high courts. The tour ended with another stop in Shizuoka, from where we returned to Tokyo.

Let me summarize some of the valuable insights I received during this trip. One of the reasons why the legal and government officers of the regions and teams welcomed my visit, wherever I appeared, was the lack of proper information in their units on SCAP policies. Although all of them requested, "Please don't quote me!" they complained without exception about the inadequacy of channels between the military government and GHQ. The legal officer of the team who wanted to reach GHQ had first to report to the region; the region reported to the corps, and the corps to the Headquarters, Eighth Army; the latter finally reported to GHQ, SCAP. Since Legal Section, SCAP, when it desired to give official directions or even just information to military government units, had also to comply with channel requirements, its communication to the teams or regions had to go to the chief of staff, who dispatched a command letter to Headquarters, Eighth Army. Usually, this headquarters translated such a command letter into its own language and sent the instructions to the corps, who, in turn, advised the regions, which informed the teams. This inexcusable army red tape meant that between the request of a team for information or direction and the receipt of an answer several months usually passed. In the meantime, the officer on the spot had to make his own determination whenever the matter did not allow delay. Furthermore, the policy of SCAP frequently had changed before the arrival of the answer, or the whole issue had become obsolete. The officers found it embarrassing that the Japanese government officials knew of SCAP directives earlier than they did. All of them said they had to be extremely cautious with regard to informal contacts. They could not, for instance, dare to write a letter to me or to other members of Legal Section with a request for advice. They welcomed the bulletin ("Legal Comments") recently given out by the Legal Section, but doubted that they could consider its contents as the authoritative opinion of SCAP. In their view, the main weakness of the organizational setup lay in the subordination of the regions to the corps. The corps commanders frequently took action that greatly affected the Japanese administration of justice, and should not have been taken at the corps level without consultation with SCAP. For example, Brigadier General Crawford S. Sams, chief of Public Health and Welfare Section, SCAP, had raised doubts as to the legal authority of the I Corps commander to issue instructions for the enforcement of the VD Prevention Law without SCAP approval.

My contacts were almost unanimous in the proposal that the Eighth Army Headquarters and corps should be restricted to technical tasks, and that within the scope of purely civil affairs, the regions should be allowed to report directly to GHQ, SCAP, where a Civil Affairs Section should be established. Fortunately, this was subsequently done, although much too late. With the establishment of the Civil Affairs Section within SCAP Headquarters, the coordination between us and the legal officers of the remaining teams improved tremendously. After that, whenever we wanted to know something we called up our colleagues in that section and got the information the next day, if not immediately. Reciprocally, the complaints of the legal officers about the administration of justice throughout Japan reached us promptly through this channel.

Another problem under discussion, quite familiar to me, was the disastrous backlog of cases in the inferior courts. There was general agreement that it was caused mainly by insufficient personnel and inadequate working conditions and facilities in the courts and procurators' offices. The system suffered from the fact that the administration of justice in Japan had always been slighted when it came to appropriations in the budget. That might have been bearable as long as the crime rate was relatively low, but had harmful consequences in a period of considerable increase of offenses because of demoralization and economic misery after a lost war. Most legal officers admitted that the judges and procurators worked overtime, and all Japanese representatives with whom I spoke emphasized this fact. There was, however, criticism of the ability of the judges to organize their work. Typical in this respect was a statement on the region in Kure. According to it, delays in the reduction of civil and criminal cases were not only attributable to the shortage of judicial and procuratorial personnel, but also to lengthy "negotiations" to obtain a compromise, postponement of trials because of insufficient evidence, excessive use of the appeal system, and reluctance in some instances to adopt new methods.

Everywhere the working conditions and facilities in the courts and procuratorial offices were extremely poor. Office space was completely inadequate and there was only an insignificant number of official residences. No stenographic help was available in the Takamatsu High Court, and no position for it was authorized. The same court had only one telephone. Although it owned two typewriters, it did not have any typist. An even more crucial problem was transportation. The individual clerical officials of the Takamatsu High Court had to travel a long time daily from their homes to the office and back again. One of them spent seven hours for that purpose, one five hours and forty minutes, while most of them commuted at least two hours. The conditions were similar in most other districts.

Partly due to these deficiencies, the authorized positions of judges and procurators were seldom filled. The vacancies among the administrative secretaries were even more striking.

Although the courts made use of release on bail, the backlog of untried criminal cases resulted in the overcrowding of prisons. In the whole area of the I Corps, which meant about half of Japan, the prison population, comprising only those inmates who served sentences after conviction, increased from 0.6 percent in November 1945 to 1.3 percent in August 1948. Another consequence of the slow law enforcement and the overcrowded prisons was that minor offenses were frequently not prosecuted. Even the procedure in the summary courts was too slow, according to the legal officers—who emphasized, however, that the main problem lay with the district and high courts.

In all my contacts with the Japanese, I stressed the necessity of imposing more rigid fines in the case of serious economic offenses, such as large-scale black marketing. I furthermore referred to the great concern of GHQ in a vigorous prosecution of tax evasion cases. The chief judges and procurators of the various high courts had been summoned to Tokyo. They had attended a meeting in the Supreme Court and in the Procurator General's Office, where they were instructed on the importance of the tax evasion cases in the light of the Occupation program. In some of the regions the procurators were advised to prosecute one serious tax evasion offense as a test case in each district court. They were, indeed, faced with a difficult problem in selecting appropriate cases, since all agreed that in the past everybody in Japan had made false tax returns. This may explain the fact that while the courts imposed high fines in some of these test cases, amounting to ten million and fifteen million yen, they were still inclined to suspend the mild prison sentence given the director of a guilty corporation. Thus the director of a sea transportation corporation was sentenced to one year in prison by the Osaka High Court for the evasion of a four-and-a-half-million-yen corporation tax, and the sentence was suspended. One chief procurator expressed the interesting view that from the standpoint of the national treasury, the so-called administrative procedure—according to which the matter is settled between the tax collector and the person subject to the tax, and in case of a false return an "administrative fine" is paid—was fiscally more advantageous than the criminal prosecution of tax evasion. The administrative fine was usually obtained without difficulty because of the bad conscience of the debtor, while in the formal criminal procedure, the procurator thought, the new requirements for evidence were so rigid that in many instances the defendant could not be convicted.

In my conversations with the public procurators, I found out that the introduction of an inquest of prosecution as a popular check on them had some practical consequences that we had not foreseen. I was told in one district that because of the law the procurators now made it a rule to prosecute every case. If they wanted to make an exception, they took the matter up in a conference of the procurators of the district, in the presence of the chief procurator. They were thus assured of their superior's approval before they refrained from or dropped a prosecution, and this way avoided unpleasant consequences if the inquest later arrived at the conclusion that the case should have been prosecuted. What the procurators were afraid of was that a successful censure by the inquest might be a black mark in their personal records. Most procurators with whom I talked thought that popular control over their functions might theoretically be a good idea, but they doubted whether the people would be able to understand the legal questions involved.

I found my previous observation confirmed that there was frequently a lack of cooperation between the procurators and the police. The police complained that the procurators went into the investigation of the cases too much, instead of leaving this function to the police, while procurators repeatedly maintained that the police were often not able to cope with a case adequately, so that the procurators had to take over. A leading procurator of a high court pointed to another place where there was lack of cooperation, namely, between the municipal police and the national rural police of the prefecture. He also commented on the relationship of the Local Public Safety Commission to the police officials. In one case the municipal police was stopped by the local commission from investigating an offense committed by a big *oyabun* (boss) of the city, and the procurators had to take over the investigation themselves.

In all districts with large Korean minorities the officers complained about the unlawful acts of the Koreans and their affiliation with the Communist party. Typical in this respect was a report for one region in which, assertedly, 90 percent of the approximately 75,000 Koreans were communists or at least "leftists." During December 1948, the legal officers of two teams spent about 30 percent of their time studying, with Japanese police, means of controlling violent demonstrations of Koreans in which a display of the North Korean flag was involved, or cases in which illegal sake was brewed or raids on tax offices took place under the guise of "livelihood protection." I had long before realized the seriousness of the problem of Koreans in Japan. There was no doubt in my mind that the decisive reason for many of them having become unruly and criminal elements of society had been their treatment as pariahs and their use as forced labor during the war. Now they claimed to belong to the victor nations, and often behaved as if they were not subject to Japanese law. They, as well as the Chinese, engaged in black market activities to a large extent.

Finally, an important question of local autonomy was brought up in our meetings. We in the Legal Section had occasionally doubted that some legislation of local entities with regard to the control of public meetings and demonstrations conformed to the civil rights provisions of the new Constitution.[3] The officers with whom I talked maintained unanimously that any check by us on local legislation would be extremely harmful to the cause of local autonomy. In their opinion the danger was not the enactment of constitutionally doubtful local legislation, but the reluctance of the local entities to enact any important legislation at

---

[3] In at least one case a municipal assembly had passed a clearly unconstitutional bylaw under pressure from the chief military government officer.

all. They were very timid in that respect, I was told, and generally restricted their law making to budgetary questions and financing. Whenever the legal and government officers suggested local legislation beyond this scope, the local authorities referred to the difficulties of financing, or raised doubt on the constitutionality of the intended matter. In the view of the officers, not very much had been changed in the subservient attitude of the prefectures and municipalities toward the Tokyo central government, which the prefectural governors consulted before they dared to have any local legislation enacted. The reason for this attitude, I was told, was not so much the tradition of the past as the financial dependence of the local entities upon the national government. The municipal authorities usually consulted with the prefectural governor before they took legislative action. Thus, in the view of the military government units, everything should be done to encourage local legislation. If in individual cases it appeared to be in conflict with the Constitution, it would be sufficient to have it challenged in the courts.

These illustrations show the variety and complexity of the problems facing the agents of the Occupation in the regions and prefectures. I feel that they have not gotten the credit for their performance that they, generally speaking, deserve. I was, indeed, impressed by the enthusiasm and competence with which young legal officers, who had never been in the legal profession, acquainted themselves with issues of law and the administration of justice. Sometimes the unorthodox idea crossed my mind that their lack of professional experience, their fresh approach to the problems, might even have been an asset.

CHAPTER TWENTY-ONE

Outbreak of the Korean Conflict

My daughter Ellen had received her B.A. at Smith College
in the spring of 1950, and it was a great joy for us when,
after a separation of three years, she joined us in Tokyo.
She was already with us when the North Koreans invaded
South Korea. The news of this event came to us as a shock,
since it was such a complete surprise. We wondered why
our intelligence was caught off guard, our own G–2, as well
as the one in South Korea. On that ominous June 25
there happened to be a large party on the roof garden of
the Dai Ichi Hotel, where the whole official American
world in Tokyo gathered in an excited mood. Among those
guests who were not connected with the Occupation, we
again met Mrs. Vining, whom I mentioned before. We had
made her acquaintance earlier, had been in her home, and
were immediately attracted by her. She writes in her autobiography that Charlotte and I "were both desperately
distressed that night by the news from Korea, foreseeing
the beginning of another world conflagration."[1] This impression was certainly right. In those first days after the
invasion I was pessimistic, in view of the incalculability of
developments. I remembered how the First World War
started in Serbia, and I was aware of the wire pullers behind
the Korean assault. I feared it could grow, avalanche-like,
into a global conflict, and nothing was more repugnant to

[1] See *Quiet Pilgrimage*, p. 255.

me than the prospect of a third world war. By and by I got
accustomed to having to live with the constant danger of
such a potentiality. The prompt resolution of President
Truman to defend South Korea through the medium of the
United Nations, and the favorable response of the UN
Security Council satisfied me.

This use of the United Nations was, indeed, included in
United States policy planning and predicated in the controversial January 12, 1950, speech of Secretary of State
Dean Acheson at the National Press Club. While he implied there that Korea was outside our Far East defense
perimeter, just as were Vietnam, Taiwan, and other Asian
countries, he added that should these areas be attacked,
"the initial reliance must be on the people attacked to
resist it and then upon the commitments of the entire
civilized world under the Charter of the United Nations."[2]
MacArthur and other critics of the administration have
accused the secretary of having encouraged the North
Korean attack by these remarks, although Dean Acheson
points out that the general himself had once defined the
defense perimeter along the same lines.[3]

During the party in the Dai Ichi Hotel I observed with
amazement how different the reaction there was to the invasion. Some officers with whom I talked—there was hardly
any other topic—greatly underestimated the task of repel-
ling the assault. I particularly remember a colonel in an
important position who almost beamingly exclaimed, "In
two weeks we'll have them crushed!"

There is ample reason, however, to believe that Mac-
Arthur was deeply shocked on that June morning when he
first learned what had happened, and that at least at that
moment he clearly saw the dangers involved to Japan and
the United States, as well as to South Korea. Whitney, in
his book, describes this initial reaction of his chief as con-

[2] See Dean Acheson, *Present at the Creation* (New York: Norton,
1969), p. 466.
[3] *Ibid.*

cern over the inadequacy of the Japan Occupation forces and of the greatly outnumbered South Korean constabulary troops, combined with condemnation of Washington, whose policy he blamed for having been an irresistible temptation to aggression for the North Koreans.[4] According to Whitney, MacArthur saw the situation as a "mess," and at that time already claimed that the United States government had no definite Asian policy.[5] After Inchon he had strong spells of optimism. When he met President Truman on Wake Island in October, a day before the Chinese interference, he expressed the view that the danger of intervention was remote and asserted that if the Chinese moved toward Pyongyang, they would be slaughtered. Nobody can be sure whether a global war would have ensued if the general had had his way, but I have concluded, notwithstanding my sympathy for him, that the president, the Department of State, and the Joint Chiefs of Staff could not be blamed for having thought it would. The subject of "the president and the general" will, however, be treated in a subsequent chapter. Suffice it here to state that MacArthur's irritation with the administration was already strong when the Korean conflict started.

I remained conscious of the explosive situation in which Japan found herself, particularly after more and more Occupation forces were sent to Korea. There was no guarantee against Japan being attacked from the air if one or both of the two communist giants entered the war. I also foresaw that with the assumption of his new responsibility as United Nations Commander, the SCAP would inescapably concentrate his efforts on defeating the enemy militarily. This would somewhat change the character of the Occupation toward prevention of subversion and of fifth columns. Thus, I anticipated, democratization would be replaced by surveillance and policing. As indicated before, these anticipations materialized, at least to some extent.

[4] See *MacArthur, His Rendezvous With History*, pp. 318ff.
[5] *Reminiscences*, p. 328.

Although this trend resulted in the disappointment of many progressive elements among the Japanese people, I find it hard to blame the Occupation for having written security with capital letters in a time of grave crisis.

In contrast to the sanguine attitude of the over-confident colonel, one of my associates in the Legal Section, a man with a family of two small children, no longer considered Japan a safe place and, after having discovered that most of our military forces had been sent to Korea, decided to quit and to return to the States.

Ellen, who as a child had experienced the outbreak of World War II in Nazi Germany, at an age when she understood fairly well what it meant, also showed a certain anxiety, and I was sorry that her start in Japan happened to take place in this atmosphere of uncertainty. It was for her to be the beginning of a period of four years during which she lived in our home with us. She followed the example of her father and became an occupationnaire, working for G–2 as a research assistant. Her assignment included analysis of political and social trends in Japan, and fast led to a successful career.

CHAPTER TWENTY-TWO

The Supreme Court Mission[1]

During the eventful year of 1950, I was fortunate enough to participate in one of the most inspiring enterprises of my official life. It brought me back, at least temporarily, to the United States, after an absence of nearly five years. I have already referred to the Exchange of National Leaders Program financed by GARIOA (Government and Relief in Occupied Areas) funds. The importance of these visits of Japanese in prominent positions, sponsored by the Institute of International Education (IIE) and organized by the various Sections of SCAP, went far beyond the objective of professional information; they were to promote the exchange of ideas and mutual understanding.

Within the jurisdiction of my division, ten missions had been carried out in 1951, including fifty-six national leaders. I may mention only a few groups: the attorney general's mission; judicial administration; administrative litigation; prosecution; law school education and standards; juvenile courts and family relations; and civil liberties. The Japanese were escorted on their tours through the United States by a SCAP official conversant with their field of interest and by an interpreter. I myself was privileged to escort the most important Supreme Court Mission.

[1] This chapter is based in part on my undated *Report: Supreme Court Mission (Project No. 117)* (Legal Section Alphabetical File, 1946–52, Box 1497, folder marked: National Leaders Program GARIOA, Project No. 117).

7. The Supreme Court Mission meets Secretary of State Dean Acheson in October 1950. Front row: Higuchi Masaru, Hozumi Shigeto, Tanaka Kotaro, Dean Acheson, Mano Tsuyoshi, Ishizaka Shuichi. Back row: William Coblenz, James P. Parker, Walter Tanaka, George Koshi, Alfred Oppler, Kishi Seiichi. (Acme Photo.)

Dr. Tanaka Kotaro, formerly professor of law at the Imperial University, member of the House of Peers and subsequently of the House of Councillors, and minister of education in 1946 and part of 1947, had just succeeded Mibuchi in March 1950 as chief justice.[2] We believed that it would be an excellent idea if he could start his tenure with a direct contact with American legal and judicial institutions. In addition, the Japanese justices could be expected to benefit from observing the independence of American judges. So a Supreme Court mission was set up, headed by Tanaka, who had an unusual international background, having studied and taught in Europe and South America.

The choice of Associate Justice Mano Tsuyoshi as the number two participant was almost a matter of course. He was probably the most dynamic among the members of the highest tribunal, and the most outspoken. As a former president of the Second Tokyo Bar Association, he was thoroughly familiar with the practical aspects of court procedure, which gave him some advantage over the scholarly but judicially inexperienced Tanaka. No greater contrast of personalities could be imagined than that between the extroverted, argumentative, sometimes aggressive, Mano, and the mild-mannered, restrained, and diplomatic Tanaka. The two men were also extremely different in their ideologies, Tanaka being conservative and Mano progressive. The latter, who, according to the grapevine, had himself hoped to be appointed chief justice, had all the professional qualifications for that office and, as I had occasion to observe, never completely overcame the sentiment that he would have done better in Tanaka's place. Whether he would have equaled him, as far as representative dignity is concerned, may, however, be open to question. I always liked to argue with him and was fond of him. To have these two

_____
[2] After my manuscript had been finished in March 1974, I was distressed to receive the news of Tanaka's death.

men together on a tour through the States appeared to be an alluring, though somewhat risky, experiment.

As a third member of the Supreme Court we selected Associate Justice Hozumi Shigeto, the oldest of the group. Like Tanaka, he was a man with a distinguished academic career, including the deanship in the Faculty of Law at Tokyo Imperial University; he was also a former member of the Imperial Academy, and for some time tutor of the crown prince. Gifted with a mature sense of humor, progressive, and international-minded, he represented the smiling and wise grandfatherly type, who had been able to grasp and accept the demands of a new era.

The fourth participant, Ishizaka Shuichi, fifty-five years old, could look back to an almost uninterrupted career on the bench. He had ample experience as a local judge, as a member of district and appeal courts, as judge of the former Supreme Court, and—since 1948—as president of the Sendai High Court. I had always regarded him as one of the efficient, though not progressive, judges of Japan. After serving as president of several other high courts, he was appointed associate justice of the Supreme Court in 1958.

Two junior judges participated in the mission, namely, Higuchi Masaru, judge of the Tokyo High Court and concurrently chief of the Liaison Section of the Secretariat of the Supreme Court; and Kishi Seiichi, also judge of the Tokyo High Court and concurrently chief of Criminal Affairs Bureau of the Supreme Court Secretariat. I knew Higuchi very well. He had formerly been in the Ministry of Justice, and I found him cooperative and painstakingly conscientious. Our pleasant contact continued when he became the chief liaison man of the Supreme Court. Kishi was known to me as exceptionally knowledgeable in criminal law and procedure (recently, he has joined the bench of the Supreme Court).

Although Tanaka, Hozumi, and Higuchi spoke and understood English fairly well, we foresaw that in the contacts with Americans, translation to and from the Japanese called for an interpreter who combined mastery of both languages with an expert knowledge of American legal institutions. I was, therefore, particularly fortunate to have with me George Koshi, who ideally satisfied this need, as the second SCAP escort. As a matter of fact, without him the Japanese judges would have been greatly handicapped by linguistic difficulties. By virtue of his bilingual ability and his familiarity, as a lawyer of my division, with the legal problems, Koshi could give a brief extract of what had been said instead of attempting a literal translation.

The mission was thoroughly prepared in Japan as well as in the United States. Since the chief justice was the most important national leader within the exchange program, and since the impression the Japanese group and the American contacts would make on each other was of considerable political significance, the Government Section was eager to make this mission a success. Kades, who was now a successful Wall Street lawyer, must in the first place be credited with the splendid planning of the program for the seven weeks' trip within the States. In a letter of March 14, 1950, General MacArthur wrote to him about the mission, mentioned that it would be accompanied by me, and called Oppler "eminently qualified to guide it due to his broad knowledge of our own practice and procedures and the structural details of the new Japanese judicial system," a bouquet which I did not fully deserve. He then asked Kades for his assistance, especially in New York State and in Washington, D.C., and remarked, "I should not call upon your assistance in this matter, as I know the pressure of your private affairs must be monumental, were it not for its great significance both to the United States and your outstanding devotion to the common objectives which both countries have sought under the Occupation."

Prior to their departure from Japan, the judges were given a thoroughgoing orientation and briefing by members of my division. We worked out questionnaires covering various subjects in which the Japanese were interested. For the understanding of the American contacts, a brief comparative reference to the situation under Japanese law was included. These questionnaires were forwarded to the Department of the Army, which distributed them to the individual American contacts. When the mission arrived, therefore, the latter were aware of its purpose and better able to understand its needs. All the credit for this laborious work of preparation is owed to my associates.

Finally, on September 27, 1950, at 3:30 PM Tokyo time, the five Japanese and we two escorts departed from Haneda Airfield on Victory Flight 34, Pan American Air Lines. After a seven-and-a-half-hour flight we arrived on Wake Island, the place of my bad luck in February 1946. Oddly enough, this barren island also saw an ominous beginning of our expedition. While waiting in the PanAm cafeteria, we were told that the engine of our plane had to be repaired. After several hours, the sergeant in charge called the names of all participants, with the exception of the chief justice, and announced that they must continue the flight on another plane at 6 AM. Then he exclaimed, "Mr. Tanaka will take a plane later!" I was furious about this ingenious idea of separating the leader from the group and have him travel unescorted. Hence, I politely informed the man that Tanaka was the chief justice of the Supreme Court of Japan and must stay together with us. This, however, did not impress him at all, and he said that he was only concerned with the safety of the passengers. I tried to explain to him that the separation of Tanaka was politically unwise, but he remained adamant. Only after I urged him very strongly to leave at least Tanaka and me together, he yielded, but I could not prevent our separation from the rest of the group.

Since our flight was scheduled only for 11 AM the next day, Tanaka and I were allowed to get some sleep. I knew from experience that no hotels were available in this locality. We were guided to a tent that served as a GI billet. There were some six soldiers in the room, most of them sleeping and snoring. Those who awakened made very surprised faces when they saw these two elderly civilians enter; they probably believed they were dreaming. We occupied a vacant double berth with linen that was far from clean. What a strange start! This was, indeed, an adventure not devised in the carefully prepared program. The chief justice proved in this unexpected mild adversity that he was a true philosopher. He took it with good humor and mumbled from time to time: "Very interesting, very interesting!"

We really did get some sleep, and after breakfast we boarded a fine plane, somewhat refreshed and cheerful. Victory 34 remained stranded. During the customs inspection in Honolulu I dropped a hint about the position of Tanaka. Afterwards we enjoyed the dinner in the airport restaurant, where the rest of the group joined us about two hours later—their plane had come to Honolulu by way of Midway Island. While we were sitting there, a tall gentleman approached our table and warmly welcomed the Chief Justice on American soil. It was Mr. Justice William Douglas, who had just returned from one of his Himalayan or Tibetan tours. When he passed the customs office, the inspector, who knew him, had said to him: "Half an hour ago the Chief Justice of the Japanese Supreme Court was here!" "Oh, I must meet him," Douglas exclaimed, and it was easy to discover us.

We landed at the Fairfield Army Base at Suison, California, where we were met by Lt. Col. G. B. Goodrick, Exchange of Persons Section, OSA, Washington, D.C., and by Lt. Col. Elwood F. Saxer of the San Francisco Field Office of the Reorientation Branch of the Department of the Army. The latter drove us to San Francisco. The Palace Hotel, where we stayed, contrasted agreeably with our Wake Island accommodations.

On the next morning the fascinating, though very strenuous and perhaps overambitious, program of orientation in the United States started. After two days in California, we proceeded by air to New York City, where we stayed for fourteen days, with side trips to Albany and Trenton. The remainder of the schedule included two weeks in Washington, D.C.; five days in Cambridge, Massachusetts; three days in Ann Arbor; brief stops in Chicago and Denver; three days in Cheyenne; and finally, three days in Seattle. After a total stay of forty-seven days the five judges, accompanied by Koshi, flew back to Japan. Having seen them off in Seattle, I flew back to Washington in order to attend the Second National Conference on the Occupied Countries sponsored by the Commission on the Occupied Areas of the American Council of Education.

The Japanese were given every opportunity to observe trial procedure in all types of tribunals—federal, state, and municipal—from the lowest magistrate court to the United States Supreme Court. They also visited the Court of Claims and the Tax Court of the United States. They were received by the Departments of Justice, State, and the Treasury. In addition, the party attended extensive lectures at various law schools of outstanding universities, as well as seminars and round-table discussions. The organization and functions of such independent administrative agencies as the Federal Trade Commission and the Securities and Exchange Commission were likewise studied on the spot. Everywhere the bar associations provided lectures and informal discussions. The Library of Congress and the Brookings Institute were also included in the program, and it was especially gratifying that we could provide the group the opportunity to attend a meeting of the United Nations Assembly in Lake Success, where they witnessed a lively discussion of the question of Korean independence and the voting of the members on various resolutions. Visits to the National Gallery of Art and to the Fogg Museum in Cambridge attended to the esthetic interests of the guests. Sightseeing tours were conducted in San Francisco, to Mount Vernon, to historical areas of Massachusetts, and to the Seattle port, as well as to Fort Lawton. Hardly a day passed without a dinner, luncheon, or cocktail invitation.

Kades was with us most of the time in New York and in

Washington. The ease and natural wit with which he handled the introduction of the Japanese to prominent personalities, most of whom knew him, was an invaluable contribution to the success of our mission. The sponsoring agency, the IIE, welcomed the group on its first day in New York through its president, Holland. Mr. James P. Parker, an attorney in the District of Columbia, accompanied us throughout the trip on behalf of the institute. He was helpful in Washington because of his many connections. He took care of the personal needs of the Japanese and was responsible for their strict compliance with the schedule. Beyond that, he rendered valuable service by successfully exploring possibilities for the Supreme Court of Japan to obtain American law books from libraries and publishers. The IIE also provided us with a much-needed second interpreter, Walter Tanaka, who had once worked for me in Tokyo. He ably assisted Koshi, and also became a kind of personal aide to the chief justice.

The most important event was, of course, the meeting of the Japanese judges with their counterparts in the United States Supreme Court. It started with a luncheon in the cafeteria of the Court. After the formal introduction by Kades, Tanaka read a speech, to which Mr. Chief Justice Frederick M. Vinson replied briefly, stressing equal justice for all. Then we attended an antitrust case. In the afternoon Tanaka, Koshi, and I were received by Chief Justice Vinson in his chambers. To my delight, Vinson expressed astonishment at the disciplinary punishment of the four Japanese Supreme Court judges on the ground of a procedural mistake. This led to my telling him the story. He elaborated on the history and number of American chief justices. Talking about the first of them, John Jay, he mentioned the initial weakness of the Court, which motivated Jay to refuse reappointment when it was offered to him and to prefer the governorship of New York. When Tanaka spoke of the introduction of judicial review to Japan, Vinson elaborated on the *Marbury versus Madison* and

Dred Scott cases. Asked how many cases the Japanese Supreme Court had yearly, Tanaka answered that each judge was in charge of four hundred, whereupon Vinson observed: "That makes six thousand!" I then explained in what instances appeal was admitted to the Supreme Court. The backlog of the Japanese Court reminded Vinson of the adoption of the writ of certiorari by one of his predecessors, William Howard Taft, as a means of relieving the burden of the Court.

On the next day, Ishizaka, Kishi, and Higuchi met Mr. Justice Tom Clark, Hozumi met Felix Frankfurter, and Mano met Black and Burton. Tanaka, again accompanied by Koshi and myself, had interviews with our Honolulu acquaintance, Douglas, and with Robert Jackson. Douglas was particularly interested in Tanaka's academic career and writings. He had read an English-language digest of Tanaka's book, *Theory of World Law*, and, after complimenting him on this work, discussed natural law with the visiting jurist.[3] He also invited Tanaka to lecture to students of the National University, of which he was the chancellor.[4] The subject of conversation with Jackson was the problem of how to deal with misconduct by radicals during trials without infringing on their right to due process of law.

On the same day on which we met the Supreme Court justices, we made a courtesy visit to the secretary of state, Dean Acheson. U. Alexis Johnson, formerly American consul general in Yokohama and subsequently undersecretary of state, and Adrian Fisher, legal advisor to the sec-

[3] Tanaka, a devout Roman Catholic, was an almost fanatical disciple of natural law. His *Theory of World Law*, written in Japanese, is a book of four volumes. References to natural law can also be discovered in his court opinions, and some decisions of his Court were influenced by this legal philosophy.

[4] The law school of National University in Washington, D.C., which has since closed down, merged with the George Washington School of Law.

retary, were also present. The conversation was very informal. The secretary talked about his experiences as a law student, and congratulated Tanaka on his recently received honorary law degree from Fordham University. Mentioning the news of the landing of our troops on Inchon, he remarked to me that General MacArthur had been "wonderfully successful." A few months later he would certainly not have said that.

I attended the solemn ceremony at which Tanaka was awarded an honorary doctoral degree at Fordham by President McGinley in the presence of Bishop MacDonald and the provost, Father Walsh. He received two additional honorary degrees, one from Georgetown, and the other from Boston University. The interest of the Chief Justice in Roman Catholicism equaled that in law. Outside the official program, Tanaka met Cardinal Francis Spellman of New York, Cardinal Edward Mooney of Detroit, and Bishop— later Cardinal—Richard J. Cushing of Boston.

The whole mission attended a lengthy series of seminars and discussions at the law school of Catholic University in Washington. Brandon Brown, the dean of the school, elaborated on the ideological sources of the American Constitution and on the philosophy of "higher laws," Tanaka's special interest. We listened to Edmund A. Walsh, vice president of Georgetown University; to Robert L. Stern, of the Office of the United States Solicitor General; to Henry F. Chandler, director of the Administrative Office of the United States Courts, and to others. Most views expressed reflected canonical philosophy. One speaker had pointed out that Western civilization was based on Roman Catholicism. This idea was then developed further by Walsh, who went so far as to assert that American democracy, as expressed in the Declaration of Independence, was not to be traced back to the Magna Carta but to natural law, to eternal principles. Walsh also attacked Oliver Wendell Holmes, who did not believe in natural law, mainly because he challenged the idea of absolute ethical rules applicable to all mankind.[5] All this appeared to me as an attempt to connect the principles of natural or divine law, as interpreted by the Catholic Church, with everything that is desirable in this world, and especially with our American system of democracy, in which a maximum freedom of the government and of the individual from ecclesiastical interference has triumphed. Whatever my own reaction may have been, I am sure that Chief Justice Tanaka enthusiastically approved of the views to which he listened and that he thoroughly enjoyed the occasion.

Finally, the big Washington program included an inspection of the United States Training School for Boys at Bladensburg, Maryland. Led by James V. Bennet, director of prisons, the Japanese had occasion here to observe a model modern juvenile penal and correctional institution. They showed great interest in the training classes for the various trades. The boys did not display the gloom that the faces of convicts in prison usually express. It was truly a showpiece and, compared to certain reformatories in New York City as they exist today, almost a paradise. The visit ended with a happy lunch in the company of the boys.

The program in New York City went on from the early morning to late at night, usually with a dinner party at the end of the day. Very often there was no rest for me when we returned to the hotel, since I had to assist the chief justice in preparing his speeches in English for the next day.

The group listened to a lecture by Frank H. Gordon, attorney-in-chief of the Grievance Committee, New York City Bar Association, and assistant to the United States attorney general, on the canon of professional ethics as the guiding principle for the conduct of lawyers. The organization of the legal profession in the United States was explained by the president. of the same bar association,

[5] See 32 *Harvard Law Review* 40, 1918.

Whitney Seymour. The Japanese saw one of America's greatest judges, Learned Hand, in action at the United States Court of Appeals for the Second Circuit, and discussed with him and Judge Jerome Frank the questions of selection of judges as well as the value of the jury system. Judge Harold Medina described the famous trial of the eleven communists over which he had presided, and a general discussion ensued on mass trials and contempt of court. The group even witnessed a murder trial by jury at the New York Court of General Sessions. Two days were spent with lectures and seminars at Columbia University. Professor Noel T. Dowling presented a brilliant and clear analysis of the power of judicial review, as exercised by the United States Supreme Court, while Walter Gellhorn elaborated on the scope of judicial review over administrative acts. Lectures of other distinguished legal scholars followed.

When our train, coming from New York, approached Trenton and the Delaware River, I did not foresee that eleven years later I would settle down in this area and make my home of retirement near Princeton. I found our visit extremely informative. After listening to arguments in New Jersey's Supreme Court, with Chief Justice Arthur T. Vanderbilt presiding, Governor Alfred E. Driscoll invited us to lunch, and then we had a two-hour discussion with him. He emphasized the fact that his state had many political and legal problems in common with Japan, since New Jersey also enacted a new Constitution in 1947. He described the developments preceding this event and dwelt on the issues of judicial independence, judicial review, selection of judges, and due process of law. Senator Bodine, president of the State Senate, participated in the discussion; so did Professor John Sly of Princeton University. In Chief Justice Vanderbilt we were fortunate enough to see another of the classical, eminent judges of our nation. In a three-hour lecture he briefed the Japanese on the judicial reforms under New Jersey's Constitution, and gave very useful advice on how to increase the efficiency of judges and to expedite trials. He appeared to all of us as the true leader of the court, who guided his associates with a firm hand.

Cambridge and Harvard! Here I was on familiar ground and happy to have a reunion with many friends. At Harvard Law School the Japanese were welcomed by Dean Erwin N. Griswold, subsequently United States solicitor general; Professor David E. Cavers, chairman of the Committee of International Legal Standing; and Dr. William S. Barnes, director of Foreign Legal Research Studies. The famous criminologist, Sheldon Glueck, lectured on the statistical and sociological aspects of juvenile delinquency; Paul E. Freund on American constitutional litigation; Zachariah Chaffee, Jr., Glueck, and Sutherland on United States Supreme Court decisions regarding contempt of court, with special emphasis on freedom of expression. Discussions on the following day with different scholars ranged from the merit of jury trials to "judicial supremacy," mistrial, probation, and natural law. To be offered so much scholarly wisdom by some of the best minds our law schools have available was a great occasion that fascinated the Japanese guests. In order to observe the teaching of law in practice, some Japanese attended classes of the law school.[6]

At the University of Michigan in Ann Arbor, we had similar experiences of an inspiring nature. Professor H. E. Yntema, well known authority on comparative law, had arranged an interesting program. We met Professor Robert Hall, director of the Center for Japanese Studies, and numerous other faculty members, including some from departments other than law. John B. Waite invited us into his home, where discussions were continued until the late evening.

[6] When we inspected the law library, Justice Mano pensively looked at the bust of Oliver Wendell Holmes, who was a kind of model for him. Since he was a frequent dissenter in the Japanese Court, he liked to think of himself as the Oliver Wendell Holmes of Japan.

Our visit to Chicago was much too short. We just had lunch there with the bar association and tea at the law faculty of the University of Chicago. It was here, possibly because of the pressure of time, that I was explicitly asked to speak about the legal and judicial reforms in Japan. While I had made it a principle to keep in the background and let the Japanese do the talking, I gave a brief presentation.

I was at first surprised to see that the program included Cheyenne, Wyoming, of all places, but as it turned out, I overcame my initial skepticism after our heartwarming experience there. The three days spent in this Rocky Mountain state, where winter and snow had started in November, were very worthwhile. It may have been the pride of the city of Cheyenne to act as host of such important guests. At any rate, this stay of the group in a place somewhat off the beaten path was so enjoyable because of an almost unbelievable degree of amicable welcome and hospitality. In this atmosphere the Japanese were not only provided with the usual briefings on courts and law, but we all had a great deal of fun. Excellently prepared by Frank Hays, formerly a colonel in the Government Section, and George Guy, also a former occupationnaire—both lawyers in Cheyenne—the program included a formidable number of social events and cheerful celebrations. On all these occasions there were speeches after the meals. Even a radio conversation was arranged, in which Tanaka, myself, and the two Cheyenne lawyers participated.

Within the official program a trial in the Supreme Court of the state was attended, and afterwards a very informal conversation with Chief Justice William A. Riner and his two associates developed. On that occasion Justice Mano, a keen observer, expressed astonishment that there was no American flag in the room, in contrast to all the other courts inspected. The Cheyenne morning papers on the next day reported that story with some excitement along the line: a Japanese judge must come to this city to wonder about the absence of the national flag in our Supreme Court! As I learned subsequently, the star-spangled banner was soon shown in the courtroom. We drove by automobile over the picturesque Sherman Range to Laramie and visited the Wyoming University Law School, where we listened to lectures of several professors.

Seattle ended our program. The group went to the University of Washington and was received by the president, Raymond B. Allen, and by John Anderson, director of university relations. On request of Chief Justice Tanaka, Dr. Allen discussed the problem of communism and academic freedom on the basis of incidents that had led to the removal of three members of his faculty. We also conversed with Dean Faulkner of the law school, and inspected the excellent law library under the guidance of Miss Gallagher, the librarian. The Seattle program included attendances of court sessions, the inspection of a law office, and a visit to Fort Lawton.

An impressive affair I wish to mention was a formal lunch to which we were invited by the Seattle Bar Association and the Institute of Pacific Relations. It was here that I delivered, on request, a comprehensive speech on the subject of our Occupation reforms. Chief Justice Tanaka and Parker also addressed the audience, which consisted of approximately one hundred fifty persons. Among the hosts, the speakers were Wilbur Zundel, president of the Bar Association, Daniel Reaugh of the same, and Mayor Devin. The atmosphere during this lunch was, in spite of its formality, overwhelmingly friendly, and I was afterwards congratulated "on the fine job you boys are doing in Japan."

I cannot sufficiently praise the generous hospitality the mission received everywhere. In my official report on the journey I listed thirty-four dinner, lunch, tea, or cocktail invitations from judges, bar associations, universities, other institutions, and private individuals. Of some of them I have a lively memory because of the conversations that followed the meals or the personalities of the participants.

Our dinner with the American Civil Liberties Union at the Park Hotel in New York combined both attributes. This was something quite different from anything otherwise offered the group. Their contacts were, on the whole, with elements of what we would today call "the establishment." Here they met one of the most original political outsiders of the nation, Norman Thomas, besides leading officials of the Union, such as Ernest Angell and Walter Frank. As a matter of course, Thomas, with his razor-sharp mind, his wit, and irony, dominated the conversation. The freedom of criticism he abundantly used impressed us all, particularly the politically cautious Japanese. He humorously told the story of his repeated unsuccessful races as presidential candidate for the Socialist party. Interesting explanations of the principles of the Civil Liberties Union, its activities, and its influence on judicial decisions as amicus curiae also were valuable to the mission.

A lunch at the Faculty Club of the University of California at Berkeley was the beginning of my friendship with Professor Albert Ehrenzweig, a former Austrian and prominent scholar in the field of conflicts of law. He showed a lively interest in my work in Japan, and a few years later we had the pleasure of welcoming him in Tokyo.

An evening dinner given by the United Nations League of Lawyers at the Army-Navy Club in Washington stands out in my memory as a huge affair. Hundreds of people connected with law and believing in international understanding were present, while Solicitor General Perlman acted as toastmaster.

An invitation by the Far Eastern expert Joseph Ballantine to his farm in Norbeck, Maryland, gave us the opportunity to have a pleasant excursion from Washington and to meet truly old Japanese hands, namely, former Ambassadors Joseph C. Grew, Stanley K. Hornbeck, and William R. Castle.

Adrian Fisher, the legal advisor of the Department of State, who had shown great interest in the mission, invited us to a lunch at Prospect House, where we made the acquaintance of Dean Rusk, then assistant secretary of state, who at first sight appeared to be quite unassuming and easygoing, and of the colorful General Snow, deputy legal advisor in the Department of State. We appreciated particularly the thoughtfulness of our host in having invited Mr. Justice Frankfurter, whose temperament and wit enlivened any party in which he was present.

The fact that I had very detailed notes on the mission has enabled me to elaborate on this subject. I wanted to show through the example of one important program how much the United States has done to promote international understanding. In the case of Japan the visit of these national leaders to the United States provided a meeting between equals, colleagues, jurists of the two worlds concerned with similar problems. The kindness and warmth with which the Japanese were received surpassed all expectations. It revealed to me not only the general magnanimity of Americans, who more easily than other nations forgive or even forget past sins, but also their conviction that the sinner had reformed, or in other words, that General MacArthur's Occupation had essentially achieved its objectives. This opinion was, indeed, repeatedly expressed to me.

The attitude of the Americans certainly also reflected the excellent impression the Japanese made on them. It was obvious to everyone who listened to Chief Justice Tanaka that he was inspired by a genuine, idealistic desire for international understanding, resulting from his adherence to natural law. Tanaka was uninhibited and moved with ease among the Americans without ever losing a certain natural dignity. To be sure, he was at that time a theoretical thinker and professorial type rather than what one would call a practical judge; but this was not conspicuous to our American contacts, so much were they impressed by his other qualities. Fortunately, Justice Mano examined everything with a pragmatic approach, and was very eager to acquaint himself with the American solution of practical problems in the administration of justice. In the discussions he was usually the one who took the initiative with questions and arguments. The experiment including in the group both Tanaka and Mano, which had appeared risky to begin with, worked well just because the two men complemented each other perfectly. Old Judge Hozumi was perhaps the most popular figure with the Americans, who loved to listen to his after-dinner stories, told in fairly good English. Professionally, as an expert in this field, he was particularly interested in all matters affecting family relations. President Ishizaka, a more elegant type of Japanese and very amiable, showed an amazing ability to adjust himself to new situations. His English, which had appeared very poor when we left, improved rapidly because he had sufficient courage to practice it. The two junior judges of the Tokyo High Court, Kishi and Higuchi, reflected modesty, courtesy, and efficiency.

The Japanese were greatly impressed by the American way of life; the width and grandeur of the American scenery; the technical wonder of the highways; the cleanliness of cities and towns; the important station of American women; and the easygoing character of the American people. They appreciated the great influence of the bar upon public life and the firm dignity of American judges, as well as the tremendous prestige attending judicial office. Many legal concepts had been known to them only in theory. To see them in practice was what the visitors needed most of all for an understanding of the Anglo-Saxon system. Furthermore, they benefited intensely from observing American court techniques, such as the setting up of the docket, assigning cases to the individual judges, and preparing and writing the opinions. In my favorable evaluation of the effect of the tour on the minds of the Japanese I was particularly influenced by the reaction of Judge Mano. Never before having been in the United States or in Europe, he had been extremely reluctant to adopt any foreign institutions and, to begin with, skeptical about the whole tour. At the end of it he appeared to be the most enthusiastic member of the group.

The Department of the Army rendered valuable assistance to the project. Lieutenant Colonel Goodrick accompanied us on our flight from San Francisco to New York. Here, and subsequently in Washington, he provided us with army transportation and took care of the necessary coordination between the escorts, the department, and the IIE. Lieutenant Colonel Saxer met us again in Seattle, where, in the absence of an official schedule, he had arranged the magnificent program we enjoyed in that city. Both officers were especially well adapted to their assignment. Their attitude toward the Japanese, far from being paternalistic, was extremely kind, reassuring, and helpful. Colonel Lou G. Van Wagoner, the chief of the Reorientation Branch in the Pentagon, kept himself continuously informed on the progress of the mission. Moreover, Mr. William Coblenz, assistant director of public information in the Department of Justice, who was assigned to help the mission in Washington, accompanied us throughout our program there and showed himself indefatigable as ready advisor and source of information about the capital.

As to the role of the GHQ escorts, George Koshi's performance as an interpreter was so brilliant that he was admired by the Americans as well as by the Japanese. The *Washington Post*, for instance, highly praised his talents. My own activity consisted mainly in explaining to the American contacts the Japanese aspect of the topic under discussion. I usually gave a very brief background summary of the legal and judicial reforms under the Occupation before the program proper started. Whenever a question of the Japanese required clarification, I pointed out the reason why it was asked and explained the actual problems with which the Japanese administration of justice was faced. Major General Carter B. Magruder, then acting special assistant for occupied areas, subsequently our chief of staff in the Far East/United Nations Command and United Nations commander, in a conversation with me at the Pentagon, kindly commended my contribution to the achievement of the mission. In a cable to General MacArthur, dated November 27, 1950, the department stated that the visitors were well received and made an excellent impression, that to a considerable degree the success of the project was due to Kades and me, and that Koshi performed the duties of interpreter in outstanding fashion. Brigadier General Keyser, SCAP's assistant chief of staff, wrote to me in January 1951 that he enjoyed reading my report on the mission in *Nippon Times*, and that he felt "positive that great good was accomplished and much credit is due you because the mission was your idea in the first place."

◇◇

CHAPTER TWENTY-THREE

MacArthur's Removal

When the mission ended, I was exhausted. Since this was my first return to the States after almost five years of absence, I had arranged a short vacation, which was combined with the official assignment of attending the Second National Conference on the Occupied Countries in Washington. It was mainly concerned with the educational aspects of occupied areas, and offered an interesting comparison of the methods applied in Germany and in Japan. On this occasion, I met my old friend, Roger Baldwin, who delivered the most impressive speech of the whole session. He was an inspiring and eloquent orator.

In Seattle I had obtained reservations for a cabin in an army transport ship back to Japan, since I expected a leisurely week aboard to give me a much-needed rest before my being swallowed again by the work in the office. When, after another flight, I arrived at the West Coast, the newspapers were full of alarming reports of the setback our forces had suffered in Korea. Fears were even expressed that the enemy might resort to bombing Japan. That was too much for me. Unable to get a clear picture of what was happening, I decided that I had to be with my family in Tokyo in this dangerous situation. Hence, the beautiful plan to return by sea did not materialize, and I again had to fly back to Tokyo. When I landed in the arms of my wife and daughter, I discovered that there was much less nervousness in Tokyo than I had found in the States.

There was no possibility of resting after the return trip and the crammed weeks in the States, since the work had piled up in the office. No wonder, therefore, that one day in March 1951 I collapsed physically and had to be admitted to the Tokyo Army Hospital. During the hospitalization of more than three weeks I underwent all kinds of tests. Never have I experienced a more thorough exploration of the cause of illness before diagnosis than while in the care of these medical doctors in uniform. When they finally reached the verdict that merely a high degree of exhaustion was involved, I felt truly reassured.

I was still confined to bed when, on April 12, the news of General MacArthur's removal from his commands hit Tokyo. My first reaction was shock and puzzlement. To be sure, his repeated press releases and other publicized statements had made it clear that he completely disagreed with the Korean strategy of Washington and the whole global policy of the administration. I had understood that MacArthur, as the military leader of the United Nations action, felt frustrated and angry because he could not destroy the enemy's "sanctuary" and prevent the masses of Chinese soldiers from crossing the bridges over the Yalu River in their thrust against the Allied forces, for whom he was responsible. This feeling of sympathy had led me to think that his abundantly shown irritation might be tolerated, in view of his great achievements as SCAP and as military commander. I was, however, not convinced that in the big issues of foreign policy MacArthur was right. At second thought, I realized that the world picture must look very different from the point of view of President Truman, who had the ultimate responsibility for the foreign policy of the United States. I also concluded with a heavy heart that even if MacArthur had been right, he had to accept the decisions of his commander-in-chief, the president. If he showed his disagreement with the president's policy publicly, it was certainly the right of the latter to relieve him. Nevertheless, and in spite of these rational considerations,

I was saddened. While I was unaware of it in my hospital bed, this sadness was shared nearly by all Japanese as well as Americans in Tokyo. It was combined with shock over the abruptness of the recall. I deeply regretted that I could not take part in the touching farewell ceremony at Haneda Air Field, when the dignitaries of the Japanese government and virtually the whole headquarters honored the departing proconsul and his family. Throngs of Japanese simple people lined the road to the port, many of them weeping; this has all been described by eyewitnesses. It seemed as if in this moment of departure the adoration for the general, flourishing in the first period of the Occupation, had been revived. Charlotte and Ellen took my place at the farewell. MacArthur shook hands with them, as with most others present. General Whitney and his colorful wife Evelyn kissed them good-bye. It would have been completely out of character had the faithful knight not followed his lord. Whitney had immediately resigned his position when Mac-Arthur's regime ended in Japan. So did Willoughby.

Truman's controversial action had the effect that the welcome due the returning hero in the States grew into something like a frantic glorification; that the Republicans of the right, other conservatives, and the men of the Chinese lobby cried for the head of Secretary of State Dean Acheson, who was considered the chief architect of MacArthur's removal, and even for Truman's impeachment;[1] that the most thorough and sometimes agonizing reappraisal of American foreign policy took place in two joint Senate committees; and that the old soldier nevertheless faded away at last. Since nobody could doubt the authority of the president to relieve the general, the controversy boiled

[1] Even among conservatives there were, however, divergent views. According to Keyes Beech, *Tokyo and Points East* (Garden City, N.Y.: Doubleday, 1954), p. 20, he heard Governor Thomas E. Dewey say on the subject of MacArthur's relief: "If I'd been president I'd have fired him a long time ago." This recalls Defense Secretary Marshall's remark that the general should have been relieved two years before.

down to the arguable question of who was right with regard to the global strategy.

There are many people who even today believe with MacArthur that the Chinese intervention offered the unique opportunity for the decisive coup against international communism. While Soviet Russia had exploded an atomic bomb the year before, it is still being argued that we had the nuclear superiority, and therefore Moscow would have thought twice before venturing into a confrontation with the United States. That would have permitted us to destroy the industrial potential of Red China "for generations to come," as MacArthur had expressed it. I think that this view was gambling with the danger of a third world war, and that it was motivated by the conception of using maximum force to destroy the enemy in a war, failing to understand the nature of the United Nations action in Korea. To start with the last point, this action had a limited purpose—as much as MacArthur hated the idea, which also was generally unpopular with the American people. It was of a predominantly defensive character, and in that situation there was, indeed, a substitute for victory. To follow the general's prescription by bombing Manchuria and even mainland China, and using Chiang's soldiers in a "fraternal slaughter," would have alienated us from our allies, and we would actually have been forced "to go it alone," not to speak of raising serious doubts about the combat readiness of those forces. Even without joining in the fighting, Russia, at that time not yet ideologically split from China, would probably have assisted the "fraternal nation" intensively with hardware and other supplies. The estimate that we could have neutralized Red China for generations appears to me dangerously sanguine. MacArthur excluded the use of ground forces in the proposed plan, and even declared that everybody who favored it needed "his head examined." Subsequent warfare in Southeast Asia has shown that the intensive bombing of North Vietnam by our Air Force failed to defeat that nation. Would not a similar failure in China sooner or later have led to the use of ground forces in spite of the alleged insanity of such action? The result would have been an open-ended bloody war, compared with which Vietnam almost appears as children's play. The number of victims on both sides would have been multiplied. Behind all these speculations, there lurks the gruesome prospect of the use of nuclear weapons against China. If we had chosen this option, we might have been able to kill or maim millions of Chinese, but it would have made us the villain of the century and might have led to a global holocaust. It is exactly the fear of this weapon and the unspoken understanding between the powers possessing it to avoid its use which has brought about an elementary change in international relations and which, we may hope, might prevent mankind from self-destruction. Unfortunately, there are elements in most nations, including our own, who have not realized that this change requires a corresponding adoption of a different ethical attitude toward war. MacArthur himself, who actually hated war, but believed that once it has started it must be won with maximum force as fast as possible, once remarked during the subsequent Senate hearings that in our times war is mutual suicide.

The memoirs of Truman and Dean Acheson show clearly that all these considerations of the Asian picture were in their minds. Besides, those responsible for our foreign policy had to take into account the consequences a full confrontation in the Far East could have in Europe, which they regarded as equally, if not more, important. By reading some of the books on the so-called MacArthur controversy, I found those explaining and defending the administration more convincing than those condemning it and supporting the stand of MacArthur. The general's reminiscences, as well as Whitney's *MacArthur, His Rendezvous With History*, disappointed me. They would have been so much more effective had they once admitted that MacArthur made a serious mistake. Instead, the master indulged in a degree of self-glorification that was completely unnecessary, since his place in history had been secured. Whitney, his alter ego, engaged in the expected adoration, which might have been touching were it not combined with somewhat weird fantasies of a communist conspiracy against his master, and with the inability to understand and respect diverging opinions. What has always amazed me in the case of Mac-Arthur was his almost fanatical conviction that he, and he alone, was right and had the solution to the most complicated world problems. I, who throughout my unheroic life have tried to do justice to both sides of a difficult problem, have sometimes asked myself whether such absolute sureness is not the mark of the genius. While it is often enough the mark of the fool or simpleton, MacArthur undoubtedly came close to being a genius. Even Arthur Schlesinger, one of his harshest, though brilliant, critics, admits that there were in him "elements of greatness."[2]

While presidential hopes may have contributed to Mac-Arthur's obstinate opposition to the admittedly not always determined policy of the administration, it can primarily be explained by his concern for his soldiers. In shouting to the world his indignation against the strategic limitations imposed upon him, and against the foreign policy of his commander-in-chief, he showed, of course, the same courage that characterized his military actions, and in this instance it was civil courage.

The poorly veiled defiance of his commander-in-chief endangered his position, as a man of his intellectual brilliance must have known. Still, besides his passionate love of country, there was another psychological motivation behind his messages and announcements. Closely connected with his pride, or one may call it vanity, which he had in common with many other great personalities, and with his mother-inspired awareness that he was a man of destiny, there was in him an urge to make himself heard in the world, to be in the limelight of publicity, to play a star role in the

[2] See *The MacArthur Controversy*, p. 258.

historical drama of his time. The best illustration of this trait was the release of his statement of March 24, 1951, in which MacArthur declared his readiness to confer with the commander-in-chief of the enemy forces in "the earnest effort to find any military means whereby realization of the political objectives of the United Nations in Korea . . . might be accomplished without further bloodshed."

It was this very action that finally broke the camel's back. Truman as well as Acheson report in their memoirs that it led to the president's decision to relieve the general from his commands. The reason was not only that MacArthur had not cleared his important message, in spite of previous explicit orders directing such clearance of public statements by military commanders. More decisively, the threatening contents of the statement was in conflict with and certain to thwart a pending project prepared and discussed with leaders of Allied governments for a diplomatic settlement on Korea. MacArthur had been informed by the Joint Chiefs of Staff of a forthcoming presidential announcement that the United Nations was now preparing to discuss conditions for such a settlement. Truman, in his memoirs,[3] characterizes MacArthur's conduct as "insubordination," and points out that "his action had frustrated a political course decided upon, in conjunction with our allies, by the government he was sworn to serve." The president was doubtlessly honest by stating his view that he himself would violate his oath to uphold and defend the Constitution if he allowed the general to defy the civil authorities.

Truman had made up his mind at this juncture, and the incident of the correspondence between MacArthur and the minority leader of the House, Representative Joseph W. Martin, with its sensational revelation in Congress of MacArthur's implied criticism of the administration, merely strengthened his conviction that the general could not be retained in his commands. Still, the president did not im-

3 See Vol. II, *Years of Trial and Hope*, 442 and 444.

mediately reveal his decision to his official advisors, but asked for their suggestions. Acheson described the spontaneous reaction of Deputy Defense Secretary Robert Lovett immediately after MacArthur's action became known. Angrily, he said: "The General must be removed and removed at once!"[4] On April 9, General Marshall announced to the president that the Joint Chiefs of Staff unanimously recommended that MacArthur be relieved of all his commands, a recommendation in which he as the secretary of defense and General Bradley, as chairman of the Joint Chiefs of Staff, concurred.[5] Although this may have been a painful decision by the military, it disproves those who blame Truman's decision on the secretary of state. To be sure, Acheson had become impatient with the patience of President Truman, and had not approved of the president's pilgrimage to Wake Island.[6] Being a very rational and legally precise man, he was probably from the beginning somewhat suspicious of the intuitive and dramatic general. Moreover, MacArthur, who as proconsul of Japan developed a singular independence from Washington (often to the advantage of the Occupation), was not the most popular figure among diplomats of the Department of State. Nevertheless, it is incorrect and unfair to say that Dean Acheson was responsible for MacArthur's removal. The reason that the isolationist men of the right tried to make him the scapegoat for the unpopular removal of the charismatic general was their disagreement with the whole trend of his foreign policy.

Although I have thus reluctantly and regretfully arrived at the conclusion that Truman was justified, even that he had no other choice but to relieve MacArthur from his commands, the administration was not free from fault in its treatment of him. To begin with, its mistakes were merely a

---

[4] Acheson, *Present at the Creation*, p. 668.

[5] *Ibid.*, p. 672.

[6] Acheson stated that the whole idea was distasteful to him; that he wanted no part in it; and saw no good coming from it. *Ibid.*, p. 590.

reflection of MacArthur's magnetic personality. For years his superiors had left him a degree of freedom and independence almost unique in the history of the federal government. He had inspired their awe as well as their admiration. His tremendous power of persuasion was often effective enough to overcome their objections to his risky plans, as happened before his Inchon landing, which dangerously enhanced his reputation of victorious hero. One has only to read his *Reminiscences* to realize that he was most abundantly praised and honored with the highest decorations. As late as on January 14, 1951, President Truman sent him a message stating that "the entire nation is grateful for your splendid leadership in the difficult struggle in Korea and for the superb performance of your forces under the most difficult circumstances." This was at a time when MacArthur had already irritated the president repeatedly. The meeting on Wake Island gave the impression of a rendezvous between equals rather than a conference between the chief executive and his commander in the field. It would have been the proper thing to call MacArthur to Washington for a discussion of the Korean conflict. Nobody is indispensable, and a few days of absence from the theater would not have done any harm. This special consideration for a man who in Tokyo was surrounded by believers and admirers could very well have weakened his consciousness of being a subordinate of the unglamorous president. The timidity some of the president's aides felt toward the general is best illustrated by Acheson's story of Defense Secretary Louis Johnson's remark on Truman's decision to order MacArthur to withdraw the speech he had prepared for the Veterans of Foreign Wars. Johnson asked "whether we dare send a message that the President directs him to withdraw the statement."[7]

It was this very prestige of MacArthur, the unique image of an ingenious military leader and the successful ruler of occupied Japan, that induced President Truman to go out of

[7] *Present at the Creation*, p. 550.

his way in his endeavor to convince his subordinate that the administration policy was correct. The president knew very well, of course, and Acheson had explicitly warned him, that the relief of MacArthur would arouse a storm of recriminations among the general's friends in Congress. One of those puzzling aspects of the situation was that the same man who in the process of the democratization of Japan had shocked the American reactionaries by his revolutionary reforms, that this "global thinker" was now closely allied to and backed by reactionary and isolationist elements. It was one of the contradictions in MacArthur's very complex nature that his progressive spirit remained limited to his Occupation assignment during the reform period in Japan. Nothing of it could be found in his uncritical admiration of Chiang Kai-shek and Syngman Rhee. The reactivation of his Republicanism was in line with his family tradition; his hatred of communism, fed by the Chinese intervention in Korea, may have led him to approve of the anticommunist campaign of Senator McCarthy. Still, it is hardly understandable that a man of his caliber did not look through the vulgar and ignoble machinations of this demagogue, and did not reject the cold war hysteria that threatened the foundations of our American democracy. This can be explained only by his delusion that he himself was the victim of a mysterious communist conspiracy that had spread even into the United States government.

Under the political conditions at that time, Truman by his action showed much courage, a quality demonstrated on several occasions of his stormy presidency. He made a very bad mistake, however, in the manner in which he relieved the Far East commander. MacArthur's reproach that "no office boy, no charwoman, no servant of any sort would have been dismissed with such callous disregard for the ordinary decencies" appears to be richly deserved.[8] No excuses for the abrupt dismissal, such as the leak of the

[8] *Reminiscences*, p. 395.

news of Truman's decision and the cutoff of communications, can detract from what appeared to be a shabby humiliation. In any case it should, and certainly could, have been avoided that MacArthur first learned of his removal through a public broadcast. Once the president had decided that MacArthur should not continue in his positions, the occasion required sensitive handling and generosity. At least the attempt should have been made to offer the general the option to resign. The mode of removal exposed the president to the suspicion that he acted in anger and irritation. It was equally ungraceful not to invite to the signing of the San Francisco Peace Treaty several months later the man who had contributed more than anybody else to befriending the Japanese. I have heard them repeatedly criticize this omission. Interestingly enough, however, the lesson of the principle Truman enforced with the dismissal of MacArthur, namely, civilian authority over military leaders, was not lost on the Japanese, who had experienced what can happen when this principle loses validity.

The drama of "the president and the general" has the flavor of a Greek tragedy in which the hero, in *hubris*, rebels against the iron rules set by the gods, but must realize that even his powerful will and noble motivation cannot overcome the barriers that make his fervently desired goal unachievable. With this comparison I certainly do not liken the president of the United States, but rather the American Constitution, to the gods. It is mainly the heroic stubbornness of MacArthur and his tragic failure to prevail over the rational policy of his superiors that revived childhood memories of Sophocles and Euripides. There was much in this proud and often incalculable semigenius that arouses our sympathy, just as the hero in the Greek drama is supposed to do. It may be my personal gratitude to and admiration of the proconsul of Japan that makes me feel that the historical verdict on this extraordinary man ought not to depend upon legal or even constitutional principles, not to mention disciplinary rules. I have no doubt it will find that his accomplishments outweighed his weaknesses and blunders. Clio—to remain in the Greek mythology—will grant him a niche among the men of destiny, to belong among whom he strived throughout his exciting life. And with this note I part from my controversial boss of the Occupation.

◇◇

CHAPTER TWENTY-FOUR

SCAP without MacArthur

After MacArthur was replaced by General Matthew Ridgway, and Frank Rizzo had succeeded Whitney as chief of the Government Section, the Occupation found itself virtually in a self-liquidating process. Drama and action were followed by toleration and laissez-faire. Supervision and controls were reduced to a minimum, depurges completed. Much can be said in favor of a relaxed policy at this time. It was based on the idea that the Japanese, who soon were to regain their independence, must learn in time to stand on their own feet instead of being continuously told what to do and what not to do. While in principle I approved of it, I clung with a certain inflexibility to the view that, as long as the Occupation lasted, we should not allow any legislation to be passed that would be irreconcilable with what we had tried to achieve. Today it may appear almost absurd that a little more than two weeks before the Occupation ended I seriously objected to the controversial Subversive Activities Prevention Bill. Under the disguise of controlling communism, it provided, among other things, for the establishment of a commission with the power to take preventive action against groups suspected of terrorist activities in the future. In a detailed memorandum[1] I ex-

[1] See my Memorandum of April 11, 1952, Subject: Bill re: Subversive Activity Prevention; Public Security Investigating Agency Establishment; Public Security Investigating Committee Establishments, Legal Section Chronological File, Box 1501.

pressed doubts about the constitutionality of this legislation, arguing that apart from the principle that no one may be compelled to incriminate himself, such fundamental human rights as freedom of association, assembly, and speech may also be violated. The weaknesses of the bill, I concluded, would aid an arbitrary administrative interference with freedom of the press and the right to associate and act collectively. The bill could well be the first step toward revival of the old Peace Preservation Law, and be used to suppress criticism and organized activities under the pretext of controlling subversives. I suggested that a safer approach to the control of subversive elements would be to make subversive activities criminal offenses, and to prosecute the individual offender in the courts of law.

I met Brigadier General G. Keyser, deputy chief of staff, a very amiable and understanding person, and Rizzo for lunch, and we discussed the matter amicably for a long time. The two chiefs were against interference by SCAP at such a late date, but they were not able to convince me; nor did I convince them of the necessity for a veto. Since Carpenter supported me, the dispute had to be settled between the two Section chiefs, and, as was to be expected, the Government Section prevailed, inasmuch as it had strong diplomatic and security arguments in favor of noninterference.[2]

Although Ridgway was a war hero, too, and stabilized the Korean battlefront, there was no hero worship for this down-to-earth personality, who lacked his predecessor's glamor but also his *hubris*. This second and last SCAP allowed freer access to his office than the first one had, and also opened the doors of his residence for social receptions of American as well as Allied and Japanese guests. I remember particularly a splendid party he and his attractive wife gave on New Year's Day of 1952. It was the first time that

[2] This legislative proposal of the Yoshida government caused the leftist parties and labor unions to stir up popular commotion, as emerged in the May Day 1952 mass demonstrations. The bill was, nevertheless, enacted into law a few months later.

Charlotte and I had driven through the gate of the fine building on the hill that had been and was again to be the American embassy. The presence on occasions like this of many Japanese government figures and of prominent Japanese from other spheres highlighted not only the change in the office of the American commander, but also the fact that the end of the Occupation and the resumption of independence by Japan were just around the corner. But it would be unfair not to recognize that the smooth transition from one command to the other and the continuity of predominantly friendly relations between the occupiers and the occupied under Ridgway would not have been possible had not the six years of MacArthur's leadership laid the groundwork for it.

To us occupationnaires the prospect of the forthcoming peace treaty meant the handwriting on the wall. The end of the job was in sight, and those who had another one waiting in the States hurried back. A kind of exodus had started, but I decided in favor of a wait-and-see attitude. Being at the end of my fifties, I had no illusions regarding satisfactory job possibilities in the United States. In addition, I found it difficult to depart from Japan at that juncture. I was very eager to observe what would happen after the nation resumed its independence, most of all whether our reforms would survive, or the pendulum would swing toward undoing the "excesses of the Occupation." I was, therefore, glad when it was decided to have me continue within the Far East Command, which remained in Japan under the Security Treaty. Maynard N. Shirven, who had been a member of Blaine Hoover's Civil Service Division in Government Section, had joined the G–4 Section of the SCAP Headquarters and was assigned to the Korean Economic Aid Division in that Section. This division was reorganized into a new separate Civil Affairs Section, called G–5, since it was realized that the manifold tasks connected with non-military problems facing the Far East Command after the dissolution of SCAP could not possibly be absorbed by a subunit of a predominantly military outfit. Something new had to be created, and different personnel, among them civilians with experience in the Far East, had to be recruited. Shirven, a man of superior intelligence, had soon become an influential member of the division headed by Colonel Walter R. Hensey, Jr., and virtually indispensable in the process of reorganization. The new G–5 Section was established on February 19, 1952, and on March 3 I joined it on the recommendation of Shirven, after I parted from the Legal Section.

These were strange days, in a twilight atmosphere. The SCAP headquarters was folding up, the Government Section was no more than a small rump organization, the other Sections were shrinking, the personnel disappearing, and the future development was in a cloud of uncertainty. One stormy day Charlotte and I saw my former boss, Colonel Carpenter, and his wife off to the Yokohama harbor.

On April 28, 1952, the peace treaty came into force, and three days later the communist-inspired riots against Americans occurred. The uncertainty was enhanced by the forthcoming change in the top command. Ridgway was to succeed General Eisenhower as Supreme Commander of the Allied Forces in Europe, and General Mark W. Clark was to replace him as Far East commander.

Clark arrived in Tokyo on May 7, and almost simultaneously the mutiny of the prisoners of war on Koje Island southeast of Korea confronted him and the departing Ridgway with an utterly troublesome situation that had to be settled immediately, on the spot. The North Korean and Chinese inmates of the camp, probably incited by political agents, had rioted and by a clever coup succeeded in capturing the commander of the camp, Brigadier General Francis T. Dodd, whom they kept as hostage for the fulfillment of their extreme demands.[3] Brigadier General Charles F. Colson, who took over command of the camp,

[3] The story of the mutiny has been told in detail by Clark in *From the Danube to the Yalu* (New York: Harper, 1954), chapter 4.

eager to see Dodd freed, accepted the conditions of the prisoners, also admitting that atrocities had been committed against them, and achieved the release of Dodd. This event, with its aspects of ridicule, was, of course, a windfall for the enemy and detrimental to the Allied cause. It was, indeed, a most unfortunate start for General Clark. The conduct of Dodd and Colson was disapproved by their superiors, and both were demoted. Dodd was blamed for his imprudence in having allowed himself to be captured, since he had been warned of the explosive atmosphere in the camp. Colson found himself in a dilemma that in recent times has faced various governments, when kidnapping of diplomats and other VIPs has become a familiar device of terrorist political opponents to enforce their will. The alternative between sacrificing the life of a human being and important national objectives is doubtlessly a most agonizing one. Giving in to the demands of the kidnapper is apt to result in encouraging the practice of obtaining hostages; it also often involves the necessity of false and humiliating admissions, which are revoked after the release of the hostage. Rejection of the demands, on the other hand, in the hope that the kidnapper will nevertheless spare the life of the victim, has repeatedly proved to be a fateful miscalculation. In other words, there is no clear-cut ethical solution to the problem, and Colson should not be censored too sternly for having decided in favor of saving the life of Dodd. Perhaps his main fault was that he yielded too fast, and that he should have tried to obtain, by negotiations with the prisoners, less ignominious conditions.

◇◇◇

CHAPTER TWENTY-FIVE

My Post-Occupation Period

Although in my new assignment I had ceased to be a missionary of democracy, the reader might expect some information on my post-Occupation activities, which kept me in Japan for seven and a half more years. A report of them could easily fill the pages of another book. Here, however, the description of my work will be merely an appendix to the main part covering my Occupation experiences and observations. I shall restrict myself to a brief summary.

ORGANIZATIONS AND PERSONALITIES

With the end of the Occupation, the SCAP organization had expired, but the American commander-in-chief in Tokyo retained his two other hats, that of the United Nations commander-in-chief (CINCUNC), and that of the commander-in-chief Far East (CINCFE). In this latter capacity, he was simultaneously the governor of the Ryukyu Islands. There he was represented by the deputy governor on Okinawa, also a general, who headed both the military units and the United States Civil Administration of the Ryukyu Islands (USCAR). The G–5 organization, which subsequently became a J–5 unit comprising members of all three branches of the armed forces, was charged with relations to the governments and the people of the three areas: Japan, the Ryukyus, and Korea. This function, technically

called a "civil affairs mission," may be characterized as the
diplomatic aspect of military activity. It requires qualities
of expertness, understanding of other nations and races,
and of moderation usually not associated with the military.
Since the maintenance of friendly international relations
is primarily a task of the diplomatic agencies, continuous
coordination with the American embassies in the now independent Japan and in the sovereign Republic of Korea was
necessary. Even with regard to the Ryukyus, where the
military kept the determining power, the manner of governmental rule deeply affected United States relations with
Japan, whose "residual sovereignty" over the islands had
been explicitly recognized by the United States. It goes
without saying that the objectives aimed at by the diplomatic and by the military authorities frequently differed.
The embassies followed principles within the framework of
our foreign policy, while CINCUNC, CINCFE, and the
governor of the Ryukyus were strongly motivated by concern with their military missions. Differences between the
two had to be ironed out in Washington.

There was initial confusion and helplessness among the
small group of officers and civilians who composed the
newly formed organization of G–5. Still, the long pre-
occupation with Japanese governmental and political affairs
benefited the former occupationnaires among us, who
rapidly grasped the problems involved in Far Eastern areas
other than Japan. Apart from Shirven and myself, another
friend and colleague from the Government Section joined
us soon, namely, Dr. Justin Williams. The first G–5 chief
was Colonel Walter R. Hensey, and the fact that he was,
unlike other so-called assistant chiefs of staff, not a general,
was somewhat disadvantageous in a military outfit. Hensey
was an intelligent and hard-working officer, not an easy
boss, and difficult to persuade when advised to make con-
cessions for political reasons. It took him some time to know
his new staff. I soon found out that he did not like intimidated yes-men, but that the best way to handle him was to

speak out frankly. He was the first in a successive chain of assistant chiefs of staff, G–5 and J–5, most of them generals and one of them an admiral. I considered Major General Daniel B. Strickler the most competent of them. He was not an officer of the regular army, but a man of considerable governmental experience, since his civilian career included the position of deputy governor of Pennsylvania. It was a pleasure to deal with this clear-sighted, sober-minded man who immediately saw the political implications of a problem and balanced them with the military objectives.

I had less contact with the top commanders, but I served under all of them until the Far East Command was dissolved in 1957. After Ridgway and Clark, John E. Hull, Maxwell Taylor, and Lyman L. Lemnitzer headed the UNC and FEC. During the Hull era the aging commander more or less left the reins to his energetic chief of staff, Lieutenant General Carter B. Magruder, who was feared as a stern disciplinarian. I had met him before in the Pentagon. Now he impressed me as a strong, perhaps somewhat humorless personality, who controlled the detailed work of his subordinates more than necessary. General Taylor held the position of FEC–UNC Commander for a very short time. I was present at the briefing when he started his new position, and admired his brilliance, his intelligent questions, and his quick grasp of the problems. Lemnitzer, who followed him as the last top commander, was generally liked because of his forthright and warm personality. He was broad-minded and had a delightful sense of humor, as I myself could observe in my few contacts with him. Once I could even persuade him to accept a version I had suggested for a message, to which he had initially objected.

My own status in the post-Occupation period underwent various changes. I was no longer a division chief, as I had been in SCAP. After some time in J–5, I became the chief of the Political and Legal unit, called Section, within the Government Affairs Branch, and had four associates, among them the able lawyers Freitag and Irving Eisenstein, working with me. Both of them joined the USCAR staff subsequently, much to its benefit. My predecessor as Section chief had been my old friend, Justin Williams. Although we did not always agree on policy questions, we not only passed the test of friendship, into which a professional relationship frequently develops, but we also had some fun by working together. Justin definitely had a political antenna, and as chief of the Parliamentary Division in SCAP's Government Section he acquired great experience in oriental political attitudes; he was also a cheerful, extroverted fellow. His approach to problems was usually more pragmatic than mine.

Dr. Sherwood Fine, our division chief, formerly a principal advisor in ESS, had the rare talent of delegating authority, because he himself was intellectually gifted enough to afford a relaxed attitude. He did not write lengthy memoranda, but his performance was outstanding when he briefed traveling VIPs. On such occasions it seemed that he mastered his subject in an almost effortless manner. The branch chief, Roderick Gillies, a former SCAP division chief in ESS, was a very different type, although he had in common with Fine a high degree of intelligence. In writing this, I am well aware that I characterize a great number of persons with whom I worked, bosses as well as subordinates, as able. But they doubtlessly were, and the organizations to which they belonged had ample reason to be proud of them. Gillies was a very reserved Scottish type, hard worker, and a clever judge of people. I found him to be one of the best listeners I ever met. He himself talked only when absolutely necessary.

When, in the summer of 1957, Lemnitzer was called back to Washington to succeed Taylor as army chief of staff, he addressed us in a farewell speech at Pershing Heights in a ceremony marking the end of FEC. We were unhappy at this for several reasons. First of all, we anticipated that with the reduction of civil affairs responsibilities the work in the remaining "United States Forces Japan" (USFJ) Headquarters would become militarized and anticlimactic for those who, like myself, had been taken over. This new organization, under the jurisdiction of the Commanding General Pacific in Hawaii, lacked the authority of governor of the Ryukyus after the establishment of the office of high commissioner with the seat in Okinawa as well as the function of CINCUNC, which was no longer exercised in Japan but directly in Korea. That left for the USFJ only the task of taking care of the relations with Japan under the Security Treaty and the Administrative Agreement. As it later turned out, our job was big, complex, and interesting enough so that we did not miss the Okinawan and Korean variety. Second, the new headquarters was not located in downtown Tokyo but in Fuchu. While this was a wise arrangement, motivated by the purpose of making American troops as inconspicuous in the capital as possible five years after the end of the Occupation, we did not like to be provincialized.

In USFJ I served as so-called International Relations Officer and, as my job description stated, worked "as principal political and international law advisor, through established channels, to COMUS JAPAN," the headquarters' commander. I experienced two commanders, Lieutenant Generals Frederick Smith and Robert Burns, both of the Air Force. They were not desk officers and, of course, not too knowledgeable in civil affairs, but had an open mind and were willing to listen to and even in most instances to accept expert advice. Burns got much publicity when he ordered an airplane back because the vacationing colonel with his wife and children on it had arranged to be given priority over several GIs on emergency leave to visit sick or dying relatives. One of the expelled soldiers phoned Burns directly from the airport, and the reaction of Burns followed immediately. If I remember correctly, the selfish colonel was also reprimanded or demoted.

In our field it was, to begin with, not the commanders' but the chief of staff's office where decisive determinations were made. Our first chief of staff, Major General Paul W. Caraway, was doubtlessly the most dynamic officer of the headquarters. A demanding personality, he understood legal problems as a former lawyer, and appreciated my work. Politically, he followed a tough line. The atmosphere in the meetings of the Consultative Group, which was designed as a means of coordinating the views of USFJ with the embassy, was sometimes frosty when he represented the military, and Ambassador Douglas MacArthur II the diplomatic point of view. Still, as a human being, Caraway was warmhearted, and I preferred him to the ambassador, who had a keen mind but certainly lacked the charismatic charm of his uncle and namesake, and who never enjoyed the popularity with the Japanese of his predecessor, Robert Murphy, or of his outstanding successor, Edwin Reischauer. After Caraway left to become high commissioner of the Ryukyu Islands, his successor, Raleigh R. Hendrix, an Army major general whose retirement was close, ceased to be the paramount figure in civil affairs matters, and this role was taken over by Vice Admiral Frederick Stelter. He directed the difficult work in headquarters on the revision of the Security Pact and of the Administrative Agreement with Japan. Intelligent, painstakingly conscientious and thorough, he listened to advice and comments from all of us before arriving at a decision on the policy to be followed by the military in the negotiations with the embassy. The knowledge of the problems he accumulated within a brief time as a result of the intensity of his explorations was exceptional. He was considerate, and showed patience with his associates. I liked him very much and am still in friendly contact with him.

The J-5 Division, which functioned as the civil affairs unit in USFJ, was occupied during my assignment by a young Air Force colonel, Lloyd Martin, who developed the capacity of familiarizing himself with complex problems of which he had never before dreamt. He symbolized the new type of flexible desk officer, ready to take over any task, however novel. Although I frequently dealt directly with the chief of staff, I had, in addition to the division chief, a branch chief as a boss. For a short time this office was held by another colonel, a friendly and judicious person. He was succeeded by Maynard Shirven, to whom I owed my assignment to G–5, FEC. We were old work companions, again and again associated as colleagues, and also personal friends. More importantly, we saw eye-to-eye with regard to political philosophy. He had a keen mind as well as the ability to express himself in a clear manner. Although he had once criticized what he called my stubbornness, he must also have respected my work, since he went to the trouble of qualifying it as "outstanding" in his efficiency report. When Shirven went to Okinawa and became the deputy civil administrator after Gillies, he was replaced by Daniel H. Blake. Bill, as we called this Daniel, was a most harmonious and patient superior. He actually did not behave like one, but rather like a friend. Politically more conservative than I, he showed sound and well balanced judgment with a good sense of humor, as if he realized that most official tension and deadline excitement were passing phenomena.

WORK ON JAPAN

With regard to Japan, my activity in the Far East Command as well as in USFJ was predominantly in the field of political analysis. I drafted weekly reports that landed in the Pentagon. They covered Japan's international relations and domestic political trends, and were occasionally different from the reports cabled by the American embassy to the Department of State. Perhaps they did not always show the same degree of optimism that often colors messages of diplomats in foreign countries. During the premiership of Kishi Nobusuke I was not so impressed by his ostensibly pro-American stance. His conservatism and advocacy of rearmament happened to be in line with United States policies of the Eisenhower presidency, but in view of the rising Japanese nationalism I remained skeptical regarding the duration of a friendship based mainly on tactical grounds and lacking truly ideological sources. I realized, however, that for the time being there was no viable alternative to supporting his regime.

During the FEC period we were overwhelmed with Korean and Ryukyuan problems, but they were frequently interlinked with Japanese concerns—as, for instance President Syngman Rhee's hostile actions against Japan, such as numerous arrests of Japanese fishermen after his arbitrary expansion of the limit of Korean territorial waters by the "Rhee line"; his unreasonable financial claims against Japan; and the dispute about the sovereignty over the island of Takeshima. Being allied to both nations, the United States saw itself faced with insoluble problems based on their truly mutual hatred, kept alive and stirred up by Rhee, who probably still suffered from the trauma of his past imprisonment and torture by the Japanese.

In the USFJ my task was to keep the commander politically informed far beyond what he received from his Intelligence Section, whenever Japan's relationship to the two Chinas and the Soviet Union, the claim of the Japanese for the return of the Kurile Islands, or internal developments within the Government of Japan and her political parties were involved. Legally, my assignment frequently required the interpretation of the Security Treaty and the Administrative Agreement, and involved complex questions of international law. After the adoption of Japanese criminal jurisdiction over members of the United States Armed Forces, the civilians employed by the United States in Japan, and their dependents, for violations of Japanese law, subtle problems sometimes arose when the right to exercise jurisdiction was concurrent, in other words when both American and Japanese laws were violated. I remember particularly the Girard case, which aroused much popular excitement in Japan and benefited anti-American elements. In this case it appeared doubtful whether the offense had been committed "in the performance of official duty," in which instance the Administrative Agreement reserved primary jurisdiction to the United States. Girard, an American soldier, had shot and killed a scavenging Japanese woman in connection with a military training exercise. The judge advocate of the Fifth Air Force, which was under the command of the same general as USFJ, in coordination with us, decided in favor of leaving the primary jurisdiction to the Japanese, who imposed on Girard a much more lenient punishment than he could ever have expected in an American court-martial.

During my last two years in USFJ, my time and that of Blake and the very able Dr. Albert Feissner, secretary of the Joint United States-Japan Committee under the Administrative Agreement, was filled with never-ending conferences under Admiral Stelter on the revision of the Security Treaty and the Administrative Agreement. In our deliberations, to which Feissner made significant contributions, we discussed all aspects of the revision in detail, in order to arrive at a headquarters position to be coordinated with the embassy. We aimed at balancing the Japanese desire for a more equal partnership with the strategic and logistical needs of the American security forces. Since most of our work was classified, I refrain from elaboration. After lengthy conferences with the embassy, the United States proposal was discussed with the Japanese government. The result was the new Treaty of·Mutual Cooperation and Security signed in Washington, D.C., on January 19, 1960, together with the Status of Forces Agreement, which replaced the Administrative Agreement.

The new treaty in several respects clearly enhanced the equality of the Japanese partner. In its Article 5 it stipulated the hitherto not pledged, though presumed, obligation of the United States to defend Japan against an armed attack in the territories under her administration. No reciprocity was demanded, but "action to meet the common danger" was made dependent upon the "constitutional provisions

and processes" of each party. This terminology was obviously designed to exclude any belligerency of Japan prohibited
by Article 9 of her Constitution. Moreover, the apprehension of a great number of Japanese lest the United States
introduce nuclear weapons into their country, start a military conflict outside Japan using its bases there, and thus
embroil her in a war, was contemplated by an exchange of
notes, which became part of the treaty. It was agreed that
"major changes in the deployment into Japan of United
States armed forces, major changes in their equipment and
the use of facilities and areas in Japan as bases for military
combat operations to be undertaken other than those
conducted under Article v [for the defense of Japan against
armed attack] . . . shall be the subjects of prior consultation
with the Government of Japan." This prior consultation in
case of certain contingencies was added to the more regular
consultation of Article 4, which provided that "the Parties
will consult together from time to time regarding the implementation of this Treaty and, at the request of either Party,
whenever the security of Japan or international peace and
security in the Far East is threatened."

In another exchange of letters agreement was reached
on the establishment of a Security Consultative Committee,
replacing a similar, already functioning body, the Japanese-
American Committee on Security. As did its predecessor, it
was to consist of the minister of foreign affairs and the
director general of the defense agency, on the Japanese side,
and the American ambassador to Japan and the Commander-in-Chief, Pacific, on the United States side. A joint
United States-Japan Committee for consulting on the implementation of the Status of Forces Agreement also continued
in operation. The original treaty had given the American
Security Forces the right to take action in case of inner
disturbances in Japan. This authorization, resented as
impairing Japanese sovereignty, was omitted in the revised
document. The latter also enabled both parties to end the
treaty after ten years. The original treaty had been silent

about its expiration, so that the Japanese felt they were bound to it forever.

Although the changes appeared to be a definite improvement of the treaty from the Japanese point of view, as may be seen by comparing the texts of the original and revised documents, the revision brought about a most serious political crisis. Already in 1959 the leftist parties, supported by labor and many nonsocialist elements, had set up a powerful organization for the purpose of systematically opposing the conclusion of a new treaty. Speeches, demonstrations, and writings had a somewhat infectious effect and, amazingly enough, even otherwise moderate leading newspapers adopted an antitreaty stance.[1]

I was no longer in Tokyo when, in the spring of 1960, the riotous mass demonstrations occurred, Kishi was overthrown after his party had "rammed" the treaty through the Diet, and the planned visit of President Eisenhower had to be canceled.

How are we to explain this strong and in part violent hostility of at least a numerous, vociferous minority of the Japanese people to a continuation of the alliance with the United States? It is perhaps too much of a simplification to look at it in terms of "anti-Americanism." Many elements of Americanism, including the more vulgar ones connected with the urban amusement world, are being adopted in Japan; there is a great interest in American literature, movies, and sport; and beneath all the negativism lies a grudging admiration. What many Japanese minded—and still mind—is the continued American presence in Japan, the superior role of the United States in an unequal alliance, the American bases in Japan and on the Ryukyus—in short, the whole dependence of Japan on the United States with regard to security, international relations, and foreign trade.

[1] For an impressive report and analysis of this opposition and resulting events see George R. Packard, III, *Protest in Tokyo: The Security Treaty Crisis of 1960* (Princeton: Princeton University Press, 1966), pp. 214-216, 219, 238-245.

All this, cleverly exploited by international as well as domestic communist propaganda, gives the Japanese, who by
nature are particularly eager to enjoy respect and prestige
in the world, an understandable inferiority complex no less
frustrating in the absence of any viable and acceptable
alternatives.

Apart from this general motivation of strong opposition
to the revised treaty, many critics pointed out the potential
dangers resulting from it. There was, first of all, the fear
of involvement in a military conflict mentioned before; it
was also argued that the mere conclusion of a new treaty
with the United States would alienate Japan's socialist
neighbors, the Soviet Union and Red China, at a time when
the cold war was still icy. Those who stressed this point saw
the decisive difference between the original and the revised
treaties as the fact that the original was more or less imposed upon Japan, since it was closely tied up with the
desired peace treaty, while the new treaty was to be entered
by a sovereign government. Those who objected to it were
against any close partnership with the United States. Far
from appreciating the protection the treaty was designed to
provide for Japan, they were convinced that such partnership with a superpower involved tremendous risks to their
country's security. Frequently, even the requirement for
consultation was regarded as increasing rather than diminishing such risk. It was argued that the consultation of the
Japanese government was meaningless unless combined with
a veto power or, in other words, unless mutual agreement
was provided for; and that a potential enemy, because of
the preceding consultation, would identify Japan with the
United States in any case, regardless of whether or not the
Japanese government had raised objections to the planned
action. Behind this whole opposition lay a great deal of
genuine pacifism, combined with unrealistic longings for
neutrality and a certain portion of national pride and even
racism. Although, because of the levelheaded leadership of
Prime Minister Ikeda Hayato and the economic recovery,

the excitement, generally limited to the urban population, subsided after the revised Security Treaty with the Status of Forces Agreement came into force, one must not lose sight of these deep-seated attitudes in any evaluation of the complex Japanese-American relations, which nevertheless have proved essentially stable.

KOREAN PROBLEMS

The principal United States mission with regard to Korea was the development and supervision of an integrated program of economic aid as a basis for relief, rehabilitation, and stabilization. This responsibility was in the hands of the economic coordinator, who had his residence in Seoul. My own activity was rather connected with the political element, vaguely defined as "to create conditions favorable to the success of the military mission." I had to observe and analyze what was going on within South Korea, the constitutional developments, governmental policies, party politics, and opposition movements. With Syngman Rhee presiding over that nation, this was an exciting preoccupation. There is general agreement that he was an indomitable pioneer of Korea's independence and an irreconcilable enemy of communism as well as of Japan. He belongs among those rare historical figures whose seemingly chimeric dreams came true—at least half true.

Neither of the great powers had cared much about the independence of the "Kingdom of the Morning Calm." When, after her war with Russia in 1904–1905, Japan made Korea a protectorate, and five years later annexed it, there was no attempt to interfere. Nobody in the foreign offices took seriously the odd little fellow who with fanatical zeal urged support for the liberation of his country from foreign rule. It was only when, during the war with Japan, the Allied statesmen who met in Cairo in November 1943, established the principle that a defeated Japan must give up the possessions that she had acquired by force, that Rhee could see the silver lining. Even then the independence of Korea was visualized only "in due course." Out of the American and Russian occupation zones, divided by the 38th parallel, developed two antagonistic Koreas after the United Nations' reunification attempts had failed. The southern Republic of Korea (ROK) was "our baby," the northern "Democratic People's Republic," that of the Soviets. Syngman Rhee did not see things as did the cautious Truman government, which always remained aware of the danger of a third world war. He hated the idea of limited war, a feeling he shared with MacArthur, and aimed at reunification of the two halves of Korea, by force if necessary. We would have liked a regime in the ROK that bore no resemblance to its communist brother beyond the 38th parallel, and in which the citizen enjoyed certain rights. Unfortunately, this was the American rather than Rhee's dream. To our disappointment, we watched him apply the same dictatorial and authoritarian methods as did his northern antipode Kim Il Sung. It is the dilemma that repeated itself in South Vietnam. The liberal doubts the wisdom of supporting an anticommunist regime that is as bad as its communist enemy, while the rulers of that regime are convinced that not only are its people not yet ripe for our advanced form of democracy, but also that individual freedoms cannot be allowed in view of the threat under which their nation lives. In light of the prevailing danger, any opposition is considered as communist, or at least as giving aid and comfort to the enemy. As long as the cold war was icy, of course, as long as we looked at communism as a monolithic power determined to destroy us and our way of life, the policy of aiding any nation that fights or is assailed by a communist state inevitably overrode the embarrassing irritation about its system of government.

Although the ROK had, under American influence, adopted a democratic Constitution with safeguards for civil rights, President Syngman Rhee ruthlessly oppressed his political opponents. In my reports, which were used for informing Washington, I had continuously to tell stories of his high-handed and obnoxious machinations. According to the Constitution, the president was to be elected by the unicameral legislature, the National Assembly. In spite of his charisma as the outstanding freedom fighter of the nation, his police-state methods and an increasing corruption in his government had made him so unpopular with the more liberal representatives of the assembly that he became truly anxious lest it would not reelect him in 1952. He therefore conceived the idea of having the Constitution amended to provide for the popular election of the president, and had those members arrested who opposed this plan. He was reelected twice, in 1952 and in 1956, but apparently things got worse. In his very old age he did not mellow; the traits that had characterized his regime—authoritarianism, corruption, and inefficiency—reached such a high degree that he lost his popularity. In 1960 he was accused of having rigged his third reelection, and he fell victim to student riots, which he had tried to repress with utmost police brutality. The United States, having lost patience with his methods, had expressed disapproval, and that may have convinced him that he had to resign. A tragic end in exile without the hopes and fervor of his young years followed. He was an excellent example of the type of leader who cannot withdraw in time from the theater of history.

I distinguish the rebel who strove for independence from the ruler who achieved it and then led his people only from one unfree condition to another. For the United Nations Command, Rhee was a hard and troublesome man to deal with, and that was true because of his undemocratic attitude not only in domestic affairs, but also in international and military fields. Even General Ridgway, who had a great admiration for Rhee's patriotism, criticized his insistence that there was a tremendous pool of Korean manpower that could be fighting for us if only we would give them arms. Ridgway's comment on this was that we knew only too well how many hundreds of thousands of dollars worth of equipment had been abandoned in flight by certain units of the ROK army during every Chinese offensive. As a matter of course, our negotiations of the armistice met with great difficulty from this man, who could not reconcile himself with the status quo, but aimed at reunification under his rule. I can, from my own observation, only confirm Ridgway's concluding characterization that "in the course of the negotiations, and before they began, his [Rhee's] intransigence, and the lusty, sometimes self-serving cries of his supporters in the United States put many thorns in our path . . . and prompted many of us privately to wish him far, far away."[2]

President Truman and his secretary of state, Dean Acheson, would have suffered even stronger vilification had they proposed the armistice on which the warring parties at long last agreed. It seems to me that in this atmosphere of incrimination, only a war hero of the prestige of General Eisenhower could have ended the Korean War on a status quo basis, just as only a De Gaulle could liquidate the Algerian conflict.

On May 1, 1952, a group of J–5 men, among them Williams and me, made an information trip to Korea. Our first stop was Pusan, the harbor town at the Southern tip of the peninsula, where our Korean Military Advisory Group (KMAG) gave us a thorough briefing. That unit was headed by another General Caraway, the brother of Paul Caraway, subsequently my chief of staff in USFJ—apparently as tough as his brother, but also as efficient. Interestingly enough, both parents of these two prominent soldiers were United States Senators from the state of Alabama.

Before the Korean armistice, Swedish and Swiss representatives, mostly officers, arrived in Tokyo on their way to Korea as members of what was to function as the noncommunist element of the Armistice Commission. A delay in the

2 See Matthew B. Ridgway, *The Korean War* (New York: Doubleday, 1967), p. 156.

conclusion of the armistice prolonged the stay of this group, and this led to the idea of keeping them entertained and offering them some information. They were invited to listen to lectures by members of our headquarters. After the first one, the attendants confessed that they had great difficulty in understanding the "American English" and asked whether they could not have lectures in German. As a matter of course, this question resulted in my lecturing to them in German on subjects such as the South Korean Constitution. Strangely enough, although this is my mother language, I found it much more difficult to lecture in it than in English, which by then I was accustomed to use in the area of my work.

RYUKYU ISLANDS

Our administration of the Ryukyu Islands involved us in many troublesome problems. First of all, there was the ambiguous international status of this territory. The peace treaty did not take it away from Japan, as it did in the case of Korea and Formosa, but left the United States an option either to propose a United Nations trusteeship under American administration, or to exercise itself, without connection to the United Nations, powers of "legislation, administration, and jurisdiction." The United States refrained from requesting the trusteeship, and Japan was quick to realize that a prospect existed for the eventual return to her of the islands. This hope was strongly encouraged by official statements of American government leaders, who explicitly recognized Japan's "residual sovereignty" over the Ryukyus, though emphasizing that as long as the tensions in the Far East continued, sovereignty must actually be exercised by the United States. The expression "residual sovereignty," first used by John Foster Dulles, means something like dormant sovereignty. While it implies an obligation to return governmental power to the dormant sovereign, the timing of such return was obviously left to the exercizer. After the

United States had transformed Okinawa, the main island, into a huge military base, the American Security Forces were eager to delay the return to Japan as long as possible, since they considered it imperative to remain the unrestricted masters over a territory so dangerously close to a potential enemy, Red China. Upon return, this mastery would be affected by the limitations of the Security Treaty and of the Administrative Agreement with Japan.

Moreover, although as a result of the base economy and the use of indigenous labor the Okinawans benefited materially from the American presence, they did not like it. The less they liked us, the greater grew their love for the Japanese, who before had looked down at them as a kind of poor country cousins, and they longed to be reunited with Japan. That produced the reversion movement. It was eagerly paralleled in the motherland, where the return of the islands became a hot political issue, cleverly exploited by the leftist parties. It developed there perhaps even more strongly than on Okinawa, since success or failure meant prestige or losing face in the international world. The early return of the militarily less significant Amami Islands in the north of the chain only increased Japan's appetite for a follow-up in the southern ones.

The reasons for our unpopularity with the inhabitants were manifold. To build our formidable defense installations, we had to requisition the land of the farmers, which was mostly all they owned, and other real property. Approximately fifty thousand landowners were affected. I was deeply involved in the long—much too long—determination of the proper legal method for such requisition and of the manner of compensation for those deprived of the use of their property. This would have been an excellent opportunity to show generosity from the beginning. Instead, it took Washington too long to abandon its budgetary approach to a problem that was political dynamite. Neither the governor in Tokyo, who was interposed in the chain of command between the deputy governor on the spot and the

Department of the Army, nor the deputy governor overlooked the importance of this issue. Although determination was finally made after the recommendation by the "Price Committee," the resentment had, so to speak, become chronic. Whether any form of compensation would have satisfied the owners, remains doubtful. What they really wanted, namely, their land back, was unattainable for the time being. The mere retention of the legal title to their property and payment of rent could not satisfy them.

Another reason for complaint was the slow pace with which the United States, that advocate of a democratic system of government, allowed the islanders to establish a form of self-government according to their wishes. To begin with, the deputy governor exercised a military dictatorship over the indigenous government of the Ryukyu Islands (GRI), with power to veto any law of the unicameral assembly. He also appointed the chief executive. The American reluctance to grant more independence than the election of municipal officials can easily be understood in light of the increasingly leftist orientation on the Okinawan political scene. This became obvious when the leader of the Okinawan People's party, Senaga, was elected mayor of Naha, the capital of Okinawa and the seat of our administration. That party represented the extreme left, and was being suspected of having close ties to the Japan Communist party. To say that this event, happening in America's advanced bulwark against communism, was embarrassing to our administration, would be quite an understatement. For many years the United States resisted pressure from the GRI as well as from Japan to permit the election of the chief executive, until it finally yielded to it. It was introduced after my time by presidential executive order as late as 1968, with the result that the candidate of the three leftist parties, Yara Chobyo, won the first election. In his campaign he had advocated "immediate, all-out, unconditional reversion" to Japan.

I was no longer in Japan when anti-American sentiment

was stirred up by the alleged storage on the Ryukyu Islands of nuclear weapons, and the take off of our B 52 bombers for Vietnam.

Whether and to what extent a political climate more favorable to the United States could have been achieved remains an open question. I do not think that the American administration on the spot can be blamed. Some of the deputy governors were efficient officers who tried hard to balance their military mission with a genuine concern for the indigenous people. Others lacked the necessary finesse in dealing with them, and were not sufficiently guided by the expert advice they received from USCAR. In my time the latter was also headed by a general officer, but otherwise consisted predominantly of civilians. Generally speaking, they were competent in their special work and dedicated to their mission of improving United States relations to the islanders. I may mention as men with whom I had close and satisfactory contacts on my five visits to Okinawa Richard Davies, the chief of the Government and Legal Department, and his young and promising associate, Freymouth. I also think that Westenberger, chief of the Public Works Department, subsequently in the Department of the Army, did an outstanding job. Two of my former chiefs, Gillies and Shirven, joined the USCAR organization later as deputy administrators. Both were first-class men and sensitive with regard to the treatment of an alien population.

For the promotion of a more satisfactory situation it would have been better to make at least the civil administrator, who headed USCAR under the deputy governor, a civilian earlier than it was finally done—after my time. Another possibility would have been to separate the governmental tasks of the deputy governor organizationally from those of the top military man on the spot and to make him a civilian. The official justification for insisting on the status quo was, however, that the military chief, if he was to fulfill his overall mission, must have the final decision also in matters concerning the GRI and its people. I felt during my activity on Okinawa that the intermediate jurisdiction of the CINCFE-governor, while probably unavoidable to keep him posted on all Far East affairs, was substantially of little value for the policy makers in the Pentagon. In the spirit of traditional comradeship, military superiors, when reporting to higher authority, hate to let their subordinates down. This habit has considerable merit when, as in the case of the governor, the headquarters of the intermediate organization is located far from the site of action. Nevertheless, the assumption that the man on the spot knows best is not an infallible axiom. Sometimes his view is narrowed down precisely because he is too near the events. Doubtlessly, the Civil Affairs Division in the Department of the Army must have found it difficult not to accept the recommendations of the deputy governor when they were supported in Tokyo. The three jurisdictions were eventually cut to two in 1957 with the expiration of CINCFE and his governorship, when the office of high commissioner was created; the high commissioner resided on Okinawa and reported directly to Washington.

In my more skeptical moods I am inclined to think that even if the generals who ruled the place had been angels of consideration and tolerance, not much would have been changed. The reason for this seems evident. We were there against the will of the people, military conquerors, not only foreigners but men and women of a different race, whose faces, clothing, and behavior were utterly strange to them, and whose immensely higher standards of living aroused their envy. As long as Japan, their motherland, was under military occupation, the corresponding situation on the Ryukyus was suffered as an unavoidable consequence of the lost war. When Japan became independent after the peace treaty, however, and foreign rule continued on Okinawa, the islanders did not easily comprehend the reason for the different treatment. Most of them were not impressed by the argument that American rule, as well as the presence of our forces with all their tremendous technological apparatus, were needed for their own protection from a communist, especially Chinese, attack. They apparently were rather afraid lest the threat was enhanced by that presence. Nor would it be realistic to have expected much gratitude for the manifold benefits they enjoyed economically and culturally as a result of American know-how, economic assistance, and promotion of education. Their ardent racial nationalism prevented the emergence of gratitude, a sentiment usually rare in the political realm.

When General Lemnitzer was governor, he received a note from an American newspaper correspondent. The latter wrote that he had recently had a conversation with a foreigner who characterized our administration of the Ryukyus as "colonial." He asked the general for his reaction to this criticism. I had to draft the answer which, of course, had to be a refutation. But I found it extremely difficult to present convincing reasons for the denial. What I finally proposed as an aswer did not fully convince myself. I pointed out that colonialism is essentially the exploitation of people of an alien nation or territory for one's own sake. On the Ryukyus, I argued, our presence and rule served the interest of the islanders; it was to protect them from possible attack and greatly benefited their well-being. Does that not sound much like the ominous "white man's burden"? The truth is that we were there and exercised power within the framework of our Far East defense policy, in other words, primarily in what we considered to be our own national interest. Our contribution to the welfare of the inhabitants was a mere concomitant of our power of government, which implied certain responsibilities to them and was not at all irreconcilable with a colonial regime. I have tried to show that the overwhelming majority of the people, with the exception of the few who earned large profits from our base economy, rejected United States exercise of sovereignty over them. Hence, I am afraid that this alien rule, unwanted by the natives, could well be labeled colonialism. I therefore wholeheartedly welcome the return of the islands to the administration of Japan. There will still be many Okinawan problems, as long as our military bases and personnel remain on the islands. For instance, the ghosts of Hiroshima and Nagasaki are still much alive, and we shall have to reckon for a long time with the fear of nuclear weapons that the Okinawans suspect to be stored on their island.

FAREWELL TO JAPAN

In 1959, at sixty-six years of age, I began seriously to plan for whatever Providence was willing to grant me of additional years of life. In the States the only possible position I might have been able to obtain would have been in the Department of the Army at the Pentagon. Having experienced before what it means to be a civil servant in Washington, I was not too eager for a repetition. I also discarded all illusions that at my age I could start an academic career and concluded, therefore, that the alternative for me was either to continue in my position in Japan until I reached the retirement age of seventy or to retire then. To stay in Japan would have been the easier choice psychologically, as postponement of important changes often is. I would continue work familiar to me in association with pleasant people. Financially, too, I would be better off, since my salary was relatively high, but the pension I had to expect was less than modest after only fifteen years of service in the government. Nevertheless, I decided in favor of retirement. First of all, I felt that if I did not want to spend the rest of my life in Japan, it was time to return to the States. After all, America was the country to which I had immigrated, and as much as I was attached to the Japanese land and people, I would not have liked to live for ever in a country the language of which I did not master. Once I was no longer part of the United States forces, this linguistic difficulty, which it was too late to overcome, would be felt as a great handicap. After having been involved for such a long time in Asian affairs, I had a strong desire to readjust myself to life in my adoptive country; but I also knew that this readjustment would grow more and more difficult with every passing year. Charlotte fully appreciated my reasons for quitting, although emotionally she, with her longing for stability, dreaded the change with all its uncertainty and the necessity of wandering again, as we had to do so many times in our married life.

Admiral Stelter was the first of my superiors whom I informed of my intention to retire. He tried to talk me out of it, but when he realized that I was determined, he expressed his regret in warm terms, and then asked me to postpone my departure at least until the new Security Treaty was completed in draft, since he did not want to miss my contribution to it. This I promised. Therefore I continued some six more months, until the beginning of November.

It was a tearful farewell for us, made harder by the honors and celebrations connected with it. In a ceremony in which Charlotte was present, the commander, Lieutenant General Burns, bestowed on me the Award for Meritorious Civil Service, the same decoration that I had received before from General MacArthur. The citation, among other commendations, credits me with having "greatly enhanced the United States Government position in Japan with the Japanese Government" and terms as "especially valuable" my "participation in high level consultations on the subject of revision of the Security Treaty and the Administrative Agreement between the two Governments."

In the office business had to be finished; at home there was the dissolution of the household, the packing and loading; and, in addition, one farewell party for us followed another. Of the numerous parties given by Japanese I will mention only two. The Supreme Court invited me to a solemn farewell lunch in the Court's official building. Not only all justices of the Supreme Court, but also judges of lower courts, including several from outside Tokyo, participated in the affair. Chief Justice Tanaka handed me a silver cigarette box with a carved inscription in the name of the Court, and read a letter of appreciation. The second party deserving mention was given by the Ministry of Justice. The guests included many officials of that office, as well as procurators with whom I had had official contacts during the Occupation. Speeches were exchanged, and one of the procurators teased me in pointing out that under my guidance the new Code of Criminal Procedure had introduced so many safeguards for the criminal offender that it was virtually impossible to obtain a conviction. Does that not sound familiar? I enjoyed this joke because I knew that when the Japanese make fun of you, they are truly fond of you. The headquarters threw, of course, a big party for Charlotte and me. Poems were exchanged, and a very fine one from the absent Feissner was read.

A friend of ours, who was an official of the British embassy, Mr. Westlake, had the kindness of arranging a big reception at that embassy in our honor. The invited guests were chosen from a list I had provided, which consisted of my Japanese as well as American friends, including a number of members of the American embassy. Finally, I greatly appreciated an especially fine gesture of Admiral Stelter. On one of our last Tokyo days he invited us for dinner, and the other guests were two couples, namely our commander, General Burns, and our chief of staff, General Hendrix, with their wives. Such military splendor of seven stars was the finale of this very unmilitary civilian's career under the generals.

When, on November 3rd, we entered the army transport ship that was to take us home, a group of Charlotte's Japanese women were standing on the pier and tearfully cried: "Good bye, Mrs. Oppler!" My own unit was represented by my dear J-5 colleague, Lt. Colonel Robert Prescott, who with his lovely wife had brought us to the harbor of Yokohama.

CHAPTER TWENTY-SIX

Concluding Evaluation

To sum up, I am inclined to believe that three reasons contributed to the success of the legal and judicial reforms:

1. Most of the pertinent legislation was enacted during the period in which the democratization policy prevailed in the Occupation, and the Japanese, under the impact of defeat and surrender, were especially open to suggestions for change.

2. The Courts and Law Division, which enjoyed a considerable freedom of action, was composed of trained American lawyers and myself, with my German judicial background, as well as Blakemore who, apart from being an American lawyer, understood the Japanese language and jurisprudence. This very composition helped to avoid the danger of excessive Americanization of the Japanese legal system. Our moderation had the effect that, while important innovations based on American practice were adopted, the character of the system was essentially preserved.

3. We made the greatest effort not to order our Japanese counterparts around, but to work with them on an equal level. Free discussion, persuasion, and compromise rather than fiat brought about agreements.

As for the staying power of the Occupation reforms, it may be said that those who expected the Japanese to turn the clock back as soon as they resumed their independence were utterly wrong. Although Japanese society cannot and never will be a replica of America, but will always adapt revolutionary innovations to traditional ways—something that nation excels in—the situation is a far cry from *plus ça change*. . . . To be sure, the desire to undo occupation reforms has existed among certain circles and within the conservative governments; in a few instances it has resulted in the correction of "occupation excesses." The trauma of defeat and destruction has, however, produced an amazingly resilient pacifism and effectively reduced, if not eliminated, the influence of the military on the government. The ideological impact of the Occupation has brought about the determination by the bulk of the people to preserve their newly won liberties. In few countries of the world does there exist a similar exercise of the freedoms of expression and of the press. Women make increasing use of their right of equality and independence now anchored in the Constitution, and citizens resolutely challenge laws and administrative acts in the courts.

The Liberal Democrats, not all of whom are reactionaries, have been plagued by factionalism. Facing inner dissension, preoccupied with economic recovery, and more recently suffering from inflation and the oil crisis, the governments may have considered it wise not to increase their problems by arousing the masses in the political and constitutional fields. Thus, since the Kishi era ended in 1960, they have shown a rather "low posture." The opposition's insistence on the maintenance of the status quo has hitherto prevented any amendment of the MacArthur Constitution, because it would require a two-thirds majority in the Diet, which the revisionists do not have. But the implementing legal and judicial reforms also remained virtually unchanged, although they could have been abolished or revised by a simple majority of the legislature. It is perhaps in the nature of fundamental human rights that once enjoyed for some period of time, they form a new tradition that can be destroyed only by extreme violence. Special interest groups for their defense become entrenched.

I refrain from further comment on post-Occupation political trends, insofar as they pertain to the legislative and executive branches of the Japanese government. I feel, however, that in light of the emphasis in this book on the judiciary, some evaluation of its overall performance will be expected of the author, however impressionistic it may be under the circumstances. The reader will certainly raise questions like the following: how do the courts, and particularly the Supreme Court, live up to their new responsibilities? Are they now a truly independent third branch of the government, and do they fulfill their mission as custodians of the Constitution? I approach these questions hesitantly and with great humility, deeply conscious that any evaluation of judicial performance depends much upon the philosophy of the critic. How different the answers will be becomes evident if we contemplate our own judiciary, for instance, the Warren and Burger Supreme Courts. Thus, the view I shall offer might be looked upon as the reaction of one personally involved in the reforms who had entertained high, and possibly exaggerated, hopes for an exercise of judicial review in the direction of a vigorous protection of fundamental human rights. I find it, however, reassuring that where I am critical my doubts are often similar to those raised by outstanding Japanese judges and scholars. What I can say must necessarily be incomplete and cannot cover more recent court decisions.

It may be presumptuous to attempt a judgment on the basis of a limited selection of cases, but in the sphere of constitutional review, with which we are mainly concerned, the decisions discussed represent, indeed, the most important findings of the Supreme Court of Japan up to a certain time, and I have been fortunate enough to have complete or partial translations into English available, thanks especially to the repeatedly cited book of John M. Maki, *Court and Constitution in Japan*, and *Law in Japan*, edited by Arthur Taylor von Mehren, as well as the publication by the General Secretariat of the Supreme Court, entitled *Series of Prominent Judgments of the Supreme Court upon Question of Constitutionality.*

There is no doubt but that the judiciary has achieved full organizational and functional independence, and has held its ground against the few attempts at interference from the other two branches. The courts have freely examined the constitutionality of statutes and administrative dispositions, and judicial review has been established firmly in Japan as a governmental function with which the legislature and the executive have to reckon. The mere availability to the citizen of challenge serves to some extent as a check upon governmental actions.

While the majority opinions of the Supreme Court are, in general, terse and strictly limited to the basic reason behind the decision, the lengthy supplementary and dissenting opinions of which the justices make abundant use show a high degree of erudition, profundity, and sophistication. Occasionally, the writers do not seem to master the art of expressing complex legal ideas in simple and clear language, but this impression may result from the immense difficulty of translation. The blend of an Anglo-Saxon type of case law with the analytical Continental approach, which was anticipated by some authors for the post-Occupation period, has not yet been achieved. In my view the analytical interpretation of statutes still prevails, although precedents unavoidably play an increasing role. Repeatedly, the grand bench of the Supreme Court overrides its own decisions, and even more often those of the petty benches. This may well create an undesirable legal uncertainty, and particularly throw doubt on the authority of the petty bench, if it is forced into the position of a lower instance instead of representing the highest tribunal. The frequent deviation from precedents can, of course, be explained by the novelty of judicial review as well as by the constant alteration in the membership of the Court due to the preference for elderly men.

As most decisions available in English translation show,

the Supreme Court of the fifties and part of the sixties was
strongly divided into a highly liberal and an outspokenly
conservative group, with a third intermediate one, a trait
it had in common with the present United States Supreme
Court. Since the majority in most cases consisted of the
conservatives, joined by some of the middle group, the
progressive justices were, as a rule, the dissenters. Justice
Mano, who during the Supreme Court Mission claimed to
be the Oliver Wendell Holmes of Japan, has to share this
glory, at any rate, with Justice Fujita. These two, who
contributed much to judicial thinking in the country and,
as may be hoped, will go into history as pioneers of future
judge-made law, were very different in temperament and
manner of expression: Mano somewhat hot-tempered and
brusque, Fujita sober and polite. Fujita's dissents in the
cases of the mass demonstration ordinances have already
become classics, with their sweeping criticism of the majority's stereotyped use of the public welfare test in the
restriction of the freedom of expression.[1] Mano's sharp pen
did not spare even Chief Justice Tanaka, whose enthusiasm
for natural law he derided in the Local Autonomy Case
with the following remark: "Unless one has the self-confidence, the logical prowess and the courage not only to
believe in natural law but also to affirm unequivocally that
any provision of the Constitution which is contrary to
natural law is void, then it is obvious that all legal problems . . . must be traced back to the Japanese Constitution
and examined as springing from there."[2] Repeatedly Mano
characterizes opinions of his brethren as "absurd," and in
the first Patricide Case his enlightened dissent declared the
majority opinion to be "complete nonsense."[3] This lack of
politeness is striking in a Japanese. The substance of Mano's
opinions shows, however, a broad historical and philo-

[1] See, for example, Von Mehren, *Law in Japan*, p. 234, note 95.
[2] The decision of January 16, 1953 is translated in Maki, *Court and
Constitution in Japan*, pp. 384ff.; see particularly p. 399.
[3] *Ibid.*, p. 138.

sophical perception. As only one example, I may refer to the *Lady Chatterley's Lover* Case, in which he cites Judge Learned Hand in disagreement with the majority's over-emphasis upon the animal element of sex, and in which he opposes its view that obscenity may exist even though the book as a whole has high artistic value.[4]

Still, what counts for the record is the performance of the majority. If any generalization is proper, it may be said that the Supreme Court of Japan has demonstrated self-restraint and caution. It has not developed anything like judicial supremacy or "overreach." From the very beginning, it has refused to act as a constitutional court, although the wording of the Constitution left this possibility open, and has maintained its character as a so-called judicial court that exercises judicial review only within the limits necessary for the judgment of a concrete legal dispute between the parties. This rule, corresponding to American practice, was first established unanimously on October 8, 1952, when the Socialist leader, Suzuki Mosaburo, requested the Supreme Court to declare the Police Reserve to be in violation of Article 9 of the Constitution.[5] The Suzuki decision was affirmed on April 15, 1953, when a member of the political opposition challenged the constitutionality of the August 28, 1952 dissolution of the House of Representatives by Premier Yoshida.[6] Consequently both decisions did not reach the substance of those explosive controversies, but Justice Mano volunteered an interesting supplementary opinion on the dissolution problem. Perhaps the Court would not have entered into the constitutional questions even in a concrete dispute between parties, but might have held that the two cases involved political issues, deciding which was *ultra vires* for the judiciary.

In the Sunakawa case we find this self-restraint in connection with the constitutionality of the Security Treaty, which the appellants also claimed to be in conflict with the

[4] *Ibid.*, pp. 18 and 19.   [5] *Ibid.*, pp. 362ff.
[6] *Ibid.*, pp. 366ff.

war renunciation clause.[7] Here the Court stated in its verdict of December 16, 1959, that because of the "highly political nature" of the treaty, the legal determination of constitutionality is, as a matter of principle, "not adaptable to review by a judicial court, which has as its mission a purely judicial function; accordingly, it falls outside the right of judicial review by the courts, unless there is clearly obvious unconstitutionality or invalidity." Justice Kotani justifiably criticizes the illogical exception the majority allows in case of obvious unconstitutionality. He calls it "a self-consoling excuse" for their basic position.

In this Sunakawa case the self-restraint was probably motivated by and is coupled with a certain pragmatic realism, which, under the circumstances, appears to be reasonable. One might have preferred an unambiguous determination that the Security Treaty did not violate Article 9 instead of the view that no clear and obvious unconstitutionality existed. Nevertheless, what I mean by reasonable pragmatism is the reluctance of the Court to interfere with historical faits accomplis, because such interference might have incalculable consequences. The same attitude may have prevented the Court from any attempt to undo the revolutionary reforms of the Occupation. A pertinent example is the Land Reform decision of December 23, 1953,[8] which dealt with the precarious question of whether the expropriated landowners had received "just compensation" for their property, as Article 29 of the Constitution requires. The majority held that they had, with four justices dissenting for fairly convincing legal reasons. But this was a situation in which the majority must have felt that considerations beyond purely legal interpretation were appropriate.

Judicial review is, after all, a balancing between the demands of governmental authority (or law and order), on the one hand, and the rights and freedoms of the individual, on the other. It is one of the most intricate and

7 *Ibid.*, pp. 298ff.   8 *Ibid.*, pp. 228ff.

sometimes agonizing responsibilities with which Japan's judiciary is saddled by the new charter. If we keep in mind the Japanese traditional disapproval of individualism as signifying selfishness, it is perhaps understandable that the Supreme Court, composed as it is of men of the older generation, appears to give preference to authority or the collective interest as against individual rights. In the majority opinions we find again and again the same pattern: the Court gives solemn recognition to the importance of the specific constitutional freedom at issue, only to continue that it is, however, limited by considerations of public welfare. In using this test as the counterbalancing weight on the scale, the Court is backed by Article 12 of the Constitution, which admonishes the people to refrain from any abuse of their freedoms and rights and to use them for the public welfare; and by Article 13, which requires those rights to demand supreme consideration in legislation and in other governmental affairs, *"to the extent that it does not interfere with the public welfare."* While the drafters of the Constitution, because of the scarcity of references to the duties of the people, were bound to set up some limitation on their rights, the choice of the public welfare standard, in light of its somewhat vague nature, might not have been fortunate. Anyway, it led to its use by the Court as a "panacea for curing the alleged unconstitutionality of the law," as Professor Ito Masami expressed it.[9] The danger exists, indeed, that a Court rigidly oriented toward law and order could under this test weaken or even emasculate the guarantee of civil liberties of the people, who then would be no better off than under the Meiji Constitution when their rights were subject to statutory impairment. Public welfare can easily be identified with common opinion or morality, an interpretation which, in the area of the First Amendment rights, would call for conformity and render unorthodox views illegal. It is for this reason that many Japanese critics of the Supreme Court prefer the clear and

[9] Von Mehren, *Law in Japan*, p. 229.

present danger test in its original Holmes version. The district courts have used it frequently, for instance in the mass demonstration cases and in acquitting persons charged with violation of the Subversive Activities Prevention Law,[10] to which I raised serious objection before its enactment.

There is no doubt but that the majority opinions reflect a strong determination to uphold the constitutionality of legislative and administrative acts by applying the public welfare test. Since the Court most often dealt with borderline cases, many American jurists will regard the underlying assumption of constitutionality as basically sound. I would, however, be less than sincere if I should hide my disappointment that in Japan, at a time when government of law was due to evolve, the majority in the Supreme Court stuck tenaciously to this assumption and did not follow the dissenters, who in doubtful cases advocated a more vigorous protection of individual rights. I do not have in mind so much the reluctance to declare legislative enactments unconstitutional, which in my view would have been proper, for instance, in connection with the prior restraint in the local ordinances concerning mass demonstrations. Mostly, the delicate question must be resolved whether a penal or otherwise restrictive law is applicable to a specific action, the performance of which the actor claims is his constitutional right. Not that I always disagree with the final results reached by the Court, but I consider the criticism of Professors Ito and Hashimoto Kiminobu, who repeatedly take exception to the balancing method of the majority, as in general well founded.[11] For instance, in the case of the abetment of a slowdown among the police, the Court observes that "such abetment does not constitute a crime in situations in which there is absolutely no danger that such slowdown activity will take place," but then declares that "the actions of the accused cannot be said to be necessarily without such danger" because of the threatening language

[10] *Ibid.*, p. 231.
[11] *Ibid.*, pp. 205ff. and 239ff.

used by the accused.[12] Justice Kuriyama, in his supplementary opinion, holds that the majority reached its conclusion that there was danger of positive harm to society on "highly ambiguous grounds." Nevertheless, he agrees with the otherwise unanimous decision of the majority. This and the absence of any dissenting opinion may be explained by what Kuriyama calls "the objective circumstances in all their aspects," including the fact that the defendant was an active member of the Communist party. If we remember that the incitement happened during the Korean conflict, when communist propaganda under foreign influences was at its height, the apprehension lest it might have penetrated the police, and therefore that the incitement might represent an actual danger, was perhaps not unreasonable. The error consists, in my view, rather in the principle—also evident in other decisions—that no crime exists only when there is absolutely no danger. In the use of freedom of expression, and particularly in instances of incitement, as well as of mass demonstrations, there exists most often some danger, but that must not be a ground for banning or improperly restricting such freedom. If it is to be truly guaranteed, speeches, writings, and assemblies need particular protection when they are disliked or even repugnant. Thus any *possible* danger in permitting them is not sufficient reason for prohibiting them, and this leads us back to the clear and present danger test.

The striking phenomenon is that in many cases the district courts as the trial courts, especially in Tokyo, have given greater weight to constitutional protection of the individual than has the Supreme Court. Admittedly, in their nonconformist posture they have frequently gone to the other extreme, as in the Sunakawa Case, when the Tokyo District Court declared the stationing of United States Security Forces in Japan unconstitutional, or when the Sapporo District Court decided that Japan was not allowed

[12] This decision of a petty bench, dated August 2, 1951, is translated in Maki, *Court and Constitution in Japan*, pp. 123ff.

under Article 9 to maintain her Self-Defense Forces.[13] Still, I find something refreshing in the unorthodox tendency of these younger judges, and it may also be promising. I have already, more than twenty years ago, publicly commended a district court for its courageous decision, which declared the patricide provision in the Criminal Code to be unconstitutional.[14] The Supreme Court reversed that decision, but more recently, on April 3, 1973, also invalidated the controversial inequality. Whether they did so on the same grounds as did the district court remains to be seen, pending the availability of an English translation.

In the Kyoto Students Case it would be unfair to criticize the Supreme Court for relying on the discretion of the university president, who imposed the disciplinary punishment of expulsion on the students; but although Hashimoto felt that the Kyoto District Court attached too much importance to the students' interests in the balancing process when declaring the expulsion excessive and illegal,[15] its decision is not only more merciful than those of the two higher instances, but can also be defended legally. To punish the students for a single offense of juvenile rowdyism with the severest possible penalty, and thus endanger or damage their whole future academic advancement may very well be regarded as an excess or abuse of the disciplinary power.

A divergence of views also existed in another disciplinary case, likewise discussed by Hashimoto.[16] A policeman was charged with illicit relations with the wife of a friend, as well as with lending money to him, a gambler, and was punished with dismissal. The Osaka District Court did not rely on the findings of the local Police Hearing Commission but independently took evidence, and arrived at the conclusion that there was not sufficient evidence that the plaintiff had committed an act unbecoming a police official.

[13] See above, p. 209, n. 2.
[14] See my article in *Contemporary Japan*, p. 39.
[15] See von Mehren, *Law in Japan*, p. 247.
[16] *Ibid.*, pp. 247–250.

The high court affirmed this decision, but the Supreme Court reversed it, holding that the dismissal cannot be called an illegal disposition in excess of the scope of the discretionary power of the person of authority. Hashimoto, emphasizing the reserved position that caused the Court to refrain from interference with the administrative action, labels the reasonableness of this decision as "problematic" in light of the facts established in the first instance.

Judicial self-restraint was used amply in the passport cases, in which the freedom to move to a foreign country, guaranteed in Article 22 of the Constitution, and its limitation by the Passport Law were involved. According to this law, the minister of foreign affairs may refuse a passport when he finds that there is danger that the applicant will perform acts that "injure markedly and directly the interests or public safety of Japan." In all three cases covered by Hashimoto,[17] the plaintiffs wanted to travel to communist countries, but were refused passports on the basis of that provision. In the Hoashi case decided by the Supreme Court in September 1958, the Tokyo District Court as well as the Tokyo High Court and the Supreme Court were in agreement that the minister's refusal was not illegal. Underlying this conclusion was the recognition, more explicit in the 1952 decision of the district court in the Matsumoto Case, that since issuing passports is connected with foreign policy, the responsibility of the Foreign Office, a court "must be extremely cautious about overturning the decision of the Minister." Such a position comes close to judicial abstention in political matters. The attitude that the administrative agency whose disposition is challenged knows best virtually amounts to an abdication of judicial review in this sphere, regardless of the merit of the decisions in the specific cases. Our Watergate scandal has taught us what may happen when the highest executive officials arrogate the exclusive right to determine when the "national security," a similarly vague term, is threatened.

[17] *Ibid.*, pp. 250–255.

Nevertheless, the caution of the Supreme Court should not be interpreted as lack of courage or exaggerated awe of executive authority. In the 1953 Local Autonomy Case it decided against the prime minister. A member of the Aomori Prefectural Assembly had been expelled by vote of the majority because of insulting remarks about his colleagues. He challenged this in the courts and simultaneously obtained an injunction from the Aomori District Court suspending the execution of his expulsion. Thereupon, the prime minister, on the assumption that he had this power on the basis of paragraph 2 of Article 10 of the Administrative Litigation Law, raised an objection to the injunction. The district court refused to rescind its injunction, and was upheld by the Supreme Court, which interpreted the above provision as entitling the prime minister only to prevent an injunction suspending the execution of an administrative action, but not to invalidate it once it has been issued. I have previously expressed doubt about the constitutionality of this provision, and today I wonder why I did not take exception to it when the law was deliberated. While the majority did not discuss constitutionality, Justice Mano, in his supplementary opinion, lucidly argued that the grant to the prime minister of the power to interfere in a judicial procedure violated, indeed, the principle of separation of powers. The majority may possibly have considered the prevention of a judicial act as the less intolerable interference than its invalidation.

There have been several other developments on the brighter side. On July 22, 1953, the Supreme Court for the first time declared a statute unconstitutional in connection with the question of whether the "Potsdam Ordinance," No. 325 of 1950, prescribing penalties for acts "prejudicial to the occupation objectives" was still applicable after Japan resumed independence upon the end of the Occupation.[18]

[18] See General Secretariat, Supreme Court of Japan, *Series of Prominent Judgments of the Supreme Court upon Question of Constitutionality*, No. 1.

As we have seen, these Potsdam Ordinances were the mechanics used by the SCAP to transform his commands into Japanese legislation. They were based on the emergency Imperial Ordinance No. 542 of September 20, 1945, which for this purpose authorized the expedient of cabinet orders instead of Diet laws. In June and July 1950, SCAP prohibited the publication of the Communist organ *Akahata* and its affiliates. The defendant was charged with such publication under Cabinet Order No. 325, on the ground that he had committed an act prejudicial to the objectives of the Occupation. The Supreme Court quashed the decisions of the lower courts and acquitted the defendant by applying Article 6 of the Criminal Code, which prescribes that if subsequent to the commission of a crime the penalty therefor has been changed by law, the lesser penalty will be applied. The rationale of this provision is to let the offender benefit from a subsequent mitigation of the law, as long as he is not yet finally convicted. It has been held that this also means that when the penalty has been abolished the defendant must be acquitted. The majority not only declared Cabinet Order No. 325 inapplicable, but also in this case found unconstitutional certain statutes which, while abolishing that cabinet order and its foundation, Imperial Ordinance No. 542, extended the effectiveness of the Potsdam Ordinances beyond the end of the occupation.

Space does not allow any elaboration of the subtle legal problems discussed by the justices. The majority was in agreement on the acquittal and on the main ground for it, namely the understanding that while SCAP Directives and the ensuing Potsdam Ordinances were supraconstitutional as long as the Occupation lasted, their effectiveness could not be extended beyond this time if their substance violated the Constitution. Hence, in such a case the laws that aimed at prolonging that effectiveness could not prevent their invalidation. Moreover, the justices of the majority concurred in the recognition that Potsdam Ordinance No. 325

indeed lacked constitutionality, and had therefore become inapplicable once the nation resumed its independence.

In other respects the views within the majority were, however, quite divergent, as the supplementary opinions show. Some justices limited their scrutiny to Cabinet Order No. 325; they pointed out that by making punishable merely acts that are in violation of directives to the Japanese government issued by the SCAP, its mandate was extremely broad in its scope without any limitation as to what particular directives it envisaged or what substance it intended to cover. "To give Cabinet Order No. 325 the effect of a statute at the time the Peace Treaty has come into force without giving similar force and effect to the existing Directives which substantiate the substance of the Order and to prescribe simply for the punishment of violation of Directives as a crime" is, in the view of these justices, "tantamount to stipulating matters which are practically impossible, thus resulting in a contradiction of the Constitution." As I understand this, they based their view on the somewhat formal point that only the excessively vague and therefore unconstitutional prohibition of violating SCAP Directives in general had been extended, but not the specific ones at issue in this case. While such reasoning avoided the need to examine the constitutionality of the specific SCAP Directives prohibiting the communist newspapers, other justices within the majority filled the vacuum left by Cabinet Order No. 325, and attacked precisely this question. They concluded that the SCAP commands established censorship, and must therefore be regarded as in conflict with paragraph 2 of Article 21 of the Constitution. Four justices, among them Chief Justice Tanaka, dissented. They raised, among other points, objections to the application of Article 6 of the Criminal Code, arguing that an offender may benefit from it only if the law is changed by a definite manifestation of the legislature, but not as a consequence of the fact that the Constitution assumed effectiveness after the end of the Occupation. To be sure, Article 6 mentions a change of the penalty by a law, but to exclude the subsequent coming into effect of the Constitution, the supreme law, from an analogous application of this provision appears to me a rather narrow interpretation of the words.

Although this decision constitutes the legal liquidation of the Occupation, its significance as a performance of constitutional custodianship should not be underrated. It is here, in the interpretation of domestic law, that the scale inclines toward the individual right as against "law and order." The fact that in this case the public welfare test has not served as a decisive counterbalance proves that the majority, uninfluenced by its understandable aversion to communism, was determined to protect clearly defined constitutional guarantees, regardless of the political creed of the person making use of them.

An acquittal along similar lines was sustained by the Supreme Court in a decision of December 20, 1961,[19] where the constitutionality of the Potsdam Ordinance regulating political organizations was involved. Article 10 of this ordinance authorized the attorney general to summon persons concerned, to hear their explanations, and to request the submission of data and other articles in ascertaining whether or not the provisions of that cabinet order were observed. According to paragraph 3 of Article 13, persons who do not comply with the request for appearance shall be punished with penal servitude or imprisonment for a period not exceeding ten years. The defendant in the case had been summoned, but failed to appear. The acquittal was based again on Article 6 of the Criminal Code. Several reasons were advanced by the justices of the majority why the demand in the ordinance for appearance and the excessively severe punishment for nonappearance violated the Constitution, so that the laws prolonging the effectiveness of the ordinance after April 28, 1952, also lacked validity in this specific instance.

[19] *Ibid.*, No. 6.

In an earlier decision of August 1, 1951, the Supreme
Court ordered a retrial in a criminal case on the basis of
indications that the police had obtained a confession from
the prisoner by the use of third-degree methods in violation
of Article 38 of the Constitution.[20]

It is my impression that in the sixties and seventies there
developed a certain loosening of the Court's self-restraint.
In the Nakamura decision of November 28, 1962, for the
second time it declared a statute unconstitutional, namely
paragraph 1 of Article 118 of the Custom Law, which prescribes the forfeiture of vessels and goods related to the
smuggling offense even where owned by a third person.[21]
Such forfeiture was held to be in violation of the property
right of the owner of the smuggled goods in the absence of
any statutory provision for notice and of any opportunity
for excuse or defense. The Court therefore invalidated the
forfeiture provision in the Custom Law as in conflict with
Article 29 and the due process of law rule of Article 31 of
the Constitution. This was another instance in which the
Court overruled a precedent. Previously, the grand bench,
in a similar situation, had rejected the challenge of the
constitutionality of a forfeiture judgment by a defendant
who claimed that a third person's property right was invaded. The dissenting opinions, which argued for adherence
to this precedent, also by referring to United States Supreme
Court decisions against allegations ex jure tertii, appear to
have considerable merit.

A defamation case decided on June 25, 1969, reveals a
more liberal posture of the Court with regard to freedom
of expression.[22] I consider it important because it was
unanimous, and because in balancing the personal honor
and security of the insulted person with the freedom of
speech of the accused, the Court gave preference to the
latter, avoiding a narrow interpretation of the words. The

[20] See Maki, *Court and Constitution in Japan*, pp. 191ff.
[21] See General Secretariat, *Series*, No. 7.
[22] *Ibid.*, No. 11.

defendant, a newspaper owner, was convicted of defamation by the two lower courts. In his paper he had stated that the publisher of another press organ had threatened a city official with exposing some corrupt act of the latter, but simultaneously hinted that this could be avoided if the official bribed him. The Court applied paragraph 2 of Article 230 of the Criminal Code, which excludes punishment when the defamation has been committed solely for the benefit of the public and regarding matters of public concern, and when the truth of the allegation is proved. A former verdict of a petty bench had ruled that the mistaken belief of the accused in the truth of his allegation does not exempt him from criminal liability, as long as the truth is not actually proved. Now the grand bench overruled this precedent and revived the fine Japanese criminological principle that no crime exists in the absence of mens rea, in other words, if the element of guilt is lacking. Since the Court recognized that the act was done with good motive for the public benefit, it held that no defamation was committed if the publisher believed mistakenly in the truth of the alleged facts, and if there was good reason for his mistaken belief on the basis of reliable information and grounds. This decision, though clearly in conflict with the precise wording of the Code, is in my view a gratifying example of a free and imaginative interpretation.

I am, therefore, glad to end this attempt at an evaluation on a more optimistic note. My respectful criticism of the excessive self-restraint displayed in other decisions of the Supreme Court does not mean that I am without understanding of its cautious attitude in the light of the unprecedented novelty and complexity of the legal problems facing it. I also to some extent sympathize with the obvious aversion of Japan's highest judges to disorder. There is ample reason to believe that as the task of judicial review, now already firmly anchored, grows more familiar, the Supreme Court and the lower courts will perform the balancing of individual versus public interests more evenly.

The combination of traditional caution with the progressive vigor of dissenters and younger judges augurs well for such equitable custodianship in the future, if it has not already been achieved.

Index

Library of Congress Cataloging in Publication Data

Oppler, Alfred Christian, 1893-
    Legal reform in occupied Japan.

    Includes index.
    1. Law reform—Japan.   2. Japan—Constitutional
law.   3. Justice, Administration of—Japan.   4. Japan—
History—Allied occupation, 1945-1952.   I. Title.
Law   342'.52'02   75-30200
ISBN 0-691-09234-6

Printed in Great Britain
by Amazon